Neuroscience of Personality

Brain Savvy Insights
For All Types of People

1.0

by Dario Nardi, PhD

Credits

Published by:
Radiance House. PO Box 691971
Los Angeles, California, 90069
http://www.radiancehouse.com

Cover design by Yehuda BenJehoshua. EEG brain maps and photographs by Dario Nardi. Photographs are blurred for privacy. All other illustrations are public domain.

Except on the opposite page, subjects' names are altered to protect their privacy.

Edited by Alison Minami

ISBN: 978-0-9798684-7-4

Printed in the United States of America

Thank You

The following persons, who are mostly UCLA students, participated in this research from fall 2006 through spring 2011.

Alana Purcell
Alex Crown
Alex Lovell
Alexis Craig
Ali Ghandor
Alice Chang
Amy Huang
Ben Barmaan
Bo Han
Brady Gibson
Brittany Ryan
Bryan Suechting
Bryan White
Caitlin O'Donnell
Carolina Romanelli
Catherine Costello
Catherine Perez
Daisuke Imai
Dana Shuler
Daniel Segal
Diana Shadbehr
Drew Morton
Evan Shulman
Gabriel Mizrahi
Grace Lo
Guy Rodgers
Hiromi Takahashi
Jacqui deBorja
Janahan Vijanderan
Jennifer Luh
Jesse Kobernik
Jon Stone
Josh Norris
Kareen Hammad
Katherine Quach
Kathryn Ek
Kecia Nason
Ligia Reyes
Maher Abdel-Sattar
Manav Sidhu
Matt Atkin
Max Schneider
Mei Chen
Melody Kasher
Michael Thompson
Mike Moskowitz
Nanae Kido
Nuper Mathur
Oisen O'Conner
Patricija Petrac
Paymon Vafa
Pedram Deraei
Raymond Beyda
Robert Martin
Ross Bernet
Sam Herskovitz
Shawn Smith
Shek Wong
Shervin Sarraf
Solaris Power
Stephanie Ng
Tanya Farshi
Tobias Divine
Travor Pratt
Vivian Vecchio
Yasha Torabi

Thank you Pam Fox Rollin for helping frame and launch my first public foray on this topic. Thank you Linda V Berens for your years of guidance and support. Thank you Linda Elliot, Belinda Lange, Susan Nash, Richard Hendrickson, Judah Pollack, Dov Pollack, Lieve Vermeulen, Gudula van Beem, Carolyn and Larry Gabbard, Clare Ayers, Sue Blair, Melody Camp, Janet Hoffman, Ravi Verma, and Jamie Johnson for your invitations, enthusiasm, and logistics. Thank you Yehuda BenJehoshua for your spirit.

Contents

1. Let's Get Brain Savvy!

Inside your brain are many keys to what make you and others tick. Imagine peering into the minds of your clients, friends, and loved-ones. Now you can!

For over fifty years, the Myers-Briggs Type Indicator® assessment has been a pencil-paper tool to better understand oneself and others through the dynamics of sixteen personality types. You may be familiar with terms like INFP or ESTJ, or with the works of Dr. Carl Jung. It's been a tantalizing start. Today, the emerging field of neuroscience is validating and building upon the work of the pioneers of personality. Neuroscience offers us a wonderful opportunity to clarify and perhaps even redefine who we are and what we are capable of. Knowing the brain lessens guesswork while promoting a valuable idea: Every person comes into this world with capabilities and potential, and together we can prosper by our different gifts.

People are waking up to neuroscience. In my workshops, I use colorful anecdotes, hands-on activities, and brain imagery to provide very specific tips for coaching and leading for individuals of all personality types. Among the tips are two big secrets: 1) Each personality type shows patterns of brain activity that strongly influence their experience, and 2) Everyone is capable of "creative flow", though what evokes that flow varies. If you get one thing from this book, it is the many ways that you and others may nurture your creative flow.

Five years ago I began a quest to better understand myself and others through brain research. I used funds from a teaching award to buy "EEG" neuro-mapping equipment. I fondly recall the first day in lab. I was excited to observe actual brain activity happening in bright colors before my eyes, as opposed to just reading about the brain. The students and I felt we were peering into a secret world. I could barely sleep for weeks afterward, and I quickly got into the groove of designing experiments and recruiting trainees. I say "trainees" for two reasons. First, young people are our future. The more I can encourage the inquiring heart of the scientific method and reveal the boons of knowledge, the better I am doing my profession. Second, though I am certified in human subjects research, I wish to focus on open-ended exploration rather than follow a pre-designed protocol, useful though that can be. I have thus designated my lab as a workshop to teach skills—to mentor trainees—rather than as a chamber to experiment with subjects.

Since the first exciting days, I have confirmed that individual differences truly matter. People of various personality types don't merely rely on different brain regions. They use their brains in fundamentally different ways. I use the ideas of Myers-Briggs and Dr. Jung because there are clear neurological and psychological similarities when I do side-by-side comparisons of two people of the same personality type. Moreover, Dr. Jung sought to transcend culturally defined notions of mind and self to offer a truly cross-cultural framework that

This Book Will Get You Brain Savvy

By reading this book, you will:

- Better understand yourself and others. We can use brain research to help move from blame to compassion when explaining behavior.
- Learn to target "in flow" and "low-threshold" activities that engage people creatively and improve their work-flow and learning.
- Identify people's struggles, stress areas, and boundary points, including "high-threshold" activities for which a person may avoid or do poorly.
- Point to the neurological validity of the Jungian model of the mind, including the ever-popular and statistically-validated Myers-Briggs personality assessment and related tools. People like to know there is science.
- Appreciate the mind/brain as a diverse, dynamic system rather than as a small set of static traits.
- Gain a bird's eye view that summarizes many key aspects of the brain all in one place, knowing that what you learn has been observed first-hand.
- Amaze people with cool insights and implications for how people operate! You may even learn which part of your head to point to and say, "This is where I'm thinking right now."

touches on and values the full human drama. At the same time, every brain is unique. No two persons are alike. Males and females differ somewhat. Culture, expertise, talents—these evoke differences too. And your brain today is not your destiny. One of my students, a senior in neuroscience, stated confidently, "I'm not nearly as logical as the other students in my classes. If it weren't for my parents, I'd be in English or history." Sure enough, I detected minimal activity in key logical reasoning centers over the two hour lab. Yet that did not deter this student from discovering how to succeed in a demanding science curriculum, likely by relying on brain regions with which she has more proficiency.

You may have noticed the book title indicates version "1.0". This is not a mere affectation. Rather, people keep asking for a book. Here it is! You will find the latest insights and implications. But know, there is more undiscovered country. Every time I gear-up another trainee (lab subject), I wonder anew if I will encounter a surprise. A new tidbit always springs up. Sometimes, that person is key to untangling a mass of prior observations. Thus, in the coming years, there will surely be a version 2.0 and perhaps 3.0. There will always be more to learn after running more labs, conducting more statistical analysis, and reading more of what others are doing. I embrace a classical scientific method, which wisely begins with lots of exploration and observation to challenge what is worth our passion. In the discipline of anthropology, where I have been located at UCLA, a first-hand observational process results in ethnographic reports. Similarly, please think of this book as a report of a very meaty and interesting pilot study, as a neurographic report.

This book is meant for everyone with a passion to understand and help themselves and others. I hope coaches, counselors, managers, parents, teachers, trainers and others will gain insight and utility. Also, I wish to suggest to fellow researchers and academics that there is value using models and methods with which they may be unfamiliar or dislike. For students of neuroscience, here is a well-organized buffet useful in any neuroscience lab! For everyone else, consider knowledge of your own mind as your rightful inheritance.

Typical Brain Research

More than ever, people are applying insights from brain research to better understand questions that have previously resisted deep investigation. Sometimes results surprise us with a counter-intuitive "Ah ha!" Other times they seem to confirm what we "already knew". Here are some typical investigative questions that brain researchers have asked and the results they have received.

In Economics

Q: Do your purchasing habits adhere to classic economic principles of maximum utility?

A: Only brain-damaged persons and trained economists answer according to classical economic theory. You read that rightly! Economists tap a specific brain region while the rest of us rely on various regions that suit our ad-hoc struggles.

In Political Science

Q: Should a political candidate focus on appealing to his/her base of voters or reach out to an opponent's base of voters?

A: Non-supporters use both emotional and reasoning centers to deny a candidate of an opposing political party. Supporters only use emotional centers to like their own politico and may completely miss the candidate's contradictions.

In Education

Q: Is there a best way for kids to learn mathematics?

A: Though several regions help with math, people use different regions based on how they learned math. Methods may be auditory, visual, kinesthetic, and so on. Some methods appear more effective than others for use in daily life.

In Psychology

Q: How do people manage their emotions?

A: This question is so complex. Let's narrow it and focus on a finer question, "How do people get angry?" When people allow negative input (criticism, etc) into their awareness, and they fail to manage their inner response by turning it into sadness, then they become angry.

In Religion

Q: Does anything special occur in the brain when people pray or meditate?

A: Yes. The average person can quiet his or her mind. Professional meditators from India are able to shut on and off at will a region of the brain that applies a boundary between oneself and the world. They can choose to feel "infinite".

Self-Leadership

People often ask, "With all the emerging brain insights, can we improve ourselves?" Yes! Doing so requires good self-leadership. I like the following short definition inspired by Isabel Myers.

Self-Leadership: Using your capabilities, softening your pitfalls, and developing your potential in order to achieve a desired outcome.

This book is your brain-savvy guide to self-leadership. Before we dive in, please take a moment to inventory yourself. As you complete each section below, consider what others notice about you as well as what you notice about yourself.

1. Your Talents/Capabilities:

2. Your Pitfalls:

3. Your Potential Growth Areas:

Now, let's take a look at ways you can identify and develop your potential!

Types, Traits, and Strange Attractors

When you hear a term like "personality type", you might be tempted to define a type as a set of fixed traits, or deny there are types at all. That would be a mistake. The word "type" is a shorthand term. It refers to a consistent pattern of activity, a stable and mutually-reinforcing set of interrelated characteristics to which a person is drawn toward. Like yin and yang, your capabilities, pitfalls, and potential growth areas intertwine. This idea might sound vague but it is scientific. In the mathematics of dynamic systems, a type is a "strange attractor". The physical, biological, and social worlds are filled with strange attractors in such diverse areas as ant colonies, climate, ecology, immunity, stockmarkets, telecommunications, and traffic. See page 168 for a peek into the strange world of dynamic systems.

Identifying Your Potential

The figure below is the raw, untamed product of nearly five years of reading and first-hand lab research to determine "what happens where" in the brain using EEG technology. The map presents the neocortex as a toolbox, a set of capabilities that people have at their disposal. With this map, you can better identify people's strengths and weaknesses. It's just a start. What it doesn't show are patterns of activity: whole-brain states that we may use as keys to development. When you learn the whole-brain states, you will be well-equipped to coach and lead. We will unpack the map's many regions and explore how whole-brain states link to the widely-used Jungian/Myers-Briggs model of personality types.

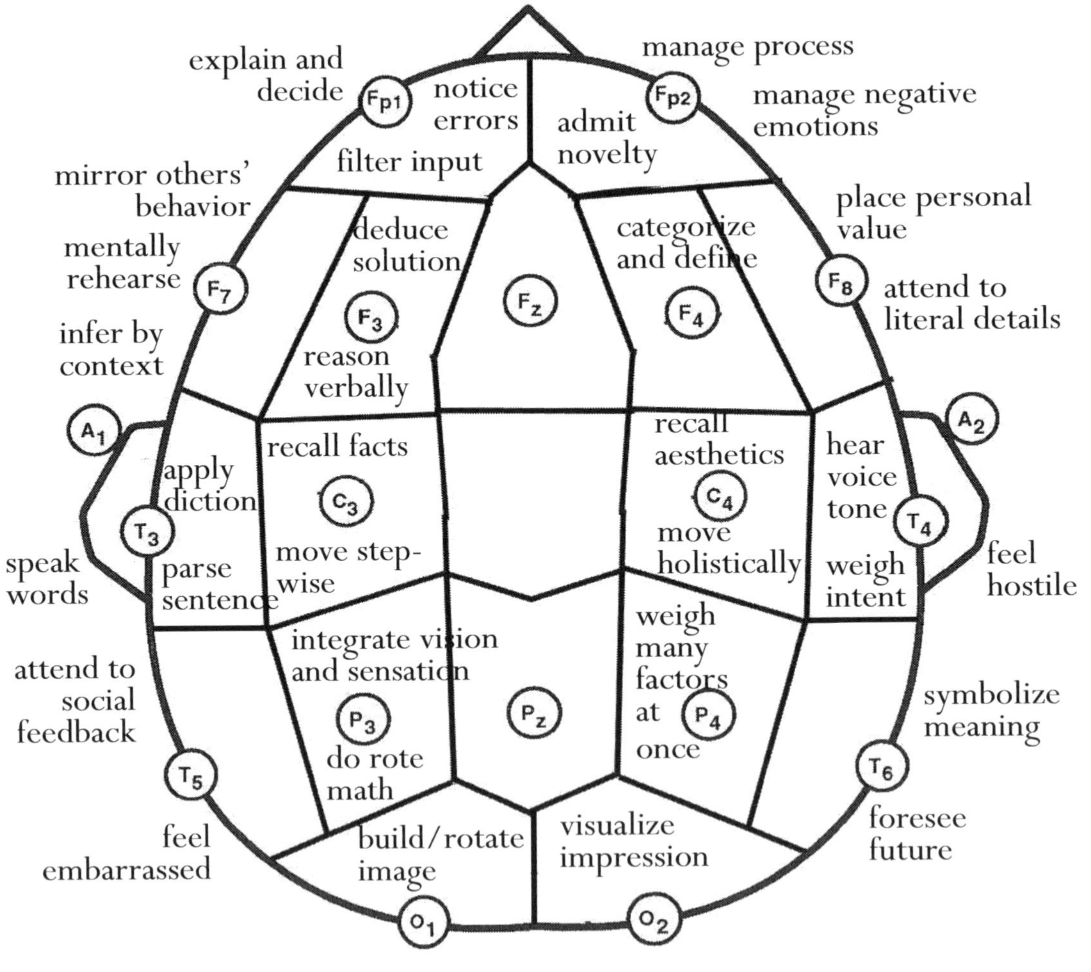

Figure 1-1: Key regions of the neocortex and associated cognitive skills.

A Sneak Peak

On the next two pages, we briefly look at two people, Maria and Ross (real people, fictional names). They use their brains quite differently.

Maria and Ross are each shown with a brain map and a skills chart. We won't get into details yet or even define terms. Instead, I will just highlight for you which regions were most active during a two-hours lab session as they tried various tasks. I also indicate Myers-Briggs types: INFP for Maria and ESTP for Ross. Chapter 5: Personality Types explains what these codes mean.

A brain map is a bird's-eye view of the surface of the brain. The triangle at the map's top is the nose while the ears are on the left and right. The map divides into numerous regions, each corresponding to a sensor on the neuro-mapping equipment. These regions mostly correspond to actual brain areas but ideally should be more fine-grained.

A skills chart is the brain map in words. You will be seeing more of these charts. To keep things simple, the chart breaks down a person's capabilities into gradations from high to medium to low. People who share the same personality type show individual variations, though trends are clear.

Maria and Ross are "opposites" in many ways, though they share some qualities. For example, both draw upon the skills of the "Chief Judge" and the "Process Manager". In fact, all people draw upon these skills, which are gifts of the pre-frontal cortex, that wide area behind your forehead that is so prominent in humans. Maria and Ross's cognitive skills otherwise differ markedly. Maria can be both precise and holistic while listening and speaking, while Ross tends to rely on deductive logic and expert classification. Fortunately, both types have average use of many cognitive skills, which act as convenient areas of overlap for them to get along.

I use terms like "Chief Judge" to make the brain's capabilities easy to understand and recall. Actual brain regions are indicated in parentheses. For example, "Precise Speaker" corresponds to region T3 on the brain map.

The maps quietly imply how to engage in self-leadership. One implication is that we can quickly engage people by appealing to tasks that trigger their favorite brain regions. For example, when we know someone is a great listener—he or she precisely hears both content and tone of voice—then we can rest easy knowing a sit-down chat will probably be highly effective. Alas, such folks are uncommon!

Maria: She relies on her deeply felt personal identity and conscience to make decisions; and she is a patient, nuanced listener with a rich, playful imagination. She meets many "selves" as a psychologist and has written and illustrated a few books that use humorous stories to help people. Her best-fit personality type is INFP, which is ~1% of the USA population.

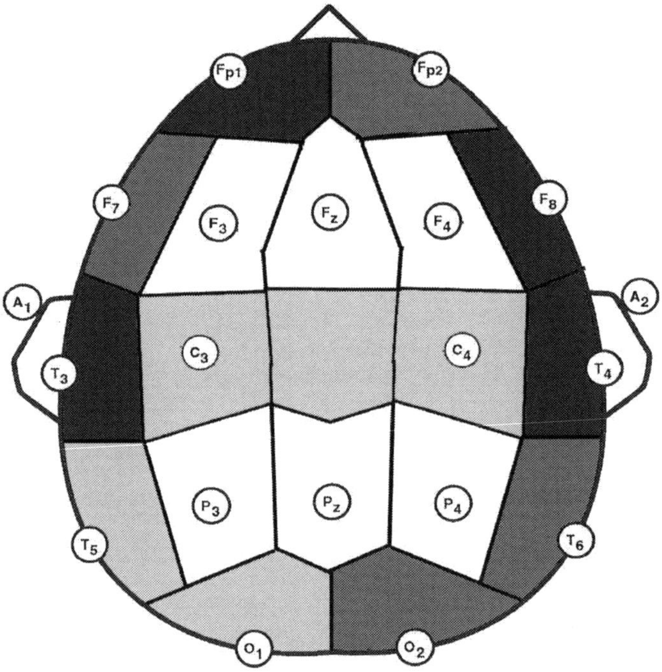

Figure 1-2: Maria's neocortex activity.
Active regions are darker here.

Table 1-1: Maria's Cognitive Skill-Set (based on her EEG results)

Activity	Skill-Set
High	Chief Judge (Fp1), Grounded Believer (F8), Precise Speaker (T3), Intuitive Listener (T4)
High-Mid	Process Manager (Fp2), Imaginative Mimic (F7), Purposeful Futurist (T6), Abstract Impressionist (O2)
Low-Mid	Sensitive Mediator (T5), Factual Storekeeper (C3), Flowing Artist (C4), Visual Engineer (O1)
Low	Deductive Analyst (F3), Expert Classifier (F4), Tactical Navigator (P3), Strategic Gamer (P4)

Ross: He is highly tactical, using deductive logic and gut feeling to pragmatically tackle situations in a hands-on way, with an impulse to take risks for big rewards. He works in finance as an investment counselor and enjoys sports of all kinds including video games and weekly poker. His best-fit personality type is ESTP, which is ~13% of the USA population.

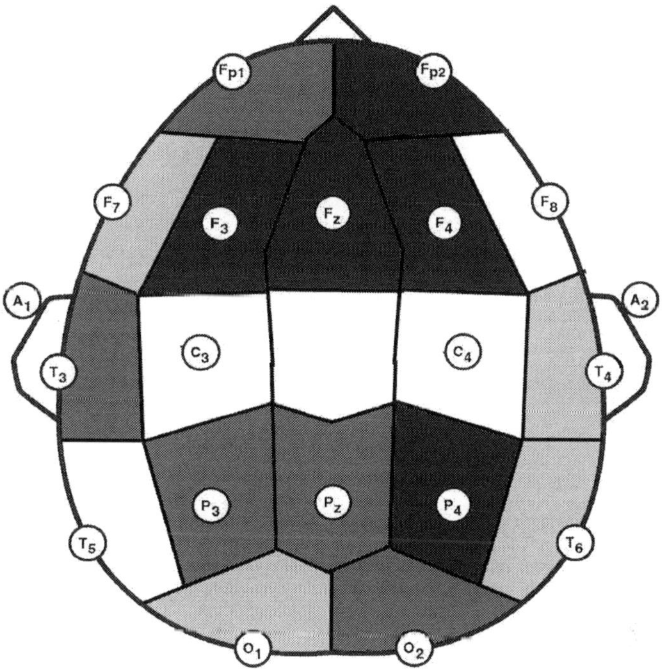

Figure 1-3: Ross's neocortex activity.
Active regions are darker here.

Table 1-2: Ross's Cognitive Skill-Set (based on his EEG results)

Activity	Skill-Set
High	Process Manager (Fp2), Deductive Analyst (F3), Expert Classifier (F4), Strategic Gamer (P4)
High-Mid	Chief Judge (Fp1), Precise Speaker (T3), Tactical Navigator (P3), Abstract Impressionist (O2)
Low-Mid	Imaginative Mimic (F7), Intuitive Listener (T4), Purposeful Futurist (T6), Visual Engineer (O1)
Low	Factual Storekeeper (C3), Flowing Artist (C4), Sensitive Mediator (T5), Grounded Believer (F8)

Global Patterns: Developing Your Potential

Sometimes the brain shows a global pattern. What activates a global pattern varies according to one's context, area of expertise, and personality type. The two figures at right illustrate important global patterns.

The top pattern occurs when all regions are dominated by a particular frequency and amplitude of electrical activity. All the regions are in-synch, dancing together. Although the image is monochrome, the EEG shows a solid color: red, orange, yellow, green, blue, or black. As we'll discover, a particularly meaningful image appears as a sustained, bright solid blue. It signals "creative flow".

Both people we met, Maria and Ross, show the top pattern. Maria gets "in-synch" when she actively listens, even on very contentious topics. When doing so, her map is a solid bright blue. She can listen with her whole neocortex for up to five or ten minutes, possibly longer! Only people of her personality type actively listen like this. It's her gift. Ross can also show a bright blue creative flow pattern. It gels when he actively jumps into solving a crisis situation or when he does physical activity such as tennis or dance.

The bottom pattern occurs when all regions are wildly out-of-synch and constantly changing. When the changes are high amplitude, I refer to a "Christmas tree" pattern. Imagine a tree decked with numerous brightly flashing lights. In contrast, when the changes are low amplitude, I refer to a "tennis hop" pattern. Imagine a tennis player nimbly balancing to her left and right, waiting for her partner to return the ball.

People like Maria sometimes show the Christmas tree pattern, even though that pattern is favored by a slightly different personality type. Certain activities such as creative wordplay coax the brain to enter this playful mode; which, as we will see, is a powerful aid for "trans-contextual thinking". Ross shows the "tennis hop" version of this pattern, typically when he is open to new opportunities. We can evoke the "tennis hop" in everyone by giving them a video game that requires quick tactical action. What does that say about Ross!

We will deeply explore these and other patterns in Chapter 3: Overview of the Neocortex and Chapter 6: Keys to the Psyche. Each of the Jungian/Myers-Briggs personality types shows a unique global pattern. The patterns strongly influence how people handle all kinds of situations as well as how people adapt, learn, and grow. Thus, each global pattern is a key to developing your potential and others' potential.

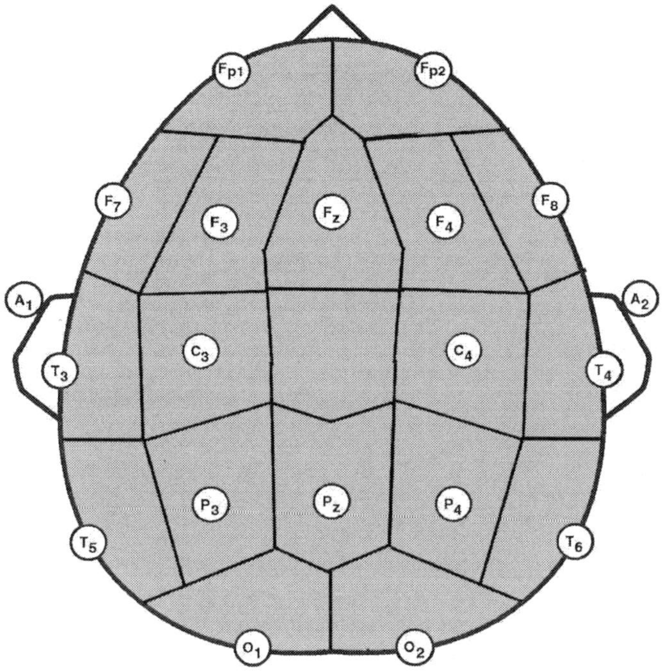

Figure 1-4: A "flow" state when regions are synchronized.

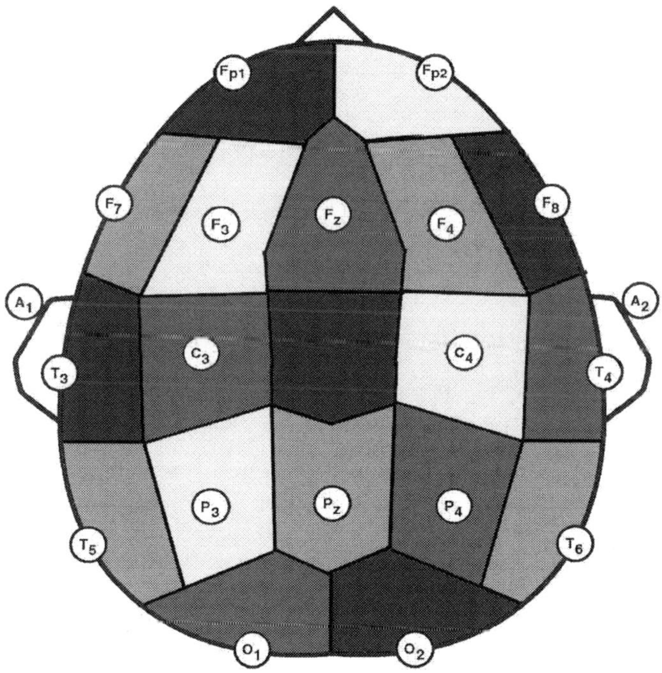

Figure 1-5: A "brainstorm" state when regions are asynchronous

Your Brain-Savvy Compass

In addition to a brain, you have a mind; also, the current context and cultural landscape influence *who* you are and *how* you are. Your psyche is the sum of all these forces. Let's explore how these forces shape our lives.

Brain: Your brain is a physical organ, a collection of neurons, glands, and other biological elements. It is wet, gooey, and fatty—it is composed mostly of cholesterol. It requires nourishment and sleep to function well; and it is physically responsive to the environment through the senses, hormone changes, motor actions, and other biophysical events. The brain is the substrate in which thinking occurs. A different substrate such as a silicon-chip robot is also possible. To use a computer analogy, the brain is hardware.

Mind: Your mind consists of data and procedures to act on that data. Procedures include abstracting, analogizing, analyzing, calculating, comparing, contrasting, deducing, inferring, matching, retrieving data, sorting, storing data, and much more. The mind includes any activity that manipulates information. Unlike the brain, the mind extends outside of us to involve interaction with media (books, etc.) and other people for collaborative thinking. To use a computer analogy, the mind is software.

Context: This is your current situation. It includes resources such as materials, money, people, and tools that are presently available as well as practical constraints such as time limits, project parameters, and other external demands. Our physical environment also presents challenges, such as how to travel from point A to point B, where to grab food, and so on. Situational challenges constantly demand our attention and have influenced the brain's evolution. We often focus a lot on situations, more than we focus on the brain, mind, or culture.

Culture: This includes shared norms, practices, and expectations of our society and organizations (school, work, etc.) Culture lurks outside of awareness while promoting assumptions about what is normal and worthwhile. Culture includes the built environment and institutions. Modern Western culture highlights achievement, consumption, diversity, education, empiricism, innovation, legalism, and so forth. It places value on science and self-help. Also notice values our culture tends to not promote much, such as honoring ancestors.

Psyche: Your psyche is the synergy of brain and mind, guided and filled by your life experiences including culture and your current situation. Consider, there is a region of the neocortex that mediates beliefs, including religious

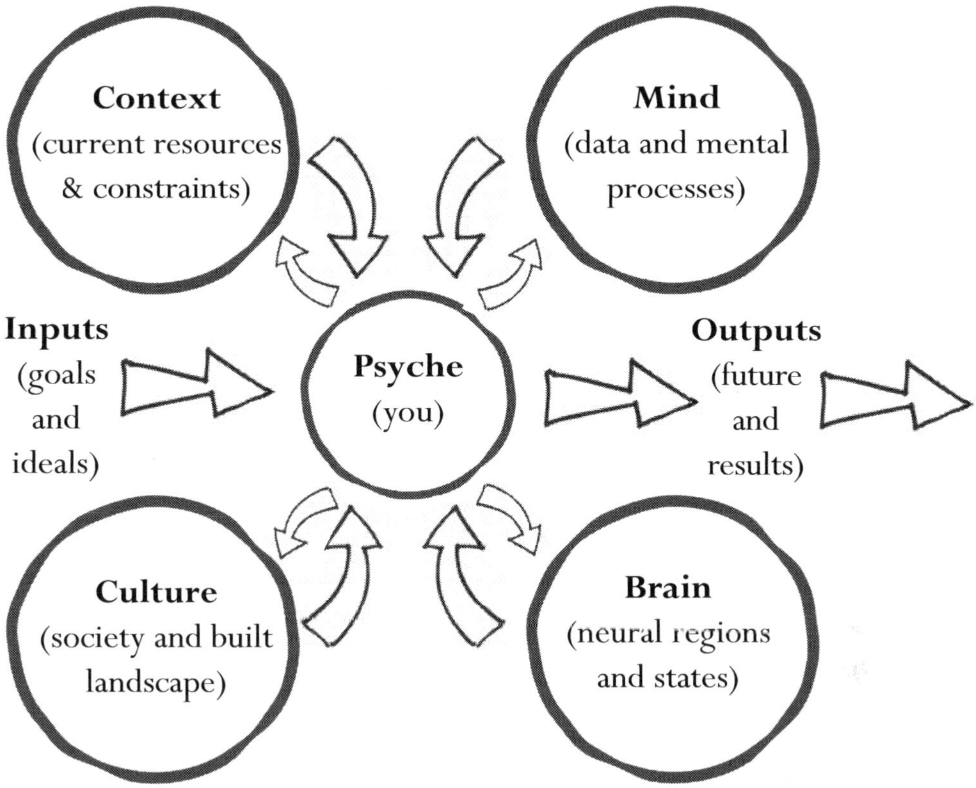

Figure 1-6: Your brain-savvy compass accounts for the rich aspects of human experience.

beliefs. You might perform a mental function such as comparing a pastor's statements to religious beliefs stored in your own brain, to check for a match. You learned about actual, specific beliefs—such as whether heaven or hell exist—from your culture and life experience; and various situations in life have provided you with opportunities to weigh and adopt some beliefs over others.

Brain, mind, context, and culture all shape each other and co-evolve. The horse shapes the rider's options while the rider shapes the horse's options. You might be born with a brain that is predisposed to a "high threshold" for religious beliefs; a lot of stimulus must occur for you to "get some religion". In turn, religious practices, such as focusing for years on memorizing over questioning, train the mind with new functions and shape the brain in lasting ways.

Those of us who study people often have big ideas about what's important. The figure above, on the other hand, is *your* compass. You are free to choose what's important to visit during your journey. Feel free to revisit this compass to help you integrate and apply what's here.

How To Use This Book

How you use this book may depend on your background.

Scientists: You will find familiar and new pieces. This book will provide you with a refreshing big picture from which much nuance may flow.

Type Users: If you use the Jungian/Myers-Briggs framework, you may feel tempted to skip ahead. I encourage you to join me for the full ride.

Everyone: This book takes you on a journey. The chapters build on each other to help you better understand yourself and others.

Agenda

Here is a brief outline of what you will gain from the rest of this book.

Chapter 2: Welcome to the Lab. Spy on a neuroscience lab in action.

Chapter 3: Overview of the Neocortex. Discover the brain's many rich facets. The "engagement curve" highlights how motivation and competence are equally important to activating those facets and unleashing our potential.

Chapter 4: Cognitive Skill-Sets. Delve deeply into the full set of capabilities that your brain's neocortex offers. We can access all of the skill-sets, but most of us emphasize or neglect a few over the others.

Chapter 5: Personality Types. Learn about Jung's model of eight cognitive processes and how it links to the widely-used Myers-Briggs assessment. Discover your best-fit personality type pattern.

Chapter 6: Keys to the Psyche. The science is in! Each of the eight Jungian cognitive processes corresponds to a pattern of brain activity that unites brain, mind, culture, and context into a comprehensive model.

Chapter 7: Natalie: A Case Study. Sit in on a live lab session. Follow along as I report on Natalie's brain activity as she tries various tasks.

Chapter 8: Insights in Action. Review essential principles and apply them to your current situation, client, or group, as practice for using the neuroscience of personality in your daily life.

Chapter 9: In-Depth Exploration. Examine the neurological data in-depth to decide for yourself about the validity of Jung's framework.

Chapter 10: Now What? Decide how to apply this book to your own life, with a focus on ethical use for personal and organizational transformation.

Appendix: Resources. Find tools to continue your journey including academic research papers, books, software, workshops, and more.

2. Welcome to the Lab

In this chapter, you get a tour of my lab. I briefly explain my methods and showcase typical tasks that subjects try. I take a humanistic (that is, non-clinical) approach. I focus on in-depth exploration and long-term observation to catch the full variety of what nature has to offer us curious creatures, and to learn what is worth studying.

I spend ninety minutes to two hours—sometimes three hours—with each subject. Every person is fascinating. With each one, I draw from a menu of tasks and split his or her time between individual and social activities. I watch an EEG monitor and the person's behavior while taking copious notes all along. I briefly interview the person after a task so he or she may clue me in on the experience. After a session, I may have come to know that person by his or her mental habits better than friends or perhaps loved-ones might after many years.

Understanding scientific inquiry ideally involves knowing the context, methods, and assumptions behind the reported results. I hope this tour will both set the stage and help explain what made the big insights possible, even though we both may wish to leap ahead to the juicy stuff!

This book speaks from my experience with fifty-eight lab subjects. That may not sound like many people. However, this is a fine number for brain research. I'm not asking people to self-report. Nor am I sticking a wetted finger into the wind to guesstimate. These days, we can actually see into the brain and measure its activities. This mitigates the need for a biblical multitude.

Neuro-mapping software is very colorful. Unfortunately, this book is not. Thus, every brain map you see here is a grayscale compression of more interesting data. The up-side: gray data points are easier to digest.

Scientific Methods

I treat my lab as a training space rather than an experimental space, and blend qualitative and quantative approaches to brain mapping. Many EEG researchers work like this. Purely conventional methods tend to hide what's interesting, and purely observational methods may suggest spurious insights. Overall, I follow a "situated" research paradigm, which opens a window to surprises.

The Conventional Research Paradigm: Here are typical steps to take when conducting experiments that focus on specific, known questions in order to locate a definitive answer. To confirm a hypothesis:

- Focus on a specific research question.
- Carefully design and vet an experimental protocol beforehand.
- Isolate each subject.
- Automate cognitive tasks for delivery by computer.
- Be quantitative, not qualitative (don't trust notes or observations).
- Analyze results statistically over many subjects to find a common region or sequence of activity.
- Take ~10 minutes per subject to complete the testing protocol.
- Link results to existing models that are already popular to help ensure your paper is accepted for publication.

The Situated Research Paradigm: Here are typical steps to take when exploring a phenomenon to learn what might be worth confirming in the future, with allowance for surprises. To explore a phenomenon:

- Focus on each person and let his or her behavior influence where to go.
- Draw up a list of questions or ideas but hold off on a formal design.
- Situate each subject in a small (friendly) group.
- Include open-ended tasks with new, live people (confederates).
- Ask a subject to share his or her self-reflections after each task.
- Note individual variations while attending to the influence of context, and analyze results statistically with an eye for differences.
- Spend significant time (an hour or more) interacting with the subject.
- Take copious notes while observing the subject and review as you go.
- Link results to various frameworks to see what fits best.

Neither paradigm is better so long as each serves its intended purpose. Since I conducted situated research for this book, the results are tentative and will require more rigorous study in the future.

Photo 2-1: Here is a social neuroscience lab day at UCLA, where I study brain activity.

Participants

I study college students ages eighteen to twenty-five. I limit myself to this age group because I want to avoid concerns about development. That is, as people mature, they may become specialized and/or more flexible in ways that muddy results. Most subjects hail from the University of California, Los Angeles. UCLA accepts applicants from among the top 1% of California high schools, a fact that might influence the kind of results I get.

The lab is popular—who wouldn't be curious?—and participation is by invitation only. I invite students based on likely personality type, high academic performance, interest in the topic, and aptitude for a laboratory experience. Thus, they participate for various reasons. I once hoped to enjoy an equal sampling of various personality types, though that is surprisingly hard.

I invite an equal number of females and males. Do men and women vary in meaningful ways? Maybe, maybe not. Like other brain researchers, I limit myself to right-handers. Left-handed people have different brain structure. Also, a subject must have hair (but not too much!) to wear the snug EEG cap.

Finally, a subject must have no evidence of brain damage or mental impairment due to lack of sleep or mind-altering drugs or alcohol, which is more likely than one might think (Adderall is a favorite stimulant). Out of curiosity, I have investigated one left-hander and one student on Prozac, a popular anti-depressant. The Prozac student presented a muted, sad neurological landscape. One summer, I recruited and tested three people at the Burning Man art festival, a highly stimulating event. I did not include these unusual cases. Ultimately, I have accumulated fifty-eight usable subjects.

A prospective subject needs to be comfortable under scrutiny in a social setting, and not discomforting to others (a pleasant odor, please). That said, I do not select for high sociality per se. In fact, many participants have ultimately settled on a preference for introversion, for example.

Experimental Set-Up

Once students are selected, they take the Interstrength Cognitive Assessment and complete an intake form (see page 152 for details and page 196 for white paper). The form helps me decide when to schedule their session and what tasks to offer during the free-form period at the end of the session. Students who indicate they are morning people go in the late morning while those who indicate they are afternoon or evening people go in the early afternoon.

The students have ten weeks to locate their best-fit personality type. The few who did not settle decisively on one type were removed from the study (see page 153 for demographic data).

The lab usually occurs in a quiet library with a pastoral view. The entire set of lab gear packs up into two boxes. Unpacking and assembling take just fifteen minutes! I have conducted most sessions on Saturdays to avoid interaction with classes and events; and more relevantly, to get students when they are likely to be more relaxed. Most lab sessions have been held during the first few weeks of each academic term. It's best not to see them stressed by exams.

A lab session starts with a form-fitting red nylon cap and multiple straps to ensure the cap remains taut. Pick-ups embedded in the cap detect electrical activity on the brain's surface. It all looks like high-tech apparel for those elves in Santa's workshop who are not entirely wholesome. Next, I inject a water-soluble gel through the pick-ups to ensure a solid connection. Finally, an assistant helps me calibrate the cap to ensure all the pick-ups are working properly.

Although the EEG guide cautions that subjects should avoid head movement at *all* times, I find that a secure cap and electrical grounding are usually sufficient to get unspoiled results.

So what exactly is EEG? Briefly, an EEG, or electroencephalogram…

- Measures electrical activity in the neocortex, the outer layer of the brain.
- Is fast, simple, and cheap.
- Measures changes in real-time (250 samples per second).
- Requires application of a tight nylon cap and conductive gel to maintain a reliable connection.
- Shows a person's next action less than a second before he or she implements that action.
- Is low-resolution and can't look into the middle or deep brain. Yet with patience and skill, it yields numerous secrets.
- EEG has been in use for over eight decades and is widely used for biofeedback and other clinical applications. It has an emerging use in games.

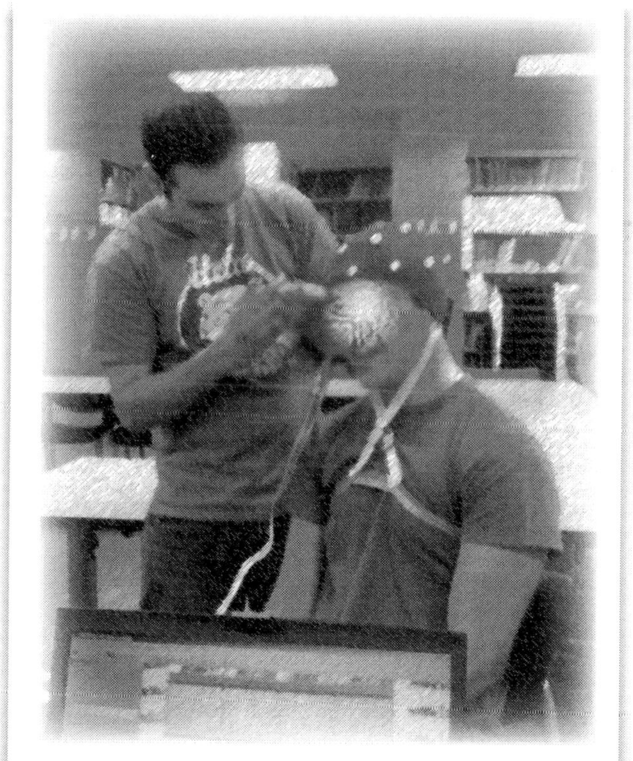

Photo 2-2: Subjects wear a snug, red, knit cap and get gelled.

Experimental Tasks

The very first task is always a series of simple exercises to achieve a "blank" EEG. One of the exercises always causes the entire neuro-map to turn solid black, indicating no meaningful activity. Here are the exercises:

1. "Close your eyes, relax and breath deeply to help clear your mind."
2. "Pick a point in your field of view and stare at it for as long as you can."
3. "Draw one circle repetitively over and over."
4. "Close your eyes, pick a word, and keep repeating it to yourself."

Here are other tasks that I have people try:

- Warm up, e.g. sign their name various ways, backward and forward with their nonpreferred hand.
- Speak and write using languages that they know or are studying.
- Play games, e.g. card games and word games.
- Perform physical tasks, e.g. juggling or tossing balls back and forth.
- Think, e.g. solving math problems and completing analogies.
- Communicate, e.g. engage in speed dating, role-play with actors.
- Recall, e.g. repeat back items on list, scene details, childhood events.
- Foresee, e.g. imagine one's life ten years from now
- Interpret, e.g. process stories, news articles, and ambiguous pictures.
- Listen to music, read a story, watch a video, and sing a song!
- Play various video games from Mario Cart to Age of Empires.
- Tell stories: e.g. tarot cards to convey a story, or recount a recent event.
- Much more.

I draw from a menu of tasks. Most tasks were designed the first weeks of the lab in fall 2006. Although I repeat many tasks from one subject to the next, I never use all of the tasks due to lack of time. I feel it is important to explore a variety of tasks and address a subject's interests. Also, over five years, I have came up with new tasks and refined others. I endeavor to spend my time with a subject this way:

- Ninety minutes of individual tasks such as solving math problems or signing his or her name in various ways.
- Ninety minutes of social tasks such playing cards, doing a role-play scenario, engaging in speed dates, and so forth.
- Thirty minutes of open-ended exploration that suits the subject's hobbies such as playing a guitar.

Typical Tasks

Short-Term Verbal Memory Task

"Please listen to the following list of words. I will ask you to repeat back the list afterward."

- duck
- avocado
- nightmare
- shoehorn
- fork
- yesterday
- transparency
- clock
- dividend

Declarative Memory Task

Please provide the names and birthdays for as many people as you can recall who are not your relatives.

Visual Projective Task

"Please look at the following illustration. What comes to mind?"

For each task, I read instructions and possibly give a handout or object to work with. I then sit back and watch his or her behavior and the EEG patterns on the computer screen at the same time while taking notes. The screen shows the person's activity in several different views at once. Each view results from a different numerical calculation method, so two views may not match. Moreover, the screen shows what's happening "now", which means I notice an event that hasn't manifested quite yet in the subject's behavior. The time lag is very short, less than a second. It is enough time for my eyes to register the event's occurrence and likely meaning but not enough time for me to respond to the event preemptively. Just as I notice the meaning, the subject speaks, acts, or otherwise shows evidence of the brain activity. This is slightly unnerving at times! Nor is this an energizing activity. Although I have done three sessions in a day, I now limit myself to one or two sessions. A brain can tire easily!

While a subject does a task, I may intervene to answer a question or direct him or her to a new step in the task. Generally, though, I minimize interaction unless there is something I would like to explore. Sometimes intervention has offered up a key possibility. For example, it is clear from the EEG that some subjects listen to me much more actively than they listen to their peers.

When a task is done, I ask the subject to self-report what was going through his or her mind. This is very important. For example, I usually offer a task that assesses how people make decisions about money in situations of risk and/or uncertainty. In theory, this should elicit activity from a particular area of the brain, region P4. This region is reportedly active in graduate students of economics. However, while it is active for my own subjects who happen to be economics majors, it is not active for many other subjects. The reason? There is a "correct" mathematical method to make the risk and uncertainty decisions, but only people who study economics know this method. So people draw upon various ways to decide. One subject showed activity in region F7, which correlates with mental simulation. During the self-report, he said he made decisions in the task by imagining he was a casino owner. This is one of many ways people have answered. If I didn't ask, I might think I was getting no clear result, or think that F7 was related to effective monetary decision making in situations

Photo 2-3: This colorful screen shows a person's brain activity in real time.

of risk and uncertainty (it's not). Failure to ask subjects what they are thinking about, along with insufficiently long sessions, is probably why EEG researchers sometimes get results that are not as interesting as they might like.

Finally, I ask for other students' input. Typically, they have been sitting quietly by me watching the EEG monitor or perhaps assisting with tasks, such as acting as opponents in a card game.

Is there an observer effect? In my experience, there can be an observer effect when the subject is watched by a large group. Once I conducted a demonstration session before an audience of several hundred conference-goers. The audience watched the EEG monitor projected onto an overhead screen. The subject was nervous until I officially ended the demonstration and continued more privately with a small group of a half-dozen. The subject's brain activity was muddy and inconclusive until she felt comfortable. Another demonstration before a class of two-dozen students frazzled a male subject. He claimed he felt comfortable but his brain activity suggested otherwise. In both cases, brain activity showed a constant muddy blue-green haze regardless of what task the subject tried. This is why I don't do public demonstrations.

When there is time and interest, I continue beyond the two-hour period to explore tasks posed by other lab students, the subject, or by me as a test-run of a new task that I might want to use in the future. All throughout, I am writing notes. A two-hour session generally results in six pages of written notes.

Most subjects also act as assistants, analysts, and ideally, someone who is a stranger to the subject. People react in surprising ways to strangers. For example, for over an hour, one subject showed minimal activity in region O1, which handles vision. I had calibrated the sensors. It was all him. Then someone new entered the room. The O1 region suddenly fired up big time but died down as the stranger became familiar. I secretly arranged with another student to invite her boyfriend to drop by. The boy was unfamiliar to the subject. When he arrived, the effect occurred again exactly as before. So many possibilities!

In a few cases I use GSR, or Galvanic Skin Response, a device that measures conductance on the surface of the skin. EEG shows a lot more varied results than GSR. Other times I run a computer-based experiment. The computer is a useful tool. I hope to use it more in the future, though it shouldn't be the only tool if the goal is to assess a variety of human abilities. For example, just as economists know that people respond to real money differently than play money, subjects' brains respond to real people and tasks somewhat differently than virtual people and tasks. I say somewhat, because while there have been a few amazingly memorable surprises over the years involving real tasks, I generally find that computerized tasks elicit sufficiently interesting responses. Perhaps people don't distinguish so much between fantasy and reality as they might hope? I will leave that for others to debate.

By the way, I am familiar with conducting formal EEG studies. In the summer of 2007, I designed and co-conducted one formal study with student Nanae Kido on the role of violence, when mixed with humor, in audio-visual media (film and television clips). Nanae wished to replicate others' published results. Studies report a lack of brain activity while watching television and also selective activation of the right pre-frontal cortex (region Fp2) in response to violence. The brief study looked at two male and two female subjects. Both males showed no neocortical activity vis-a-vis violence even while watching a clip of the Texas Chainsaw Massacre, while both female subjects showed activity as predicted in region Fp2.

When a session ends, I like to review the written notes and summarize them verbally to help myself remember key points for later, and then type up a report at home. One term I was slow at typing reports! Why did I procrastinate? I have gleaned from observing several subjects an interesting observation: Some people's brains embrace detailed reviews while others suffer it. Ultimately, I've compiled a thick journal of what I call "neurographic reports". That term is inspired by "ethnographic study", a traditional practice of anthropologists.

Confounding Factors

Here are some variables that likely affected subjects' brain activity.

- Time of day vis-a-vis subject energy level
- Variations in testing protocol
- Brain age (effects of maturation)
- Equipment calibration
- Drug/alcohol effects
- Left-handedness or unusual brain anatomy
- Brain injury or congenital defect
- Prior exposure to certain experimental tasks
- Life distractions
- Other, unknown factors

3.
Overview of the Neocortex

This chapter provides a broad overview of the neocortex, that quintessentially human layer of our brain.

We start with anatomy: the brain's two hemispheres and the four lobes within each hemisphere. Along the way, you will visit sixteen distinct regions of the neocortex. These regions are the meat and potatoes to sustain you for the rest of this book. The next chapter goes into even more detail about them!

The presence of sixteen regions is by chance. There are other EEG devices that are sensitive to twenty-four, sixty-four, or even two-hundred fifty-six regions! Thus, when we talk about regions, you may wonder why certain cognitive skills go together; just remember that the EEG equipment is limited. If the equipment had higher resolution, we could make finer distinctions. That said, with patience and awareness, EEG offers wonderful insights.

Beyond anatomy, we will explore neurological patterns. Foremost are global patterns that occur across the whole neocortex, such as when all regions are in synch or out of synch. These global patterns don't readily show themselves. It takes patience and a subject-focused approach to experimentation to evoke them. We will also learn about brain waves, circuit patterns, states of consciousness, and what might be among the most important pieces, the "engagement curve". This curve highlights how important motivation and competence are to leverage your brain's potential.

By the way, everything in this book holds for right-handers. If you are left-handed, there is a 50% chance that your brain is simply a mirror image of a right-hander's brain. The other 50% of you shows unusual brain organizations, which might explain the rumor that creative folks are lefties.

The Brain

The brain is a complex electro-biochemical system. It consists of multiple layers and interconnected modules. The figure below offers a side view of the neocortex, which is the outermost layer of the brain that is visible from the outside.

The neocortex is the newest and most cognitive layer. It is responsible for numerous mental processes including decision making, sensory perception, motor control of the body, language, and consciousness thought. This book focuses on the neocortex.

Older interior regions are important too and help with emotions, memory, and bodily functions such as breathing. Fortunately, a lot of this interior activity trickles up to the neocortex, which processes the activity along with its other duties. This is why, for example, you can consciously alter your breathing rate even though you normally don't need to.

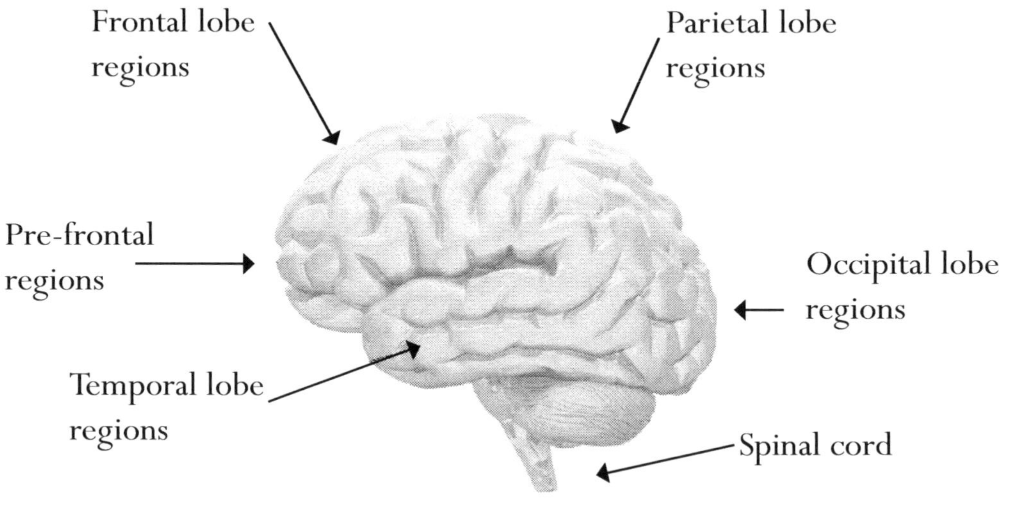

Figure 3-1: Major parts of the brain, as seen from a person's left side.

The neocortex is highly wrinkled, which grants it more surface area, and multiple fissures divide it. A key fissure separates much of the brain into two hemispheres. Lesser fissures further divide the neocortex into lobes, each of which is home to various smaller regions that handle specific cognitive tasks such as logical deduction, mimicking others, noticing tone of voice, and so on. We will focus on these small regions. Now, let's explore the neocortex!

Two Hemispheres

The brain has two hemispheres: left and right. Generally, the left hemisphere handles the right side of the body, including the right eye, ear, hand, and foot; while the right hemisphere handles the body's left side. The left hemisphere is dominant for people who are right-handed. Reverse the situation for left-handers. Whichever hemisphere is dominant is the more verbal, linear, and analytical side; while the other is more holistic, spatial, and nonverbal. Here are brief descriptions of the two hemispheres for a right-handed person.

Left: This hemisphere is more verbal, linear, and analytical. It is adept with words, numbers, facts, diagrams, steps, and deductive reasoning. It is skilled at making decisions and delivering explanations.

Right: This hemisphere is more holistic, spatial, and nonverbal. It is adept with tone of voice, patterns, reasoning through parallel constraint satisfaction, impressions, and induction. It is skilled at managing processes.

As you will see, these broad generalizations about the two hemispheres are generally unhelpful. We will focus on the brain's many smaller regions, as summarized on the coming pages and fully detailed in the next chapter.

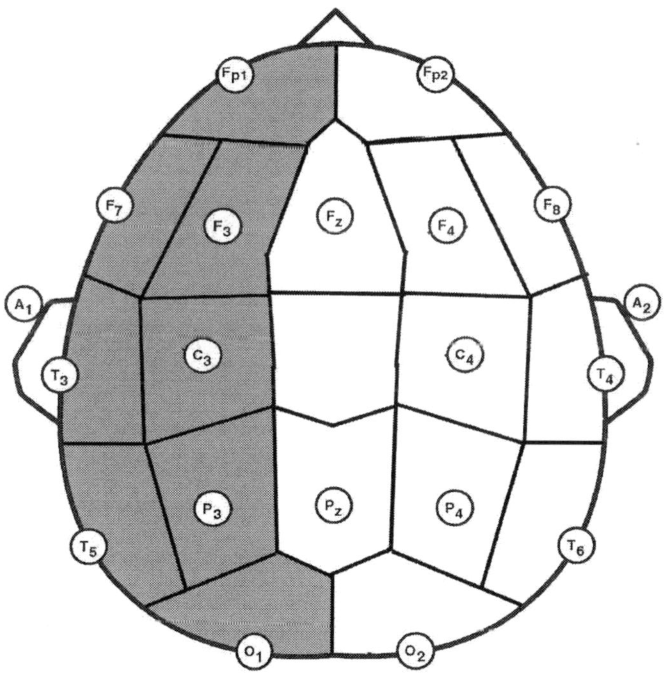

Figure 3-2: The brain has two hemispheres and consists of numerous regions.

Pre-Frontal Regions

Two key regions preside at the front of the brain, beneath your forehead just above your eyes. These important regions are part of the frontal cortex, though researchers often highlight them separately. Both regions are highly active for everyone and act as managers for much of the brain's other activities. People habitually use one region more than the other, though highly complex tasks quickly engage both sides. Here are brief descriptions of these two regions.

Fp1: This region is active when a person gives an explanation, picks among options, or explains a meaning. When a person says, "My reason is...", "I am picking...", or "I think that because...", this region is likely active. This region also acts as a gate keeper to screen out negative information that might distract us emotionally.

Fp2: This region is active when a person deals with novel information or when noting he or she has reached a point in a process. For example, when asked to brainstorm, a person generates ideas and this region activates just before he or she says, "I can't think of anything more." This region also admits negative input and mutes our emotional responses so we can reflect on the input.

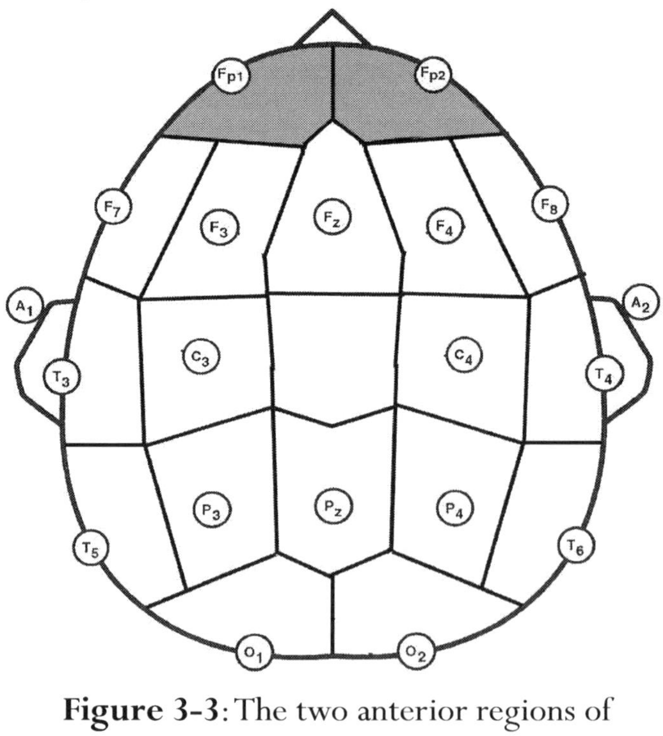

Figure 3-3: The two anterior regions of the neocortex act as supurb managers.

Frontal Regions

The frontal regions stretch from the hairline toward the center-top of the head as shown in the figure below. They handle various high-level cognitive activities. Here are brief descriptions of four key frontal regions.

F7: This region helps us mirror others' behavior, especially their physical behavior. We also use this region to engage in mental rehearsal and infer likely details according to context. What words go well with "traffic"?

F3: This region helps us linearly derive solutions using verbal/symbolic reasoning. For example, if A=B, and B=C, then logically A=C. Using this region is like moving (and perhaps backtracking) along the branches of a tree.

F4: This region helps us categorize and define concepts in a holistic way, using a spatial-kinesthetic best-fit. For example, this region would help us instantly know whether a dolphin better fits in the mammal or fish category.

F8: This region helps us evaluate people and situations in terms of personal importance along a spectrum from like to dislike (that is, values we hold regardless of context). This region also helps us attend to literal details rather than inferring based on the situation.

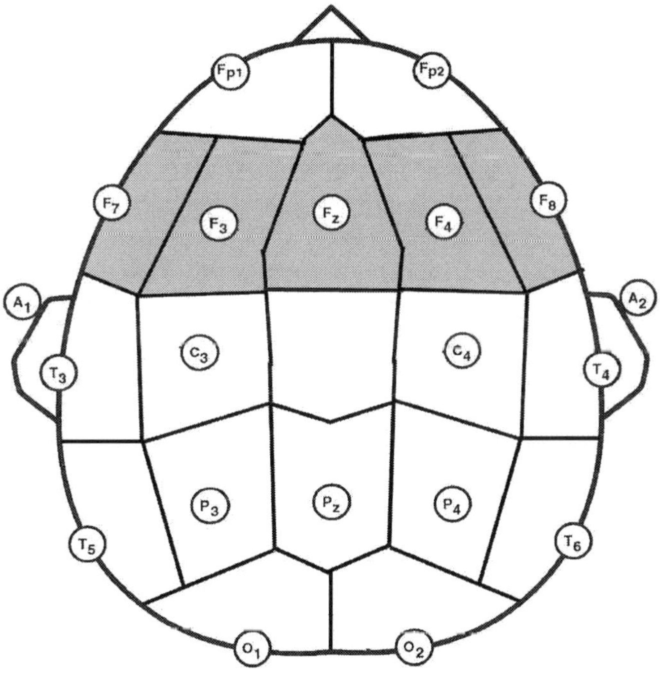

Figure 3-4: Four key regions of the medial and posterior frontal lobes.

Temporal Regions

The temporal regions sit by and behind the ears, as shown in the figure below. Here are brief descriptions of four key temporal regions.

T3: This region takes an analytical approach to spoken language. It helps us focus on specific words, correct grammar, proper usage, and effective diction. Using this region, we focus on content over delivery.

T4: This region takes a holistic approach to language, mainly focusing on tone of voice and other affective qualities of speech. Using this region, we focus on the style of verbal delivery rather than on content.

T5: This region helps us act in a socially appropriate manner. While using this region, feelings of embarrassment or shame encourage us to quickly and appropriately meet (or otherwise respond to) others' social expectations. This region also appears to help men recognize and analyze faces.

T6: This region is active when we say the word "will", as in "this is what will happen." This region helps us know what will occur in the future by projecting how a situation will play out around us. Also, it helps us give a symbolic meaning to images. It appears to help women recognize and evaluate faces.

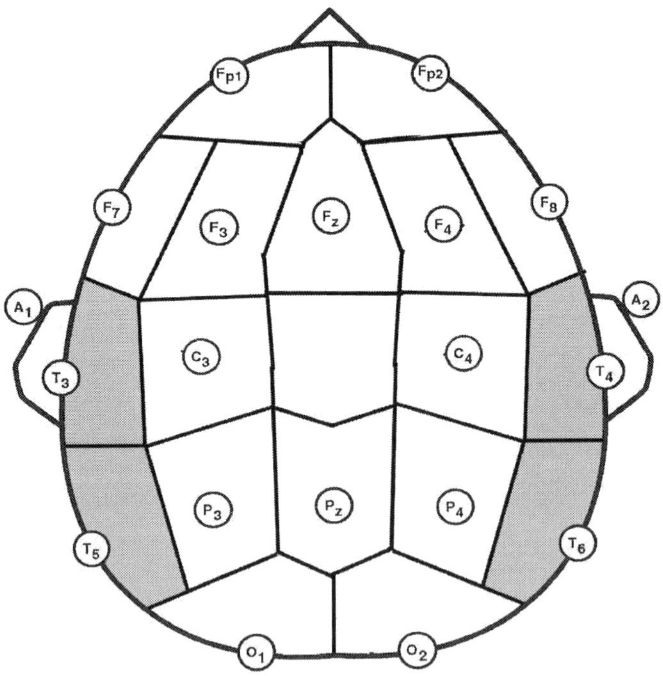

Figure 3-5: Four key regions of the temporal lobes

Parietal Regions

The parietal regions sit at the top of the head, as shown in the figure below. These regions handle memory, motion, sensation (taste, touch, temperature, etc), mathematics, and reading. Our memory regions work "batch style". They "upload" a whole memory into consciousness and then hand it off to us for use by other regions. Here are brief descriptions of four key parietal regions.

C3: This region attends to motion and sensation on the right side of the body. Also, it helps us recall facts (dates, percentages, proper names, etc.) and physical action steps.

C4: This region attends to motion and sensation on the left side of the body. Also, it helps us recall aesthetic qualities and whole-body experiences.

P3: This region integrates visual-kinesthetic data. It is involved in object identification, motor skills such as aim, and mathematical calculating using a grid. For example, it helps us name objects by touch while blindfolded.

P4: This region helps us holistically weigh the numerous pros and cons of many uncertain or risky factors or options at once to arrive at a single result. For example, how are the odds when you play a particular betting game?

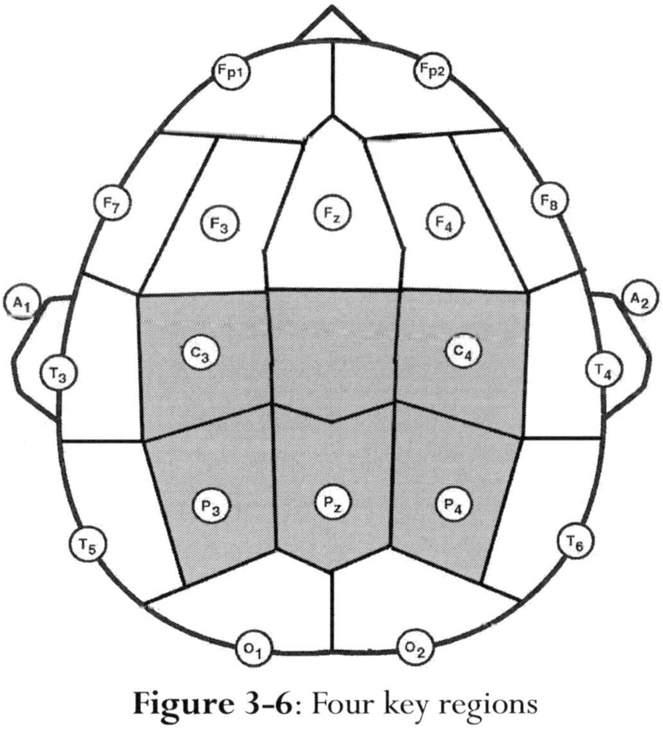

Figure 3-6: Four key regions of the parietal lobes.

Occipital Regions

Two occipital regions sit at the back of the head as shown in the figure below. Both handle vision. Vision is highly complex. As light hits the eyes, nerves send information to the occipital regions for processing. Simple dots of color are disambiguated as people, objects, and spaces. This region also judges distance, evaluates brightness and dullness, adjusts what we see to account for ambient light levels, and much more. As we develop in early childhood, we learn to "see" objects as whole units. For example, we see the letter "A" rather than two diagonal lines and one horizontal line. By the way, a mass of neurons represents exactly what hits the eye, though the "image" is positioned upside down! Here are brief descriptions of the two key occipital regions.

O1: This region handles images that enter through the right eye. It can manipulate images analytically. It works somewhat like an auto-cad program to help us rotate, measure, explode, construct, and deconstruct objects.

O2: This region handles images that enter through the left eye. It interprets images in a holistic way. It is comfortable with photographs and artwork. It works like an art critic to help us process abstract visual impressions.

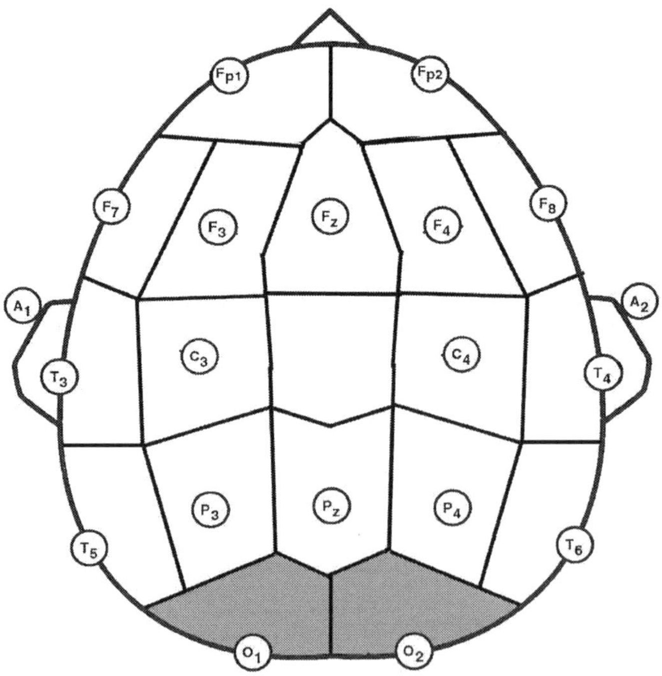

Figure 3-7: These two posterior regions of the neocortex lie in the occipital lobe.

More Views!

In addition to a bird's-eye view of the neocortex, we can take other views to observe brain activity. The two figures below show complementary views. The top figure uses bar graphs that emphasize the volume of activity (amplitude) in all sixteen regions. The bottom figure shows what just one region's activity really looks like: a mass of waveforms, often with one feature slightly dominating others. When I refer to a particular kind of activity, I refer to what predominates.

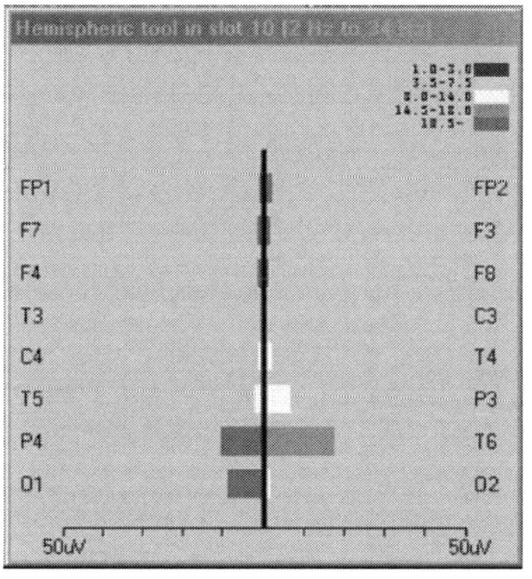

Figure 3-8: This "hemispheric" graph shows high activity in regions P3, P4, T6 and O1.

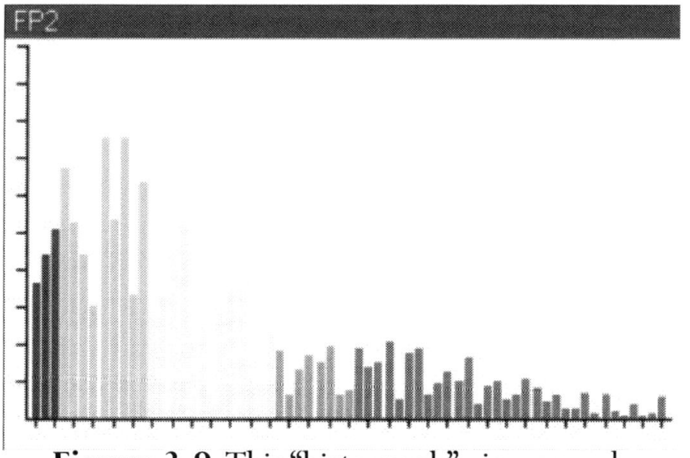

Figure 3-9: This "histograph" view reveals the full range of activity in just region Fp2.

Brain Waves

Your brain is an electronic device. Yep! Neurotransmitters provide biochemical action. Simultaneously, your brain shows electrical patterns that behave like waves. Consider brain activity like waves on a beach.

Frequency: This refers to how often the waves come. High frequency means many waves in a short period. The waves come fast. In contrast, low frequency means the waves come slowly.

Amplitude: This refers to how big the waves are. Low amplitude means the waves are short, while high amplitude means the waves are tall.

Look at the four figures on the facing page. In Figure 3-10, delta waves roll like a calm ocean. Occasionally there is a blip. Later figures show higher frequencies. In Figure 3-13, beta waves roil like frenetic, choppy waters.

The table below summarizes activity bands that my EEG machine afforded me along a color spectrum. Since this is a monochrome book, I will show results using the shades indicated in the far-right column.

Table 3-1: Bands of EEG Activity

EEG Color	Wave Band	Hertz	Typical Indication*	Shade (this book)
Black	Delta	0.0 - 0.5	Asleep	White
Blue	Delta	1.0 - 3.0	Resting	White
Green	Theta	3.5 - 7.5	Alert	Light Grey
Yellow	Alpha 1	8.0 - 14.0	Active	Dark grey
Orange	Alpha 2 / Beta	14.5-18.0	Energized	Black
Red	Beta / Gamma	18.5 - 40	Excited	Black

* Overall behavior and energy level.

Brain regions activate—increase in frequency and amplitude—by how people approach a task. Here are two key points to remember.

Active Regions: Particular regions “light up” on the EEG when we engage in activities that are at least somewhat challenging and motivating for us. As challenge and motivation increase, the amount of activity also increases.

Quiet Regions: These regions are not in use or are handling routine tasks such as signing your name. Also, regions are quiet in the face of hopelessly difficult or boring tasks that we give up on, or perhaps don’t even wish to start.

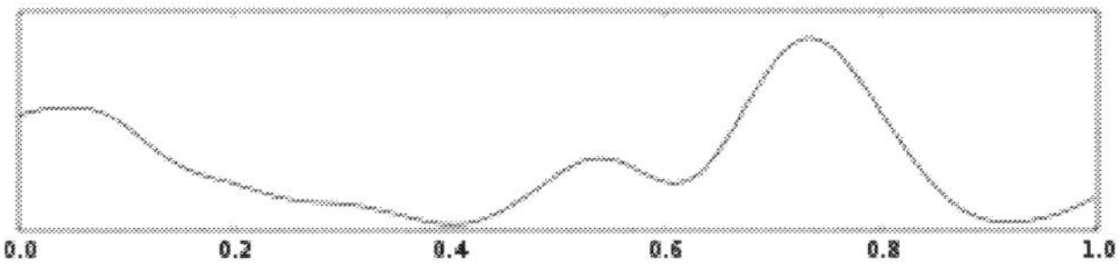

Figure 3-10: Delta Waves: Highly relaxed (1.0 - 3.0 Hertz)

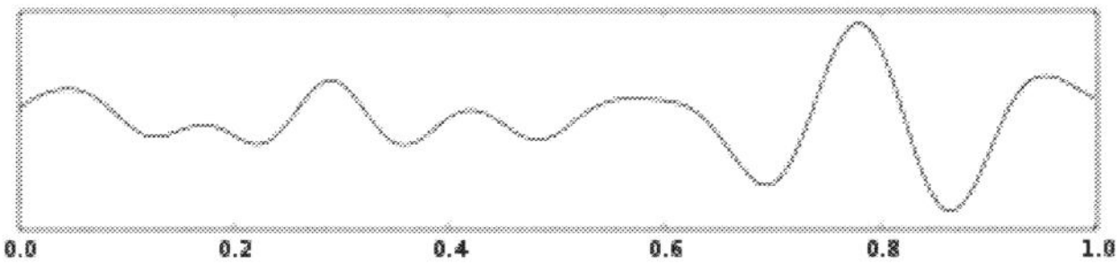

Figure 3-11: Theta Waves: Low intermediate activity (3.5 - 7.5 Hertz)

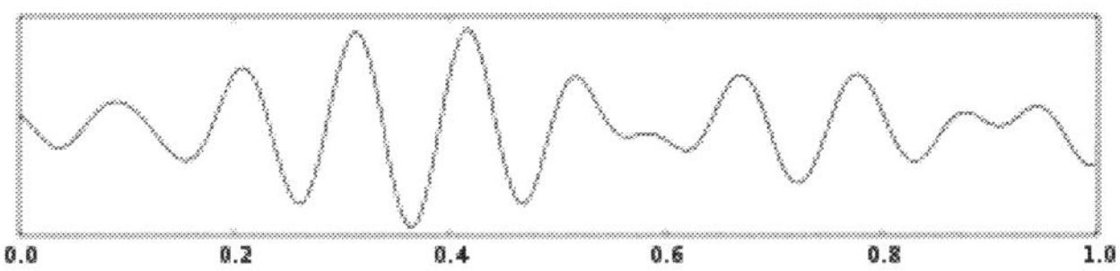

Figure 3-12: Alpha Waves: High intermediate activity (8.0 - 14.0 Hertz)

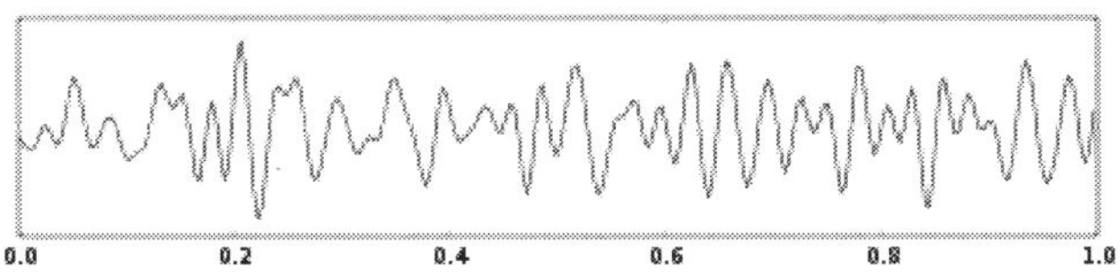

Figure 3-13: Beta Waves: Very active (18.5 - 40 Hertz)

Threshold to Activation

Each region such as T5 or Fp2 has a threshold that varies from person to person. When the amount of stimulus falls below a region's threshold, that region is less active and typically shows delta waves. Conversely, when the amount of stimulus exceeds the threshold, that region is more active and shows theta, alpha, or even beta waves. This is why two people, when pressed with the exact same stimulus, show more or less activity in the same region. For example, persons with a low T5 threshold are highly attentive to social feedback and easily embarrassed, while those with a high T5 threshold will not be unless really pushed.

Table 3-2: Sensory Stimulus Versus Brain Activity

Amount of Stimulus	Person A (low threshold)	Person B (high threshold)
A little	Some activity.	No activity.
A moderate amount	More activity.	No activity.
A lot	A lot of activity!	Sudden activity!

Micro-States Versus Macro-States

EEG typically shows "micro-states": transient patterns that last fractions of a second, or perhaps a second at best. For example, when a person solves a multiplication problem, various regions engage, and even a simple act of "carrying the one" will show itself, though it will typically show too quickly to document. It is truly very unusual for a particular region to remain still at a particular frequency and amplitude while other states keep varying.

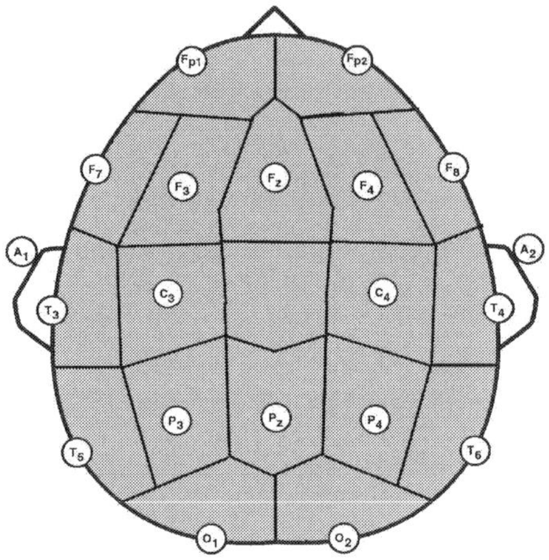

Figure 3-14: A "flow state" when regions are synchronized.

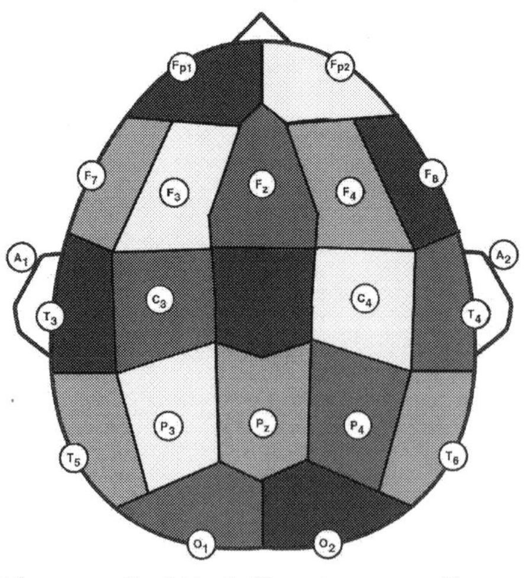

Figure 3-15: A "brainstorm" state when regions are asynchronous.

We can prompt people with activities that engage their interests and really excite their minds. We slip a conductor into a room full of random musicians! When we do, one particular frequency band may easily dominate over all regions of the neocortex for periods of one to two seconds, and sometimes up to two or three minutes. I will refer to this phenomenon as macro states or global states.

During a synchronized macro state, all regions are also at maximum amplitude. This means all regions are engaged to work together or at least get to work in a consistent manner. This is a state of "flow".

Now, what's happening in each macro state? The table at right lists six synchronous states, one for each frequency band; plus two asynchronous states that offer unique benefits. One macro state (orange, at 14.5-18.0 Hz) has yet to present itself more than once or twice, and for no more than a second, offering few clues to its role.

Table 3-2: Macro States

Color Band	Correlations
Synchronous States	
Black	This state presents itself as solid black with near-zero amplitude and indeterminate frequency. It may easily occur when you meditate, watch television, or sleep deeply. Otherwise, this state is unusual.
Blue (Delta)	This state occurs when we are awake and calm. It may easily occur when we busy ourselves with an activity for which we have creative expertise, whatever that expertise is. We might also enter this state when we are copacetic, open to whatever comes next.
Green (Theta)	This is a dissociated state, when we shut out bodily sensations and emotions, promoting an objective third-person experience. It may easily occur when we focus on problem solving, lose a game, don't like someone, or argue using reason.
Yellow (Alpha)	This is an associated state, when we admit and focus on bodily sensations and emotions, promoting a subjective, first-person experience. It may easily occur when we win a game, like someone, or listen to our favorite music with eyes closed.
Orange	Not observed to date.
Red (Beta)	This state occurs when the neocortex is hyper-stimulated. It may easily occur when we learn the rules of a promising new game, attend a festival of lights and sounds, experience an "Ah-ha!" moment of insight, or see someone attractive. The brain may take time to "come down" from this excited state.
Asynchronous States	
Mixed (low) "Tennis hop"	This state looks black but on closer inspection all regions are rapidly varying between color bands at 2-5 Hz. This state may easily occur when we play video games, or are alert but bored, or are waiting to respond to an uncertain outcome.
Mixed (high) "Christmas tree"	All regions are wildly out of synch and each region keeps changing in frequency and varying between mid and high amplitudes. This mode occurs when we engage in transcontextual thinking (see page 98 for details).

Creative Expertise

Among the various global states, a solid bright blue pattern (delta waves) comes to the fore when we do an activity requiring our expertise, whatever that might be. Often, that expertise involves creativity, such as singing or writing. In this state, every region is at high amplitude and in synch. On the outside, the person is calm and relaxed, yet also energized and highly focused. Here are activities that I have observed move a person into a state of flow:

- Acting by following a highly rehearsed scene.
- Describing the ultimate meaning of why people live or die.
- Drumming a familiar beat.
- Handling a dramatic crisis in a role-play scenario.
- Listening intently to someone else, or only to an authority figure, or only to women or men.
- Pointing while talking, or using a finger as a guide while reading.
- Remaining calm in a social situation.
- Reviewing the past.
- Searching for a creative solution to a novel problem.
- Singing a unique song while playing guitar (the person is a professional singer). Singing someone else's song did not evoke flow.
- Tossing a ball back and forth with a partner, or juggling multiple balls.
- Visualizing dancing (the person did ballet for fifteen years).
- Visualizing the future (with desire for accuracy).
- Winning a hand of cards.

Researchers may easily miss patterns like these when experimenting, particularly if they are not focusing on a person's passions. However, I spend ninety minutes or more with every subject—a wide window of opportunity. Moreover, when the usual lab tasks are done, I probe his or her interests, from playing drums to arguing politics. Doing so invites these patterns to appear.

With a pinch of luck, a person may show a global pattern for two or three minutes, unwaveringly. Less frequently, a person remains here up to ten minutes, theoretically longer! Once a flow starts, a person may stop for a while and then re-start; and flow may be selective, such as when listening to a particular person or type of person. Seeing this pattern is a high point on any lab day!

As we'll see in Chapter 7, a person's personality type and area of expertise both strongly influence what evokes this pattern.

Circuit Patterns

You might wonder how the brain's regions interconnect. They link much like a tangled tree or elaborate highway system. There are narrow branches and wide trunks, slow lanes and speedways. Neural activity often dances around the neocortex following a predictable route. The figure below shows one typical route. The route jumps from T3 to P3 to F8 to Fp1. The person:

1. Listens to words spoken by himself or others, then...
2. Integrates visual and kinesthetic data, either to complement the verbal data or to focus his mind (P3 regulates our sense of personal boundaries).
3. Evaluates the inputs in terms of strongly-held personal values.
4. Decides what to do and explains why.

This particular pattern correlates with two personality types (ENTJ and ENFJ) that are both known as quick and decisive with an in-charge style. Not surprisingly, this route affords rapid consideration of data to make decisions. A possible pitfall: the person may perform slowly or poorly when faced with tasks that don't fit the sequence, a known challenge for these two personality types.

Most people show a sequence or route when performing a repetitive task such as solving multiplication problems or sorting objects. These patterns are challenging to track in real time and often resist statistical analysis.

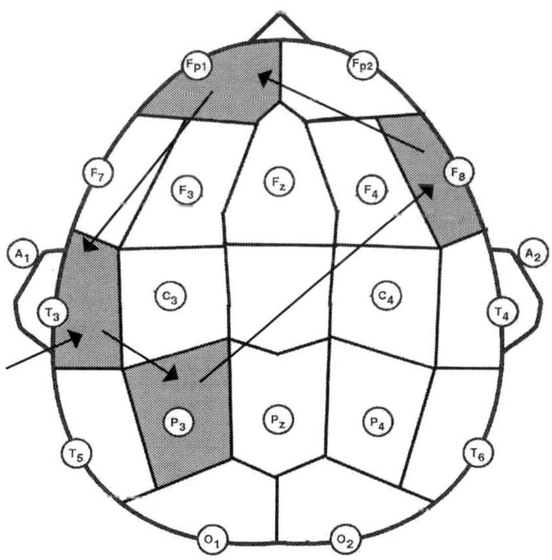

Figure 3-16: A "circuit" of activity involving four distinct regions.

The Engagement Curve

People's brain activity rises when they engage in tasks for which they are competent and motivated.

Engaged = competent + motivated

Specifically, as the graph below illustrates, brain activity increases progressively as motivation and challenge to one's competence increase. However, when a task's difficulty surpasses a person's competence and motivation, brain activity drops, suddenly and drastically, as the person gives up.

A great example is a simple three-part exercise. Please:

1. Sign your name normally.
2. Sign your name backward with your non-preferred hand to earn a prize.
3. Sign your name in the Farvu language.

A commonsense hypothesis says that signing your name with your preferred hand in your native tongue should evoke little activity, while signing backward in another alphabet (or a fake alphabet) with one's non-preferred hand should evoke much more activity.

This hypothesis proves partly false. It addresses competence but not motivation. Low motivation overrides high competence, and vice versa. Moreover, there are many founts of motivation: interest in the task, a desire to please (or not), the weight of serious consequences, and so forth. For example, one lab subject wrote his name backward in Arabic with his non-preferred hand. This task showed no brain activity compared to normal signing. Why? As he said, he knew none of us in the lab could read Arabic, so his penmanship didn't matter. In later chapters, we will explore how motivation links to personality type.

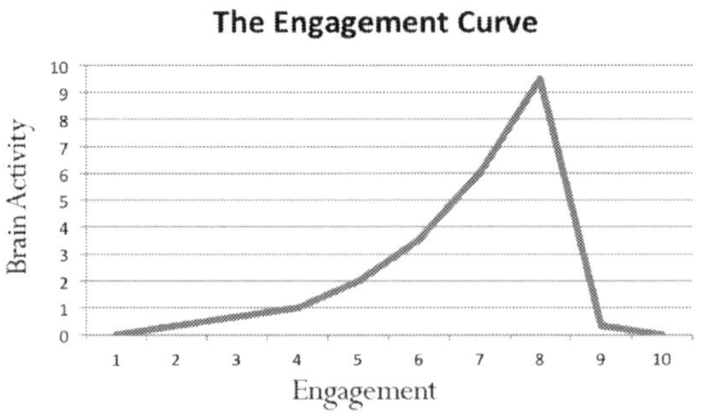

Figure 3-17: More engaging tasks evoke more brain activity, up to a point.

Anatomy of the Triune Brain

Nestled underneath the neocortex are two less conscious and more primitive layers. These layers handle essential functions that often feed upward into the neocortex and back, especially to the prefrontal regions. In ideal circumstances, the neocortex allows us to exert conscious will over the lower layers. However, when we are stressed, signals from those lower layers tend to overwhelm us.

The figure below shows the triune brain: the neocortex on top, the limbic system underneath, and the cerebellum further down by the brain stem. Here are brief descriptions of the lower layers.

Brain Stem and Cerebellum: This ancient structure handles essential functions like breathing and coordinates the brain with the larger nervous system that runs throughout the body. The cerebellum coordinates muscle action and integrates patterns of movement so that appropriate signals are sent to appropriate parts of the body. It ensures good posture, equilibrium while walking, and even execution of memorized routines such as piano finger movements.

Limbic System: This middle layer of the brain includes structures such as the amygdala, hippocampus, and thalamus. You may have heard of these. They regulate numerous functions that are mostly primal and unconscious including:

- Attachment and pair bonding, such as an infant to its mother.
- Body language, including sexual signaling.
- Deeply-seated prejudices and superstitious feelings such as fear of the dark and aversion to toxic-looking substances.
- Encoding of information from short-term memory to long-term memory.
- Instinctual reactions such as the fight or flight response.

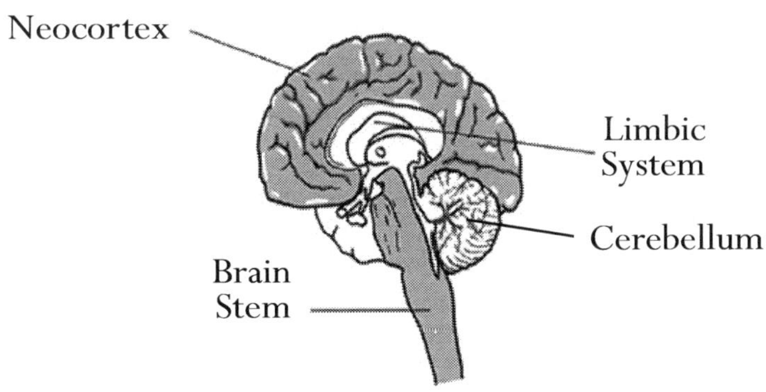

Figure 3-18: A cut-away view of the brain's three layers, seen from the left-side.

• Raw emotional responses such as anger, disgust, and fear.
• Sexuality, including sexual orientation and many gender-specific behaviors and sexual attractions, such as to youthful, symmetrical faces.
• Wakefulness, sleep, dreaming, and other states of consciousness.

Sometimes, the limbic system's hum-drum activities trickle up to the neocortex, such as memory retrieval appearing as brief blips on the EEG monitor in the central regions C3 and C4. But often this does not occur.

Research is still defining the limbic functions and to what extent they may be innate to our species, dependant on one's genes or nine months in the womb, and/or and formed in early childhood. Once "programmed", these functions seem to be fixed for life and can only be overcome though conscious force of will regardless of what learning occurs in the neocortex.

The Neocortex: The neocortex is not a single sheet neatly divided into geographic zones as earlier diagrams in this chapter suggest. Rather, the neocortex consists of six layers (labeled I to VI).

The figure below shows these layers. Neural connections run vertically, linking deeper layers up to the brain's surface. The connections also run horizontally, linking different regions to ensure that the formation and activation of neural patterns is contextually appropriate and not just stimulus-response. We can change our neural wiring as we learn throughout life, though learning most easily occurs before age thirty.

EEG technology detects changes in electrical activity at the very surface, which means the EEG is not showing the activity of specific cognitive functions; rather, it shows the evidence of activity of all six layers beneath a region. This is yet another reason why puzzling out the neocortex is both art and science.

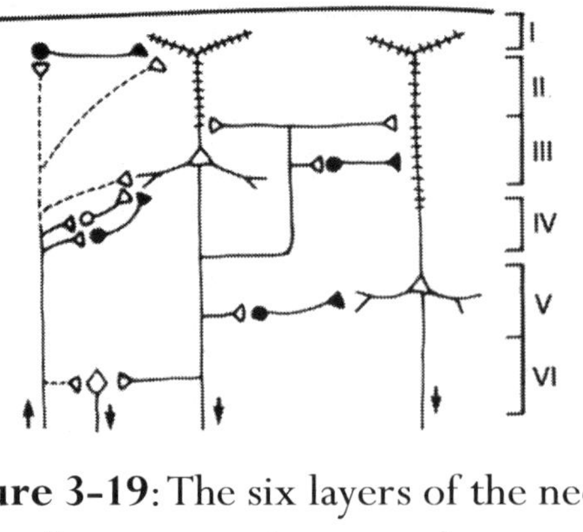

Figure 3-19: The six layers of the neocortex form a complex neural network.

4.
Cognitive Skill-Sets

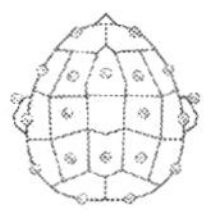

This chapter provides in-depth descriptions of sixteen regions of the neocortex, as shown in the table below. The descriptions are based on 1) what is reported in the brain literature, and also 2) what I have personally observed in my lab.

Table 4-1: Sixteen Neocortex Regions

Region	Skill-Set	Region	Skill-Set
Fp1	Chief Judge	Fp2	Process Manager
F7	Imaginative Mimic	F8	Grounded Believer
F3	Deductive Analyst	F4	Expert Classifier
T3	Precise Speaker	T4	Intuitive Listener
C3	Factual Storekeeper	C4	Flowing Artist
T5	Sensitive Mediator	T6	Purposeful Futurist
P3	Tactical Navigator	P4	Strategic Gamer
O1	Visual Engineer	O2	Abstract Impressionist

The names of the cognitive skill-sets will help you remember and understand how they can be useful to you in daily life. The regions are not personality types! Everybody uses all of the regions, which are workhorses of the mind. For example, region F3 helps us do logical deduction, which anyone might practice. That said, people show more activity in some regions than others. I would not be surprised to learn that people focus on activities and roles—and otherwise organize their lives—around the regions they prefer to use most.

As you read, you will be asked to estimate your aptitude with each skill-set on a scale from minimal (1) to average (3) to exceptional (5).

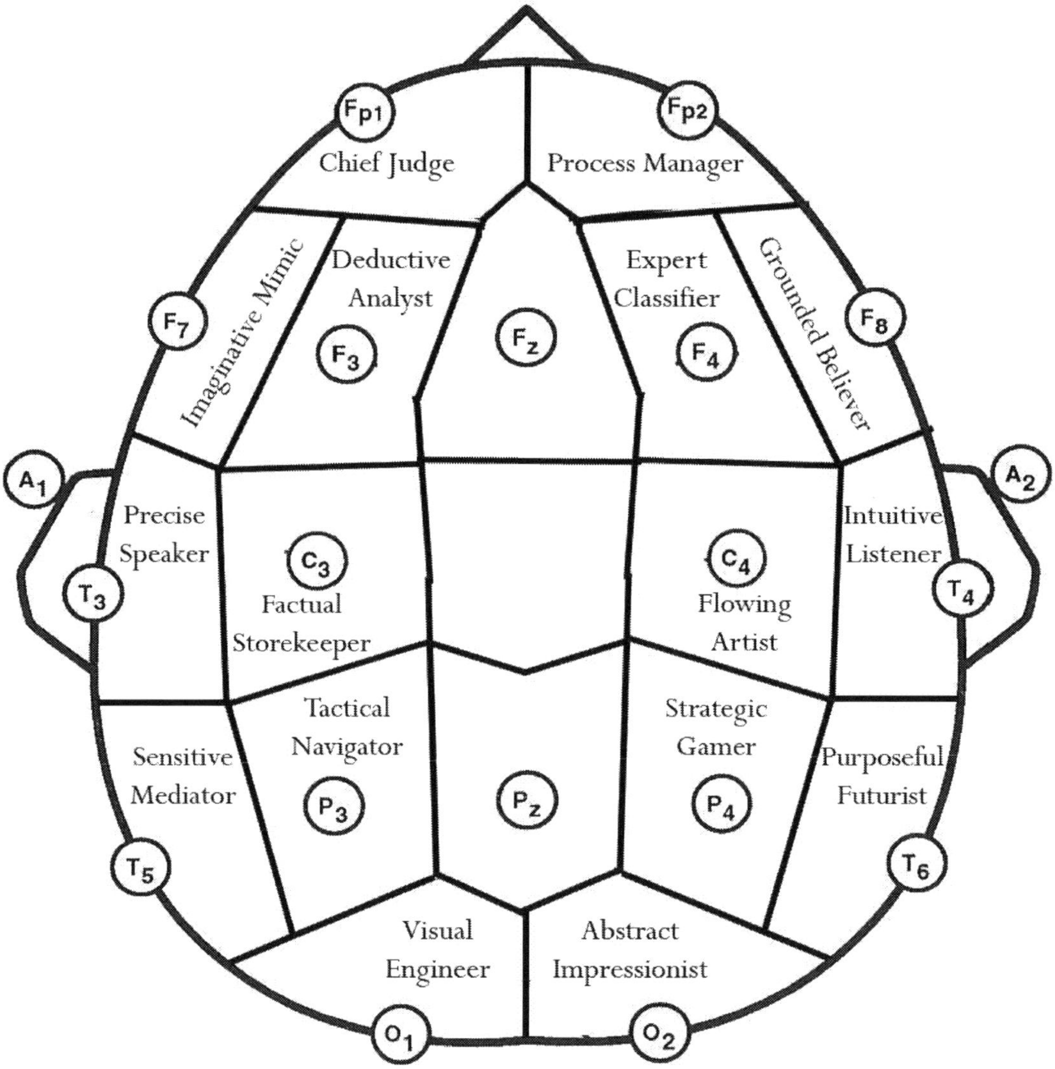

Figure 4-1: Sixteen cognitive skill-sets identified in the neocortex using EEG.

The various regions of the neocortex handle tasks in a similar way for all of us who are right-handed (a lefty's brain map may be the mirror image or have a unique layout). However, people vary greatly in how much stimulus will activate a region. Also know, linguistic or behavioral cues such as a favorite word or head nod often accompany the use of regions that are easily activated.

Region Fp1: The Chief Judge Skill-Set

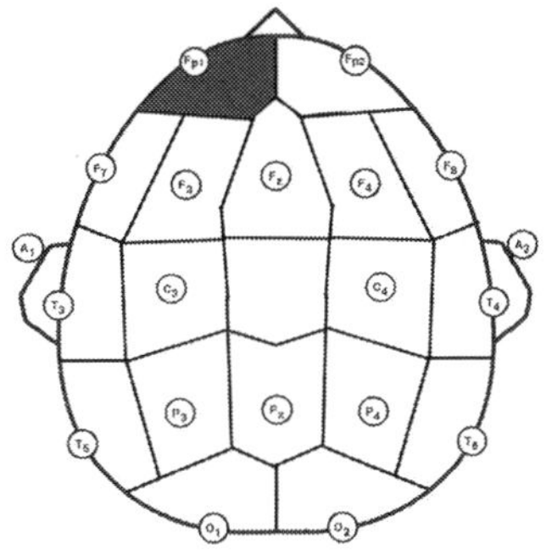

This region sits just above your left eye, behind your forehead, in the left frontal lobe. It is active when you:

- Provide a reason.
- Decide between options.
- Detect an error.

This region is like a high-powered executive, ship's captain, or court judge. It collects and integrates information from all other regions to make and explain decisions. People use this region when they say, "I think this because…" or "I pick that one". It literally lights up just fractions of a second before we speak or act. We may verbalize our reason or decision, or we may keep it to ourselves. Either way, the results come rapidly and with confidence. This region can help us concoct reasons that sound plausible or actions that look doable. It also detects errors and deviations from the norm, signaling when something is not right.

This region activates to help us ignore unwanted ideas that are negative or undesirable so that we stay happy and positive. When we hear criticism, take in violent or depressing content, or are exposed to a disruptive idea, this region may easily come into play, directing our attention elsewhere. In a study by Ginette Blackhart, this region lit up when people decided to skip an introspective task. The task asked them to explore how a sad story they just read applied to their own lives. Conversely, this region was less active for people who introspected. Thus, it seems that happiness comes at the price of willful ignorance!

Statistically, more people use this region than any other. Those who underuse this region may be slow to make decisions, struggle to provide explanations, and/or have difficulty noticing errors or screening out negative input. Also, criticism or unpleasant ideas may easily move them to sadness, anger, or fear.

Using this region may frustrate us sometimes. Using it feels confident and quick, but its actual performance may be poor—a bad choice or illogical explanation—particularly when relying on it to ignore unwanted information.

Your Turn: Estimate your aptitude for this region: 1 2 3 4 5

Region Fp2: The Process Manager Skill-Set

This region sits just above your right eye, behind your forehead, in the right frontal lobe. It is active when you:

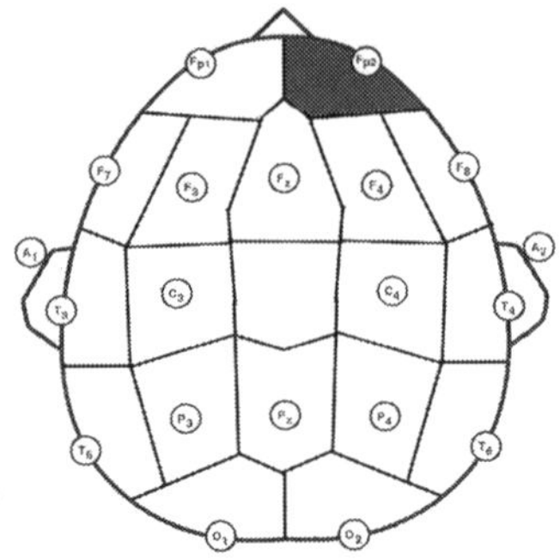

- Notice which step you are on in a task.
- Perceive that you are done brainstorming.
- Consider a new or unpleasant idea.

This region is like an ever-vigilant (but hands-off) facilitator or taskmaster, letting you know when to start, stop, or try again. It gets active when we are exposed to new information and helps us process that information in a productive way. People use this region when they say, "I'm done" or "I can't think of any more ideas". It fires fractions of a second before we note where we are in a process. Broadly, this region helps us track whether we are at the beginning, middle or end of a task. For an open-ended activity like brainstorming or re-living a memory, it suggests stopping points but is flexible. You are welcome to keep exploring. Unlike region Fp1, this region is not very verbal or directive, and it may quietly allow other regions of your brain to do their thing until it is time to move on.

This region helps us explore and deal with information that is counter to what is typical or desirable. When we hear criticism, take in violent or depressing content, or otherwise receive disruptive data, we can use this region to delve into that information, considering its meaning and how it applies to us; simultaneously, it helps regulate our emotions so that we remain calm rather than getting angry. In one study, this region lit up for people who decided to explore how a sad story they read applied to their own lives. This suggests that sadness and depression may be a price we pay for introspective living.

People who under-use this region may be impatient, preferring to focus on decision-making; and they may get side-tracked or erupt with bursts of hostility when called to grapple with odd or unpleasant input.

Using this region may frustrate us sometimes. While using it, we likely are ineloquent. Also, over-using this region may lead us astray as we delve into negatives or endlessly try a task without making decisions.

Your Turn: Estimate your aptitude for this region: 1 2 3 4 5

Region F7: The Imaginative Mimic Skill-Set

This region sits behind that depression on your left temple. It lies in the left frontal lobe. It is a multi-talented and very important region. It is active when we:

- Infer based on context.

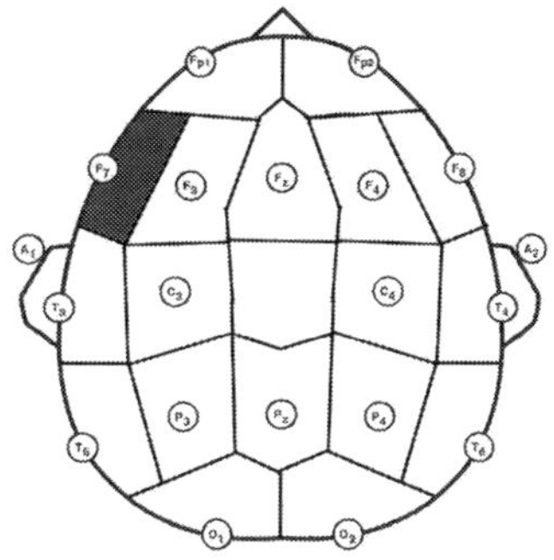

- Imagine another place or time.
- Mirror others' behavior.
- Ask "maybe" or "what-if".
- Mentally play out a situation.

This region is home to "mirror neurons", which are special cells. Using these cells, we can watch a person perform a task or behave in a certain way and then mimic that person to quickly learn the task or act as if we are like him or her. These cells also fire when we imagine doing something but don't actually act. This region acts as our mind's very own Star Trek "holodeck", a place where we can play out real and fanciful events.

Here's how it works: We select a context, which might be the immediate situation before us, a future event such as an upcoming test or race, or a historical or imaginative context such as a childhood birthday party or ancient Rome. Then we play out the simulation, perhaps asking "what if?" This region does its best to supply details and simulate what would likely happen. Thus, we can use this region to make sensible guesses. Consider the words "car", "road", and "flat tire". Now imagine a larger scene, or several scenes. Perhaps an accident occurred. Who or what else is in the scene? How do people feel (don't reason the answer, just play as-if)? This region can also supply you with additional words that fit the implied context, such as "traffic", "ambulance", or "rain".

This region is not analytical, though we may feel like we are analyzing as we explore a myriad of scenarios. Simply, it helps us make smart guesses based on context and imitation. People who use this region with skill are able to quickly build rapport with others and make insightful guesses about people without having any particular reason or theory in mind. Their mental simulations simply "reveal" what they need to know.

People who under-use this region may display a lack of empathy, find it hard to learn by imitation or inference, puzzle over others' motives, dislike what-if questions and brainstorming, and/or feel challenged to think "outside the box".

Using this region may frustrate us sometimes. Using it can be fun and provide ideas for why people act as they do. However, our inferences may be wrong. Moreover, while this region provides an appearance of empathy and rapport, the act of mirroring others does not mean we truly care.

Your Turn: Estimate your aptitude for this region: 1 2 3 4 5

Region F8: The Grounded Believer Skill-Set

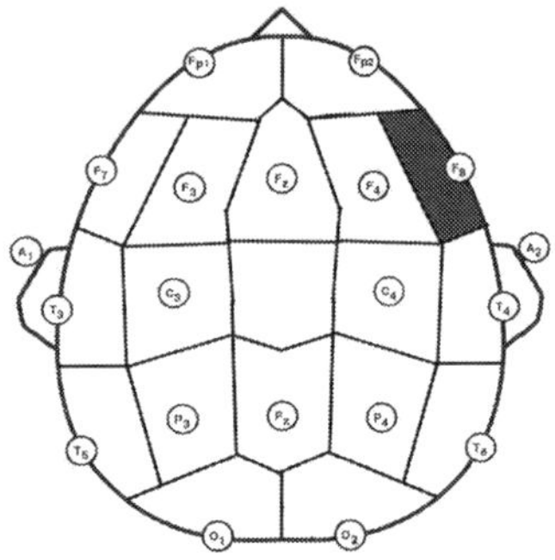

This region sits behind that depression on your right temple. It lies in the right frontal lobe. It is home to several different functions. It is active when we:

- Recall exact, literal details.
- Say a word or phrase with strong emphasis.
- Identify what we believe.
- Rate how much we like or dislike something.
- Ignore context.

This region gets active when you say what's important to you in life. A musician, when talking about music, might slightly *emphasize* words like "guitar" or "my song". Similarly, consider friends and relatives. Say their names and what you like or respect (or not) about them. Who do you like more? Or consider, what are your values? Can you name them? Everyone has words or phrases that predictably light up this region. The actual words vary by individual. Knowing these could provide great insight into the people and events that have likely shaped a person. By the way, people tend to show more activity here when mentioning the parent of the same sex regardless of how pleased they are with that parent. Also, for some people, this region is really active when they focus on what they dislike or don't believe, rather than what they like or believe!

This region guides our speech and behavior to fit what we have grown to identify as important and worth believing in, including religious convictions, personal values, and loved-ones. This region also helps us recall literal details. You may wonder how beliefs and details relate. Consider, this region lies opposite region F7. Just as F7 allows us to think contextually, this region ignores context. When someone or something is truly important and worth believing in, then that importance transcends context. Most of us have had the experience of easily and accurately recalling what we care about! Baseball fans easily recall reams of baseball data, for example. So in general, while some people may have a head for details and yet lack ideological conviction, or vice versa, there is a natural link between what we recall in detail and what we set as always valuable. The box on the next page about autism goes into more detail about this link.

People who under-use this region may have difficulty accurately recalling details, or they may lack grounding in a lasting identity of solid attitudes and beliefs. To them, everything is contextual and therefore relative. They may value

Autism and Regions F7 and F8

Interestingly, autistic persons tend to show low activity in region F7 and high activity in region F8. They find it hard to mirror or learn from others socially, and they often find it challenging to make inferences. For example, if asked what word might go with "lake" and "woods", they might say "dolphin" instead of "cabin" or "fishing" like most people would. Yet autistic persons also tend to recall minor details with high precision. If shown a photograph of a lake in the woods, they more accurately recall the photograph's details compared to the average person. Most people tend to recall details poorly because they guess-timate details according to context, relying on what they imagine "should be there" rather than relying on what was literally there. For autistic persons, this penchant for detail does not translate into exceptional ideological convictions, suggesting that beliefs and details are close neighbors, sharing a duplex building so-to-speak, rather than living together.

the act of holding values more than attending to the details of those values.

Using this region may frustrate us sometimes. It can lead us astray when we focus on beliefs over evidence, or focus too much on details over a big picture.

Your Turn: Estimate your aptitude for this region: 1 2 3 4 5

Region F3: The Deductive Analyst Skill-Set

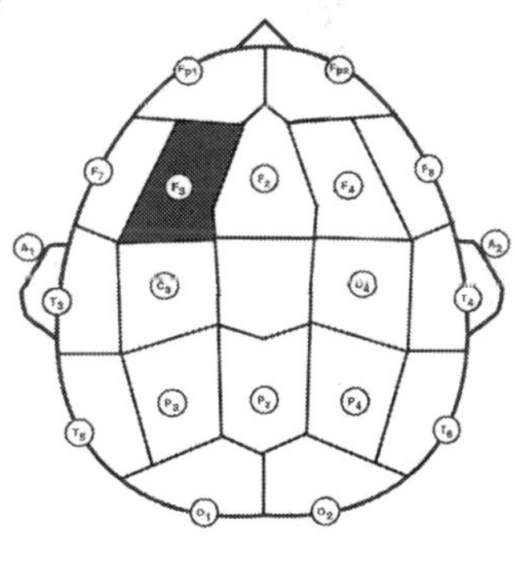

This region sits between your forehead and the top of your head, on your left side. It lies in the frontal lobe. Coincidentally, it's the spot where right-handed people often scratch their head when trying to think! It is active when you:

- Make logical deductions.
- Backtrack or otherwise correct your thinking due to a reasoning error.
- Follow a chain of reasoning.

We can use this region to make a series of logical deductions. For example, "If A equals B, and B equals C, then A equals C." That said, this region is a lot more complex than a simple syllogism suggests. Using this region is like climbing around a tree of many branches. We start at the trunk, and each logical deduction carries us along a branch to a new spot on another branch, until we reach the last branch and hopefully deduce an accurate conclusion. When we use this region, the deductive process generates conclusions for us, whether we like them or not. Often we will need to backtrack to go in a more accurate direction. This region also sits by key brain sites for speaking, making it very verbal, though we don't need to speak out loud to use it. Simply, use requires that we think in words or symbols (math, etc.) in a linear way and keep checking our logic at each step. Thus, this region requires more work than many people are trained for. In psychological experiments, people often say they are "logical" without fully appreciating what's required. Using F3, we don't just make-up reasons as we might using region Fp1. Truly, we deduce them.

People who under-use this region may falter at deductive reasoning. A majority of people show less activity here than in other regions, suggesting that under-use is common. Moreover, regions like Fp1 and T3 can easily provide an illusion of sound thinking and accurate speech. Thus, a deficit may not show up in daily life unless the person works in a discipline that relies on deduction.

Using this region may frustrate us sometimes. Accurate logical deduction takes work and patience for backtracking and self-correcting. Moreover, even when the reasoning is sound, a thought that is logical won't necessarily match empirical evidence.

Your Turn: Estimate your aptitude for this region: 1 2 3 4 5

Region F4: The Expert Classifier Skill-Set

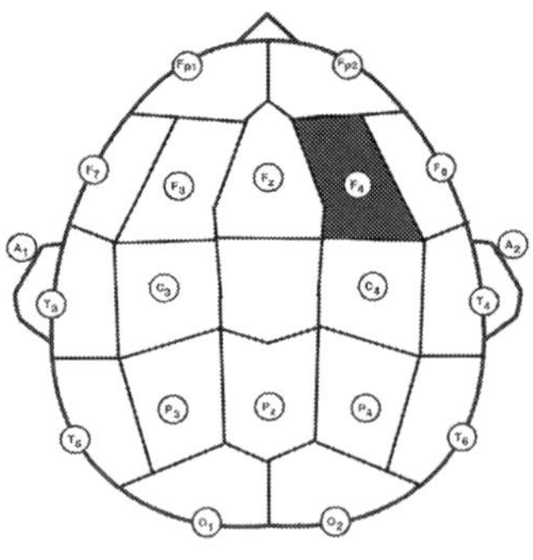

This region sits between your forehead and the top of your head, on your right side. It lies in the frontal lobe. It is active when you:

- Categorize a person, place, thing, event or idea.
- Have a sense for how well a concept (e.g. dog, traffic, justice) fits a particular category.
- Link two concepts together.

We use this region to classify and define concepts, which include just about anything and everything. For example, is a dolphin a fish or a mammal? Is a particular cell specimen cancerous or benign? Or is your new colleague a competitor or an ally, according to some definition of these terms? To understand this region, imagine a wall of mailboxes for an apartment building. Each box is assigned to someone. You can use this region to place various arriving letters into the correct boxes or notice when a letter is in the wrong box. This region isn't eloquent like region F3. It doesn't get involved in grammar or crafting sentences, yet it knows labels such as "marine mammals" very well.

This region is also holistic. A concept comes in and this region evaluates it against all possible categories. Also, it often has a spatial or visceral quality, such that when we categorize something incorrectly, we may feel uncomfortable, like trying to force a square peg into a round hole. This region requires time to develop skillful use. Having coherent categories is a sign of expertise.

People who under-use this region may find it difficult to accurately categorize and define concepts, which can pose a challenge in any discipline that requires expertise. For example, a doctor must be able to correctly diagnose conditions to prescribe the right treatment or she may cause more harm than good. Like region F3, a majority of people do not utilize this region as much as other regions. When we do not learn clever categories for concepts, then we may say a dolphin is a fish because we are missing, or have mis-labeled, our "mailboxes". To use a metaphor, a mailbox may be spacious enough to house a guppy, but doing so is a cruel mistake!

Using this region may frustrate us sometimes. Firstly, it takes training or years of experience to build up an accurate landscape of categories. Also, using this region can get us into trouble when we stray beyond our expertise and apply categories to subjects with which we are unfamiliar.

Your Turn: Estimate your aptitude for this region: 1 2 3 4 5

Region T3: The Precise Speaker Skill-Set

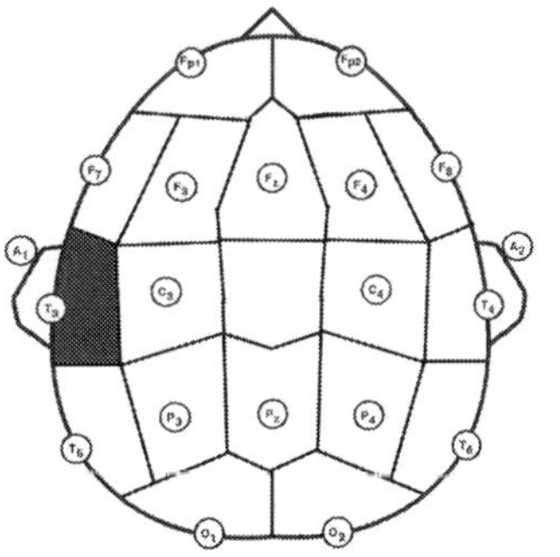

This region sits around your left ear in the left temporal lobe. It is active when you:

- Speak words.
- Compose complex sentences.
- Attend to proper grammar and word usage.
- Listen to other people's words.

This region handles words, both your words and those spoken by others. It lies next to and feeds into key brain areas that process spoken language. It concerns itself with proper word choice, grammar and usage, and other technical elements of language. When you use this region to listen to people, you listen for how they use their words and focus on content in general. Consider the difference between, "he visited the house" and "he stayed at her house". There is a slight but critical distinction between the words "visited" and "stayed"; moreover, the choice of "the" over "her" is a minor change of meaning. This region does not handle tone of voice or other aesthetic qualities of language.

We use this region to handle any tasks we've learned to do by speaking. For example, if you were taught to do mathematics by saying numbers to yourself, then you are likely using this region to do math! A big challenge: this region handles both listening and speaking. Thus, if you tend to talk to yourself in order to think (solve math problems, etc.), then you will likely find a noisy environment seriously distracts your thought process. When this happens, you may find that you cannot think clearly and interact with others at the same time.

Although the spoken word feels essential to human activity, some people do not use this region much. They don't talk to themselves. They may think in symbols or pictures or even sensations. Similarly, when someone else starts talking, they may quickly tune out unless they judge the content as highly relevant.

Using the region can frustrate us sometimes. The ability to use words in a precise way is not related to thinking logically. Though some reasoning regions like F3 are close by, others like F4 and P4 are far away and mostly nonverbal. Fine speech can provide an illusion of reason. Also, we may get caught up in selecting just the right grammar or split hairs about the meanings of sentences.

Your Turn: Estimate your aptitude for this region: 1 2 3 4 5

Region T4: The Intuitive Listener Skill-Set

This region sits around your right ear in the right temporal lobe. It is active when you:

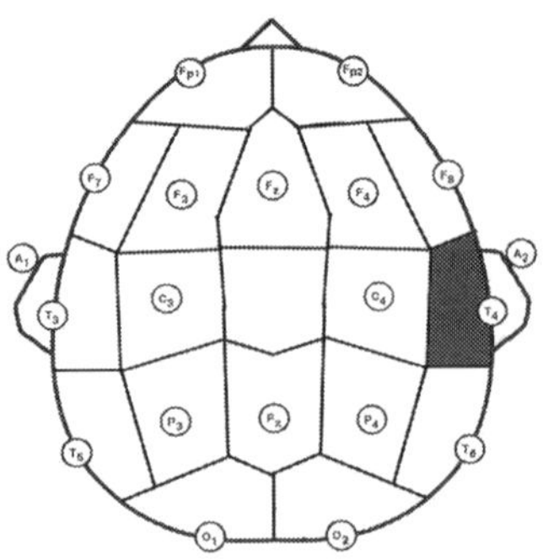

- Notice someone's tone of voice.
- Hear when something "resonates" or "speaks" to you personally.
- Feel someone is speaking in a phony or false way but cannot say why.
- Speak with powerful affect.

This region handles tone of voice and other affective qualities of sound and voice. It lies next to regions that handle personal identity, belief, and aesthetic sensibilities—all phenomena that are often hard to articulate yet easily conveyed through affect, particularly one's tone. When we use this region, we mostly focus on how something is said rather than the specific words used, though this region does respond to specific words that resonate with our beliefs and identity. This region would likely light up when a musician hears the word "music" because of the word's importance to that person.

This region is more critical for social interaction and language than some folks might imagine. For example, someone might say, "I love you" with genuinely deep affection, or with off-handed sarcasm, or in a perfunctory robotic way. Similarly, consider how shallow or misleading e-mail can be. Though e-mail can communicate many words, people tend to resort to brief asides or emoticons such as a smiley face or winking face in order to convey the tone of what's said. Without those cues, we may easily misinterpret what others say.

Accounting for others' intentions shows here. We can focus on someone's motivations, such as noting that a criminal suspect is guilty of bad intent even through he was caught and ultimately failed to get away with his crime.

This region holds a dark secret. It is home to irritation and hostility. This region becomes active when people get annoyed or outright angry and cannot subdue their anger, particularly when they hear an offending word. Normally, we rely on regions Fp1 and Fp2 to help us manage our emotions, where Fp1 provides happiness (but we remain ignorant) and Fp2 provides sadness (if we take time to introspect). When neither of these regions is working for us, the result is anger when criticized.

People who under-use this region tend to miss voice tone, both out of their own mouths and from others. They likely rely on analyzing word content and thus think they understand what is said, but may miss key information such as how the speaker feels about them, or whether a statement was a joke or for real. The person may also use a monotone voice, dispiriting or confusing his listeners.

This region can sometimes frustrate us when we respond intuitively to words, but the content of the words is misleading or factually wrong. We might be led to believe what someone says just because it "sounds good" or has been carefully framed to speak to our values.

Your Turn: Estimate your aptitude for this region: 1 2 3 4 5

Region C3: The Factual Storekeeper Skill-Set

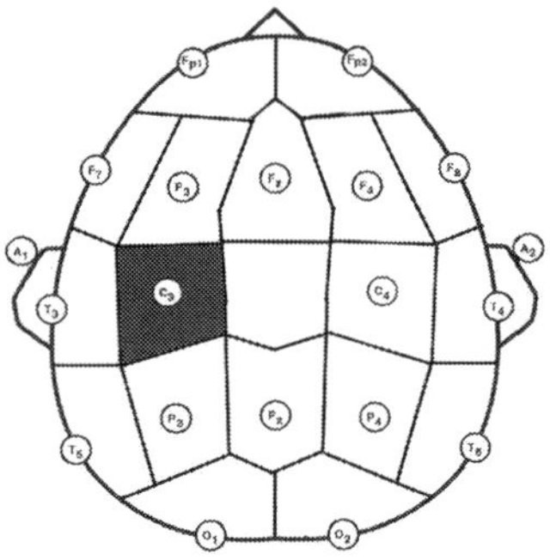

This region lies near the top of your head, on your left side. It lies in the somatosensory region of the left parietal lobe. It is active when you:

- Remember a fact.
- Retrieve a memory that contains specific information such as a date or time.
- Recall a sequence of action steps.
- Prepare to move your body's right side, such as to move your right hand.
- Skillfully draw charts, tables and diagrams.
- Attend to sensations on or within the right side of your body.

This region handles sensations and motor movement of the body's right side. Sensation includes both touch and internal sensations (called proprioception) such as pain or hunger. Strenuous activities, such as manual labor and dancing, and some sedentary activities such as sewing or drawing, engage this region. Sadly, a lab environment offers few opportunities to move around. Multiple studies confirm that this region is organized using a homunculus. That is, neurons are laid out in a way that mimics the actual bipedal layout of the body, with neurons handling the face, neck, chest, arms, hands, torso, legs, feet and so on.

This region may also activate when you retrieve factual memories like birth dates and textbook knowledge that can be discussed such as what year Columbus first arrived in the Americas. If I were to ask you to name various American presidents or recall how many windows are on the front of your house, there is a good chance this region will briefly reflect the fetching of data from your "memory storekeeper", which is a region called the hippocampus that lies deep down in the brain rather than in the neocortex.

It is important to know that this memory works "batch" style. Imagine two ways to watch a movie clip on the Internet. Either you completely download the clip and then watch it, or you stream it in, watching it as it downloads. The former is called "batch" and that's how the brain works. When you wish to recall a memory, this region retrieves the whole memory for you, or at least a sizable chunk. This retrieval occurs in a jiffy! Then this region goes quiet as you use the memory. Similarly, with regard to motion, the act of moving does not, in and of itself, activate this region. Instead, this region prepares you for such movement, especially if you require precision or are trying a new move. For example, if you have never juggled a ball or shuffled a deck of cards before, then this region will briefly activate fractions of a second before you do so.

Although deep areas of the brain handle much of memory and motion, this region gets involved. Often, memory and motion are more closely linked than many people realize, particularly when we need to recall facts related to body motion such as dance steps. Reflect on how you pose your body when you learn something. Do you find that sitting, with pencil in hand, suddenly releases some facts that weren't so available when you were standing? Thus, how we pose our body when we learn affects how we best recall facts.

People who under-use this region tend to easily forget or confuse facts. Some may have difficulty using the right side of their body and may show poor hand-eye or hand-foot coordination, such as difficulty executing dance steps.

Sometimes this region can frustrate us when we find we cannot recall information with the speed or accuracy that we may like.

Your Turn: Estimate your aptitude for this region: 1 2 3 4 5

Region C4: The Flowing Artist Skill-Set

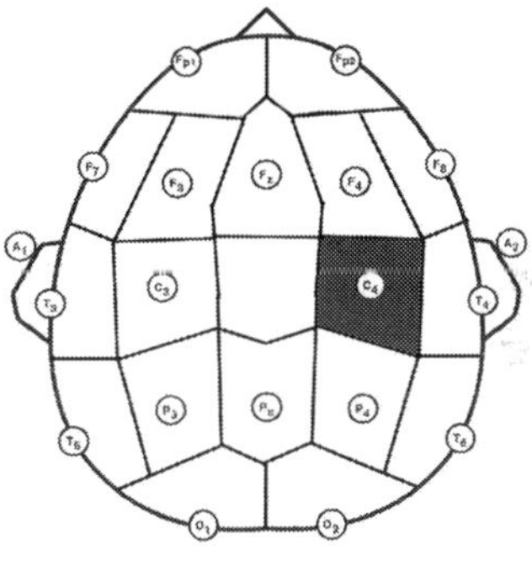

This region lies near the top of your head, on your right side. It lies in the somatosensory region of the right parietal lobe. It is active when you:

- Remember a beautiful place.
- Retrieve a memory based on aesthetic qualities.
- Recall whole-body affect.
- Prepare to move your body's left side, such as to move your left hand.
- Skillfully draw realistic, free-hand illustrations.
- Attend to sensations on or within the left side of your body.

In most ways, this region is the mirror image of region C3. It attends to the left side of your body rather than your right side. It is also organized like a little homunculus, with neurons neatly laid out from head to toe, with more neurons devoted to the more sensitive regions of the body. Like C3, it gets involved when you access memories. That said, this region lies in the right hemisphere and is more holistic. If region C3 becomes active when we recall factual data like someone's birthday, then C4 becomes active when we recall the most beautiful place we have ever visited. The word "beautiful" is a lot less precise than a calendar date! Fortunately, region F4 is next door and ready to check whether a memory falls into the beautiful category.

This region is also home to fluid body motion and affect, which is no surprise since region T4, which handles tone of voice, is also next door. Imagine dancing to rock music by improvising moves rather than following steps. When done well, the improvised moves are in synch with the rhythm of the music and not predictable. This region helps the dancer maintain an elegant, entertaining style. Generally this region also gets active when we need to use both sides of our body rather than our preferred side. For example, playing a piano usually requires two hands, each coordinating but doing its own moves. One of the clearest ways that this region gets active is when we draw, whether we do precision drawing for realism or more abstract drawing for cartoons and such.

People who under-use this region often show poor artistic skill and perhaps lack smooth body motion. After primary school, education tends to steer people away from these skills; and when these skills are not highly valued in a society, an adult may not miss much. Lab experiments demonstrate that small harmless electrical bursts to the left hemisphere can suddenly allow regions in the right hemisphere such as this one to become more active; people suddenly gain (or re-gain) artistic ability for several hours until the effect ends. This suggests that many of us may have more access to this region than we realize.

This region is entirely nonverbal and thus can be tricky to identify or express what is occurring under its watch, which may frustrate us at times.

Your Turn: Estimate your aptitude for this region: 1 2 3 4 5

Region T5: The Sensitive Mediator Skill-Set

This region lies a few inches behind your left ear, but not yet to the back of your head. It lies in the left posterior temporal lobe. It is active when you:

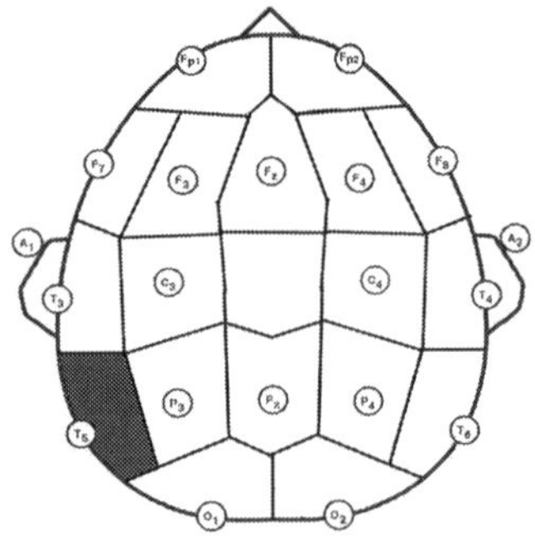

- Notice others' input about your social behavior.
- Are curious what someone thinks of you.
- Adjust your behavior in order to appease or conform to others' expectations.
- Feel embarrassed.

Like region T7, this region contains "mirror

neurons", clusters of special cells that help us imagine what others are up to and respond to their input appropriately. If F7 is about mimicking or imagining people's physical actions, this region focuses on social behavior.

When we use this region, we focus on others' judgments regarding the appropriateness of our behavior. When someone scowls at you, shows you a pleasant smile, utters a reprimand or compliment, or otherwise provides you with feedback, you can respond in several ways. First, you might simply note the person's feedback and choose to ignore it. But more likely, using this region, you adjust your behavior to get more positive feedback or to change the negative feedback into a positive. This region actively encourages us to change our behavior by supplying us with feelings of embarrassment and possibly shame. We might also blush or feel flustered. Calling attention to blushing or other reaction promotes this region's activity even more, in a spiral of ever-greater self-consciousness and embarrassment. This region is not just about pleasing people we care about; it attends to strangers' expectations and input. Thus, using this region tends to assure pleasant social relations, perhaps at the expense of one's own needs and desires. People who use this region a lot tend to be highly sensitive to others and easily insulted or elated.

This region can activate when we know we are being watched but haven't yet received feedback and wonder what others are thinking. For some people, this region is most active when they wonder like this; activity then stops once they receive the actual feedback. They are attentive to what is not said and are unlikely to adjust their behavior to social expectations.

Studies suggest this region helps men but not women to distinguish other people's faces in analytical way. Women rely more on region T6 instead.

People with low activity in this region tend to either not notice others' feedback or simply choose to not respond. That said, few people are entirely immune to social feedback; and when this region does come into play for them, its output may be so profuse that it spills over into neighboring regions. One neighbor is region P3, which facilitates one's sense of self. A person who is normally an "independent free thinker" may suddenly find herself blushing, highly self-conscious, and perhaps somewhat uncoordinated.

Sometimes this region can frustrate us. It is challenging to "just ignore" input when this region is encouraging us to conform.

Your Turn: Estimate your aptitude for this region: 1 2 3 4 5

Region T6: The Purposeful Futurist Skill-Set

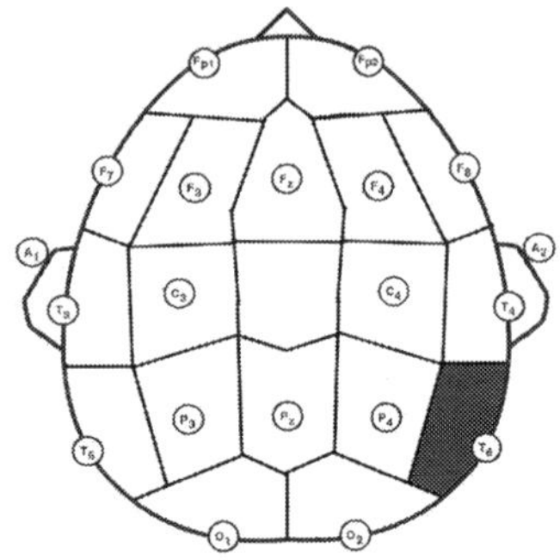

This region lies a few inches behind your right ear, but not yet to the back of your head. It lies in your right posterior temporal lobe. It is active when you:

- Say the word "will"; as in, what will occur in the future.
- Imagine yourself within a complex system.
- Notice abstract spatial-structural relationships.
- Assign a symbolic meaning.
- Envision your future.

This region lies next to region P4 and is diametrically opposite region F7. It is similar to both these regions but is highly future-oriented and relational. It activates when we pick a location, time or system and insert ourselves into it. For example, this region lets you know what "will" occur at your workplace tomorrow. Unlike region F7, this skill-set is not about acting "as-if" or dreaming up a fantasy. Nor is it about planning an outcome. Instead, it aids us seriously, offering predictions that will likely occur in actuality. Saying "I will..." really encourages activity in this region to foresee our future.

This region is holistic as it notices and weighs many abstract spatial relationships at once. Imagine exploring an architectual model of a city with its many parts, layers, and details. Then focus on the spatial arrangements of the buildings to find patterns. Now, instead of a city, consider a model of the psyche or an organization or culture. This region is nonverbal and cannot, by itself, explain insights and predictions. Its offerings thus seem obvious or mysterious.

This region also gets active when we consider symbolic meanings, such as what an icon, photo, musical score, or piece of clothing symbolizes. It's unclear how this fits with the future-oriented quality of this region, though symbols are a great way to holistically represent complex situations when we lack words and analytics to explain ourselves.

Studies suggests this region helps women but not men to distinguish other people's faces in a holistic way. Men rely more on region T5 instead.

People who under-use this region may be surprised by how their lives unfold. They fail to predict and deal with future events. Under-use also shows up when people confuse what *will* happen with what they hope to happen.

Using this region can be frustrating sometimes. It is mostly nonverbal and lies next to region O2, which handles abstract visual impressions. Thus, using this region may evoke only symbols, vague visual glimpses, and a few words. Also, though it focuses on foreseeing the "right" future, it can assure nothing.

Your Turn: Estimate your aptitude for this region: 1 2 3 4 5

Region P3: The Tactical Navigator Skill-Set

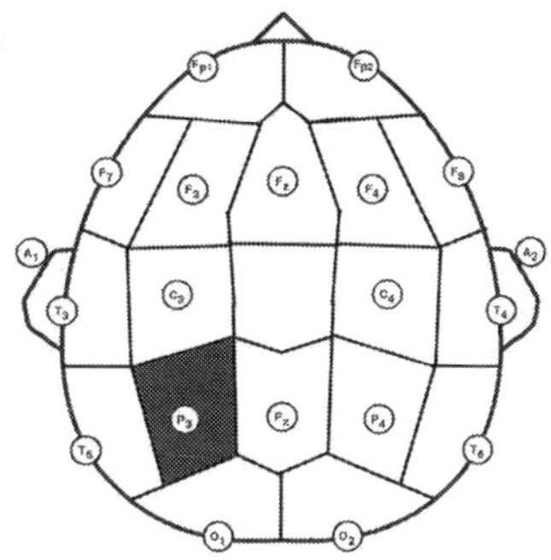

This region lies between the middle and back of your head, on your left side. It lies in the left parietal lobe. It is active when you:

- Identify tangible objects.
- Use physical and visual cues to move your body.
- Attend to where you end and the rest of the world begins.
- Work a problem using rote memorization.

This region is the seat of the physical sense of self in the environment. Specifically, it really helps us integrate visual and kinesthetic cues to guide how we move our bodies. When there is a lot of activity in this region, we experience the world as a giant grid of space in which we can see and act. It's a wonderful resource for physical activities that require tactical moves. For example, a basketball player must track himself, teammates and opponents, the ball, guidelines on the floor, distance to the net, and so forth. The better this region works, the faster we integrate a multitude of visual and kinesthetic inputs in order to act with rapid precision. The act of tossing a basketball into the net while opponents are moving at the same time is perhaps a high point when using this region. Unfortunately, EEG does not yet allow us to watch people's brains as they play sports, so this is speculative. Perhaps in the future! Where I do see similar results is when subjects use a finger to guide their reading in order to focus themselves; or to solve math problems by navigating a mental grid, such as moving through a times table. In fact, studies associate this region with skillful math performance.

Beyond sports, this region defines for us where we end and the rest of the world begins. Experiments show that professional meditators are able to decrease activity in this region and shift activity to other, frontal brain regions. This may explain ecstatic feelings of "losing one's sense of self" and "merging with the universe" during meditation.

This region helps us identify objects. It may get active when we handle mystery objects while blindfolded or view oddball images like orange-colored apples.

People who under-use this region may be somewhat clumsy or unaware of where they are and how their motion affects others. They may have poor aim or balance, or poor ability to predict the trajectories of objects around them. Some may even inappropriately intrude in other people's physical space.

Using this region may frustrate us sometimes. People who over-rely on this region may feel highly self-protective, with a strong boundary or defensive stance between themselves and others.

Your Turn: Estimate your aptitude for this region: 1 2 3 4 5

Region P4: The Strategic Gamer Skill-Set

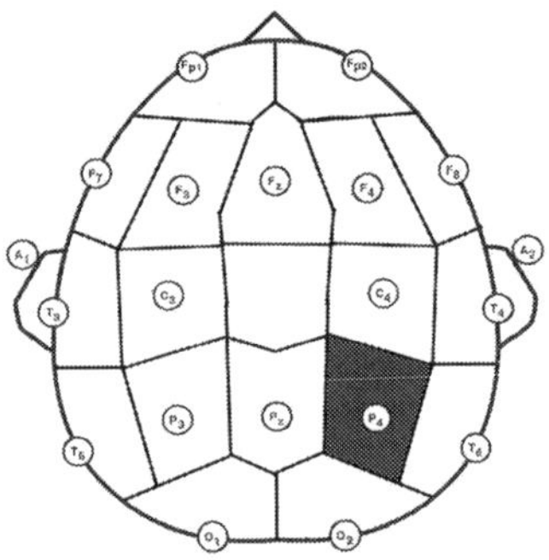

This region lies between the middle and back of your head, on your right side. It lies in the right parietal lobe. It is active when you:

- Weigh numerous pros and cons.
- Calculate and compare various risks versus their likely rewards.
- Objectively evaluate many factors at once.
- Locate and apply leverage (influence).

This region helps us grapple highly complex problems in a comprehensive, strategic way that simultaneously considers numerous risks, uncertainties, rewards, and outcomes. For example, if you are in mixed company and are wondering whether to tell a particular joke, you might use this region to quickly assess whether the overall impact will be good or ill in light of your audience's probable values, how much people have likely had to drink, any likely repercussions that might occur, the apparent demeanor of your host, and so forth. Notice how much uncertainty is embedded in this situation! Little, if anything, is taken as precise or absolute. Instead, it helps us weigh many pros and cons at once to arrive at intuitive solutions.

Economists often study this region. In experiments, they ask people to solve economics problems. Maybe a card game offers a 25% chance to win \$10 or a 75% chance to lose \$3. Set aside personal circumstances such as whether \$10 means much; do you consider this a sporting game to play? When testing people who are trained to answer these questions, this region activates. It appears to be responsible for weighing odds, risks, and uncertainties in an intuitive holistic way. This region may also aid us to solve a system of equations—a collection of two or more mathematical expressions that share variables—in a simultaneous way. It is no surprise that, as with region P3, studies associate this region with skillful math performance.

Besides helping us strategize game scenarios and math problems, this region helps inform us where leverage points may lie to steer those games closer to our benefit. For example, we might seek to change the odds above more in our favor, with a 30% chance to win $10 or a 70% chance to lose $3. This region considers nudging and gut intuitions as well as the numbers. Like region F4, it has a spatial quality and may make "calculations" based on the relative weight of different options. As a metaphor, each factor is like a planet with a gravitational pull, with some factors having far more pull than others. We can evaluate the sum of pulls from all directions to arrive at an average or best fit.

Like regions F3, F4 and P3, a majority of people do not utilize this region as much as they could. For example, because most people are not savvy with economics, they tend to use other regions. When presented with a gambling scenario, a person might wonder how a casino owner would answer, invoking region F7, rather than solving the question strategically.

Using this region can frustrate us sometimes, because not every activity in life is nicely resolved as a game of chance.

Your Turn: Estimate your aptitude for this region: 1 2 3 4 5

Region O1: The Visual Engineer Skill-Set

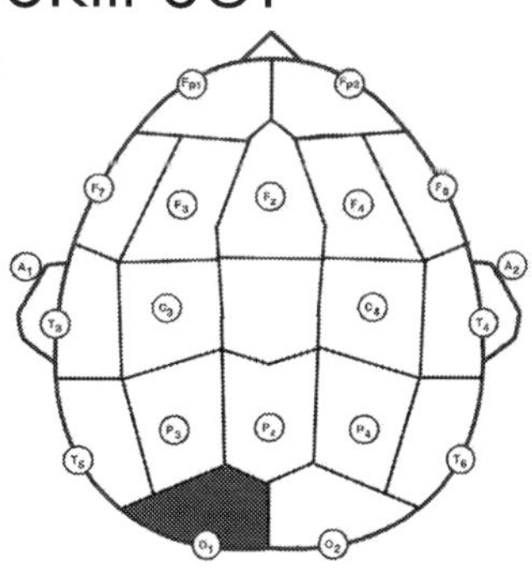

This region lies at the back of your head on your left side. It lies in your left occipital lobe. It is active when you:

- Read a chart or diagram.
- Visually disassemble an object to visualize its components and how it works.
- Visualize how elements of an object will fit together to form a structure.
- Mentally rotate an object in your mind's eye.

People are highly visual. Consider what a camera registers: the impact of light on film, or a film-equivalent. That's it. A camera cannot discern where one object ends and another begins because it does not know about depth, changes in lighting, distance, and so forth. Imagine a kitchen floor of black and white tiles. The camera doesn't know whether the black tiles are holes, black boxes on the floor, or what. It can't even consider these options. Our common sense notions of vision are so potent, it is hard to imagine not being able to see!

When we really use this region, we go beyond its usual gifts. People who rely on this region are natural engineers and architects, able to mentally rotate objects, follow charts and diagrams with ease, and project how building elements will fit together in their mind's eye. They look at a chair and precisely see a piece of furniture in all of its component parts and the exact functionality of those parts. In fact, these folks may prefer to refer to charts and diagrams over other media because they find these so easy to use. They will also think spatially; for example, when searching for a lost object they will scan the environment in a methodical way so that they cover every nook without wasting effort. To some extent, this region can compensate for or mimic deductive reasoning, which is associated with region F3. The person visualizes problems using Venn-diagrams, tree-structures, and similar means in order to reason through problems visually. The result can be just as precise and perhaps faster, though not all problems lend themselves to visual representation.

While many people make active use of this region, others are challenged to understand charts and diagrams, which appear like a foreign language to them. This is an obstacle to mastering many technical and practical problem-solving tasks that rely on visual thinking.

Using this region can be frustrating in a paradoxical way. We may visualize an object very precisely in our mind's eye, down to measurements and interlocking parts, yet completely lack the words to explain what we see.

Your Turn: Estimate your aptitude for this region: 1 2 3 4 5

Region O2: The Abstract Impressionist Skill-Set

Location: Right occipital.

This region lies at the back of your head on your right side. It is active when you:

- View a photograph or painting.
- Sense how colors, shapes, and other elements fit aesthetically.
- Notice or set the theme of an illustration or a photograph.
- Gain an impression of a person's character from their appearance.

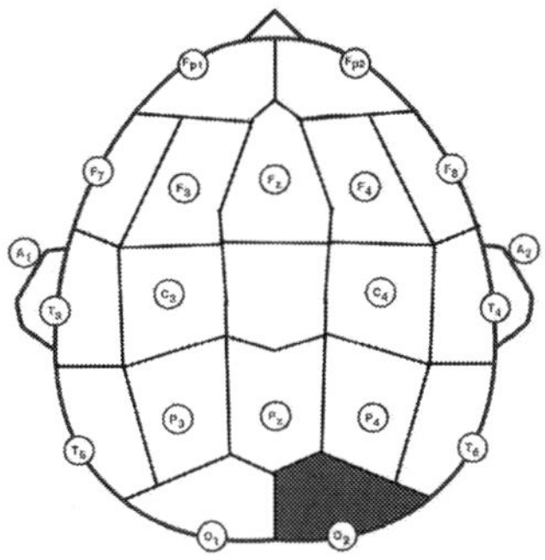

Like region O1, this region is incredibly visual. Unlike O1, it is imprecise and holistic. It concerns itself with visual themes: the various inter-relationships of elements that convey an image's overall balance and meaning. Rather than rotate or measure an image in your mind's eye, as region O1 does, this region allows us to consider many possible arrangements or themes at once to locate what best fits the image, whether we are creating it ourselves or trying to understand someone else's creation. Also unlike region O1, this region does not need to labor itself to consider all elements and sub-elements that comprise an image. Rather, a person who is skilled with this region can review and sort many images at a startlingly rapid pace. If region O1 can engineer for functionality, this region can provide breathtaking composition.

We may use this region to size up and react quickly to a person or place. This may be its original evolutionary benefit. Just as tone of voice can carry a lot of meaning about a person's character and intentions, the way a person presents himself or herself visually can convey a lot of meaning before we interact. While this region does not focus on meaning making or facial recognition, it gives us "a thousand words" at a glance about everyone we meet, every object we notice, and every place we visit. We instantly detect a theme that may or may not resonate with us. Some people describe the sight of ugly design as physically painful while the sight of elegant design sends them to heaven. This suggests how O2 may link to other brain regions to provide a kinesthetic response to visual input. However we find a view, other regions are needed to provide words and suggest actions in response to what we see.

People who under-use this region may be hard-pressed at "art appreciation". Photographs and pictures do not "speak" to them. Good design, they know not. Rather, they gravitate to environments that are functional, socially acceptable, and/or in-line with their values. Similarly, and more detrimentally, some may be slow to evaluate people and places visually.

Using this region can be frustrating sometimes. Visual sensibilities, abstract themes, and compositional skills are hard to explain. One's inchoate impressions of a person based on his or her look is equally challenging.

Your Turn: Estimate your aptitude for this region: 1 2 3 4 5

Table 4-1: Cognitive Skill-Sets Check List*

Region	Skills	Rating
Fp1	Chief Judge: Focus on explaining, making decisions, noting errors, and screening out distracting information.	
Fp2	Process Manager: Focus on process, either step-by-step for tasks, or open-ended creative brainstorming, or both.	
F7	Imaginative Mimic: Mirror others' behavior, pick up skills by observing others, and make imaginative inferences.	
F3	Deductive Analyst: Follow a chain of logical deductions and backtrack to correct thinking due to reasoning errors.	
F4	Expert Classifier: Accurately place concepts by testing them against many categories at once to find a best-fit.	
F8	Grounded Believer: Evaluate people and activities in terms of like or dislike, and/or recall details with high accuracy.	
T3	Precise Speaker: Focus on content of the spoken word, attend to proper grammar, usage, enunciation, and diction.	
C3	Factual Storekeeper: Easily memorize and execute steps of movement (dance steps, etc.), and/or recall facts.	
T4	Intuitive Listener: Focus on voice tone and other affective qualities of sound. Speak in a holistic way to influence.	
C4	Flowing Artist: Draw, paint, dance or otherwise use your body in a flowing, spontaneous, and/or artistic manner.	
T5	Sensitive Mediator: Attend to how others respond to you and alter your behavior to get more desirable results.	
P3	Tactical Navigator: Integrate physical space, motion, and visual clues to move skillfully through the environment.	
P4	Strategic Gamer: Weigh many pros and cons, risks and uncertainties at once in order to finesse complex situations.	
T6	Purposeful Futurist: State what will surely happen in the future, and/or apply a symbolic meaning to a situation.	
O1	Visual Engineer: Mentally rotate, measure, arrange, assemble and explode objects with a focus on functionality.	
O2	Abstract Impressionist: Notice holistic themes, patterns, and relationships in photos, paintings, and similar images.	

* Use this table to record your proficiency with the various cognitive skill-sets.

5.
Personality Types

Self-leadership often involves new experiences, so let's start with an activity to exercise the mind. Refer to the drawing below as you do the two activities that follow:

1. Look at the drawing. Notice the shapes, shadings, and placement of images on the page. Just allow your eyes to explore where they will. Now, what tasks or opportunities for action do you see in the drawing?

2. Why do you suppose apples were chosen as a stimulus to explore personal growth? Brainstorm as many ideas as you can. Now what potential is there to use the ideas you have generated in some other part of your life?

These activities exemplify cognitive processes that we all use to some extent in daily life. The first activity asks you to look at the drawing in detail and see "what is". The scene suggested a course of action, such as picking the apples.

When we are highly attentive to our physical environment, we see and can act on the opportunities before us. The second activity asks you to imagine "what might be" and link your ideas to other situations. When we are attentive to patterns and interactions, we can open ourselves up to new innovative possibilities.

Now reflect. Which activity was more fun? While you were trying each one, did you experience an increase or a decrease in energy level? Which activity felt more like how you do things? Which felt easier? Asking questions like these helps us identify what motivates and challenges us.

In this chapter, we explore a powerful tool: Carl Jung's dynamic framework of eight cognitive processes. Everyone can use all eight, and we each have a non-arbitrary pattern of preferred use. Your pattern is your "personality type".

Dr. Carl Jung

In the 1920s, Swiss psychiatrist Carl Jung observed "functions" of human nature—cognitive processes that people use to gather information and make decisions. He described ways people relate to the world around them and to themselves.

Maybe we actively make decisions based on personal values—this involves talking with others and acting on our values, not just thinking about them. Or maybe we enjoy engaging the world around us directly through the five senses, trusting our gut instinct. Or maybe focus on some other process. Whatever our preference, we use cognitive processes actively to get from one moment to the next within the larger systems of life—our environment, our use of tools, our relationships with other people, and our culture.

Early in his career, Jung proposed that people can orient themselves to the external world (extraverting). This is the world of people, places, objects, and actions. Alternatively, people can orient themselves to their own inner world (introverting). This is the world of thoughts, feelings, memories, and imagination. Often times, extraverting shows up when we initiate activities and interactions, while introverting shows up when we wait for others to initiate and then respond. Jung believed that people have a preference (akin to handedness) that influences their behavior, and the difference between the two orientations lies in where we focus and recharge our energy. Since Jung's time, psychologists have validated his proposition in various ways using both paper-pencil assessments, psychometric data, and brain research.

Four Functions

Beyond extraverting and introverting, Jung identified four basic "functions". A code letter stands for each function.

In any situation, we can focus our attention and access information using either of the following functions:

- **Sensing (S)**—Focus on tangible data, what is known (the past and present), and practical means. This is tangible, experiential awareness.
- **Intuiting (N)**—Focus on concepts, patterns, potential (the future or atemporal), and "what-if". This is symbolic, conceptual awareness.

Also, we can make decisions and get organized using either of the following functions:

- **Thinking (T)**—Decide and organize based on objective criteria, logic or model-based reasoning, and impersonal principles.
- **Feeling (F)**—Decide and organize based on social appropriateness, values, and importance or worth to self and others.

Our smallest acts may involve all four functions. All four are needed, valuable, and available to everyone.

A Total of Eight Cognitive Processes

We can use each of the four functions in either the external world (extraverting) or our internal world (introverting). Thus we use a total of eight cognitive processes.

A common notation is used to name the processes: the capital letter that stands for the process (S, N, T, or F) plus a lowercase "e" or "i" to indicate the orientation. For example, Se means Extraverted Sensing; that is, sensing engagement of the outer world. Fi means Introverted Feeling, or feeling evaluation made quietly within oneself. And so on. "N" is used for intuiting because using the letter "I" might be confused with introverting.

The table on the next page summarizes these eight processes. You can use the table to rate how each process may fit you, from "not me" to "a lot me". Also take a moment to notice how the table is arranged to highlight similarities and differences. The next chapter will go in-depth, describing how each process correlates with particular neocortex regions and whole-brain states. In the meantime, use the table and keep reading to get a sense of what Jung's theory is all about.

Table 5-1: The Eight Jungian Cognitive Processes*

Extraverted Processes	Introverted Processes
Perceiving—how we access data and focus attention	
Extraverted Sensing (Se) *"Immersing in the present context."* Respond naturally to everything tangible you detect through your senses. Check what your gut instincts tell you. Test limits and take risks for big rewards. Not me ☐ ☐ ☐ ☐ ☐ A lot me	**Introverted Sensing (Si)** *"Stabilizing with a predictable standard."* Carefully compare a situation to the customary ways you've come to rely on. Check with past experiences. Stabilize the situation and invest for future security. Not me ☐ ☐ ☐ ☐ ☐ A lot me
Extraverted Intuiting (Ne) *"Exploring the emerging patterns."* Wonder about patterns of interaction across various situations. Check what hypotheses fit best. Shift the dynamics of a situation and trust what emerges. Not me ☐ ☐ ☐ ☐ ☐ A lot me	**Introverted Intuiting (Ni)** *"Transforming with a meta-perspective."* Withdraw from the world and focus your mind to receive an insight or realization. Check whether synergy results. Try out a realization to transform yourself. Not me ☐ ☐ ☐ ☐ ☐ A lot me
Judging—how we organize and make decisions	
Extraverted Thinking (Te) *"Measuring and constructing for progress."* Make decisions objectively based on evidence and measures. Check whether things function properly. Apply procedures to control events and achieve goals. Not me ☐ ☐ ☐ ☐ ☐ A lot me	**Introverted Thinking (Ti)** *"Gaining leverage using a framework."* Detach from a situation to study it from different angles and fit it to a theory, framework, or principle. Check this fit for accuracy. Use leverage gained to solve any problem. Not me ☐ ☐ ☐ ☐ ☐ A lot me
Extraverted Feeling (Fe) *"Nurturing trust through giving relationships."* Empathically respond to others' needs and take on their needs and values as your own. Check for respect and trust. Give and receive support to grow closer to people. Not me ☐ ☐ ☐ ☐ ☐ A lot me	**Introverted Feeling (Fi)** *"Staying true to who you really are."* Pay close attention to your personal identity, values, and beliefs. Check with your conscience before you act. Choose behavior congruent with what is important to you. Not me ☐ ☐ ☐ ☐ ☐ A lot me

* Feel free to rate yourself for each process on a scale from not you to a lot you.

Cognitive Preference

Jung observed that everyone has potential access to all eight cognitive processes but that we each prefer one as dominant—playing a lead role—with a second process playing a support role. An everyday metaphor is hammering a nail: our lead hand uses the hammer while our other hand holds the nail in place.

Sign your name here

____

Now sign your name again using your other hand:

____

Did you notice that writing with your dominant hand took little effort and that more concentration was required with the other hand? Similarly, you prefer some cognitive processes, and just as you can use your non-preferred hand, you can and do engage all eight cognitive processes at different times and levels of proficiency.

Our two preferred processes allow us to do perceiving and judging, introverting and extraverting. We seem to have a built-in preference for one of the four perceiving processes and one of the four judging processes. Similarly, we tend to use one of our two preferred processes for introverting and the other for extraverting.

For example, maybe you prefer Introverted Intuiting (Ni) in a lead role with Extraverted Feeling (Fe) in a support role, or maybe you prefer Extraverted Sensing (Se) in a lead role with Introverted Thinking (Ti) in a support role. Or maybe you prefer some other pairing. Whatever the arrangement, your two preferred processes allow you to perceive and decide, introvert and extravert.

For every pairing there is an "opposite". For example, Ni-Fe opposes Se-Ti. Jung observed patients over many years. He proposed that during mid-life in particular, people explore the opposite processes. More recent research suggests there are "true opposite" pairings. For example, the true opposite of Ni-Fe is Si-Te, and the true opposite of Se-Ti is Ne-Fi. These true opposites bedevil us and may represent life-long cognitive deficits.

All said, the pairings tap into sixteen possible personality type patterns.

Sixteen Type Patterns

Dr. Jung's ideas first became widely known through the work of Isabel Myers. You may be familiar with the Myers-Briggs Type Indicator® (MBTI®) questionnaire, among other questionnaires, which provides a four-letter personality type code (ESTJ, INFP, etc.) to help people discover which of sixteen personality type patterns fits them best.

The MBTI® questionnaire is the most widely used and most heavily researched and published personality assessment in the world (see www.capt.org). Its current incarnation, Form M, is strongly validated by statisticians. It was not designed to directly assess Jung's ideas but it is a good predictor.

Each four-letter type code such as INFP or ESTJ represents two preferred processes. For example, INFP has Introverted Feeling in the lead role and Extraverted Intuiting in the support role. I will not explain the somewhat convoluted coding system. Trust that there is a method to the madness! The type descriptions on the next eight pages include the four-letter type codes for readers familiar with that construct.

Temperament—Core Needs and Values

Dr. Jung's ideas also became popular through the work of Dr. David Keirsey. Keirsey revitalized an age-old framework of four temperaments. Temperament theory goes back twenty-five centuries to the Greek physician Hippocrates. Keirsey proposed that each temperament was home to four of the sixteen personality types. Types within a temperament gravitate to the same core needs, values, talents, contributions, and self-concept.

Later, Dr. Linda V Berens updated and refined temperament as a theory of motivation. This book uses her terms and descriptions, with her permission. She names the four temperaments and groups types under them like this:

Catalyst™ Types		Stabilizer™ Types	
INFJ	INFP	ISTJ	ISFJ
ENFJ	ENFP	ESTJ	ESFJ
Theorist™ Types		**Improviser™ Types**	
INTJ	INTP	ISTP	ISFP
ENTJ	ENTP	ESTP	ESFP

Table 5-2: The Link Between Type Codes and Temperaments.

Like the Myers-Briggs assessment and Jung's cognitive processes framework, temperament theory is validated statistically.

Temperament is useful because it describes holistic qualities: it names people's core needs and values, describes how people go about getting their underlying needs and values met, and how they tend to reshape their environment and grow. Moreover, each temperament is a pattern of interrelated qualities. What does this mean? Consider, temperament proposes that the Stabilizer and Theorist temperaments both value "structure". What kind of structure? The kind fits with their other values. Stabilizers also value stability, group membership, and logistics. Thus, the Stabilizer temperament values structure that maintains stability, encourages membership in a group, and ensures logistical success. In contrast, the Theorist temperament values a different kind of structure, one that is conceptual and strategic—a mental structure, interest in the underlying organization of nature, or a methodology that insures competence.

All of us have the needs and values of all four temperaments but one is "home base"—the one that comes naturally to us, the one we go to when we are under stress, and we cannot seem to live without. It is the pattern we are most drawn to and find satisfying. Often, we dislike one temperament—we avoid or remain suspicious of it.

Temperament has been statistically validated using the Interstrength Temperament Assessment. To learn more, see *Understanding Yourself and Others, An Introduction to the 4 Temperaments-4.0* (Linda V Berens, Radiance House), 2010.

Finding Your Best-Fit Personality Type

The upcoming pages briefly describe the sixteen type patterns. Each type is a set of interrelated characteristics: a name, two cognitive processes, a cloud of unique themes, and various temperament-related qualities.

Each two-page spread describes four types on the right and their shared temperament on the left. Remember to read and evaluate each type as whole.

There are several ways to locate a best-fit type. First, you may browse at random and try on various types to see what fits best, as you might while shopping for shoes. Alternatively, you can use your results on page 74 as a starting point to focus on certain types before exploring the rest. Finally, you might sort by temperament. When a particular temperament resonates with you, consider all of the types under it to find a best-fit. Then consider the other types.

Improviser™ Types

Here are essential qualities of this temperament pattern.

Motivators: Adapting to the moment, freedom to act now, making an immediate impact, opportunity, and daily variety.

Primary Contribution: Handle crisis situations.

Needs/Values: The core needs are to have the freedom to act without hindrance and to see a marked result from action. People of this temperament highly value aesthetics, whether in nature or art. Their energies are focused on skillful performance, variety, and stimulation. They tend toward pragmatic, utilitarian actions with a focus on technique. They trust their impulses and have a drive to action. They learn best experientially and when they see the relevance of what they are learning to what they are doing. They enjoy hands-on, applied learning with a fast pace and freedom to explore.

Talents: People of this temperament tend to be gifted at employing the available means to accomplish an end. Their creativity is revealed by the variety of solutions they come up with. They are talented at using tools, whether the tool be language, theories, a paint brush, or a computer. They tune into immediate sensory information and vary their actions according to the needs of the moment. They are gifted at tactics. They can easily read the situation at hand, instantly make decisions, and, if needed, take actions to achieve the desired outcome.

Learning/Adaptation: Use trial-and-error, variation on a theme, and hands-on tools to "find a fit".

Self-Concept: People who identify with these types often say the following about their personality.

- *"How I am depends on context and what's needed. What's important is that I'm flexible to handle whatever comes up."*
- *"There are varieties of people, but we're still all pretty much the same."*
- *"There are no temperaments, types or patterns."*
- *"One's self is strongly influenced by the many events, encounters, and experiences we have in life."*

Not like me ☐ ☐ ☐ ☐ ☐ A lot like me

Analyzer Operator™ • ISTP	Composer Producer™ • ISFP
Lead Process (Ti) ***Introverted Thinking***—Analyze a problem using a framework, and find an angle or leverage by which to solve it. **Support Process (Se)** ***Extraverted Sensing***—Take tangible action relevant to the moment and current context. **Unique Themes** Actively solving problems. Observing how things work. Talent for using tools for the best approach. Need to be independent. Act on their hunches or intuitions. Understanding a situation. Taking things apart. Making discoveries. Sharing those discoveries. Unsettled by powerful emotional experiences.	**Lead Process (Fi)** ***Introverted Feeling***—Choose and stick to what you believe is congruent with your personal identity. **Support Process (Se)** ***Extraverted Sensing***—Take tangible action relevant to the moment and current context. **Unique Themes** Taking advantage of opportunities. Stick with what's important. Talent for pulling together what is just right. Creative problem solving. Building relationships. Attracting the loyalties of others. Being their own true self. Have their own personal style. Play against expectations. Struggle with nurturing their own self-esteem.

Promoter Executer™ • ESTP	Motivator Presenter™ • ESFP
Lead Process (Se) ***Extraverted Sensing***—Take tangible action relevant to the moment and current context. **Support Process (Ti)** ***Introverted Thinking***—Analyze a problem using a framework, and find an angle or leverage by which to solve it. **Unique Themes** Taking charge of situations. Tactical prioritizing. Talent for negotiating. Want a measure of their success. Keep their options open. Enjoy acting as a consultant. Winning people over. Caring for family and friends. Enjoy exhilaration at the edge. Disappointed when others don't show respect.	**Lead Process (Se)** ***Extraverted Sensing***—Take tangible action relevant to the moment and current context. **Support Process (Fi)** ***Introverted Feeling***—Choose and stick to what you believe is congruent with your personal identity. **Unique Themes** Stimulating action. Have a sense of style. Talent for presenting things in a useful way. Natural actors—engaging others. Opening up people to possibilities. Respect for freedom. Taking risks. A love of learning, especially about people. Genuine caring. Sometimes mis-perceive others' intentions.

Stabilizer™ Types

Here are essential qualities of this temperament pattern.

Motivators: Upholding long-standing traditions, duty and obligation, group membership, safety and security, and structure and stability.

Primary Contribution: Support day-to-day continuity.

Needs/Values: The core needs are for group membership and responsibility. People of this temperament need to know they are doing the responsible thing. They value stability, security, and a sense of community. They trust hierarchy and authority and may be surprised when others go against these social structures. People of this temperament prefer cooperative actions with a focus on standards and norms. Their orientation is to their past experiences, and they like things sequenced and structured. They tend to look for the practical applications of what they are learning.

Talents: People of this temperament are usually talented at logistics and at maintaining useful traditions. They masterfully get the right things in the right place, at the right time, in the right quantity, in the right quality, to the right people, and not to the wrong people. They know how things have always been done, so they anticipate where things can go wrong. They have a knack for attending to rules, procedures, and protocol, including best-practices to ensure change is implemented in a way that maintains stability. They make sure the correct information is assembled and presented to the right people.

Learning/Adaptation: Memorize, practice, practice more, and look to authority for guidance and proper form.

Self-Concept: People who identify with these types often say the following about their personality.

- *"What's important is what roles a person fulfills, such as mother, brother, manager, and so forth, and whether we fill our roles responsibly."*
- *"Who we are is influenced by our upbringing, ethnicity, and religion."*
- *"I don't like the idea of classifying people; it's discriminatory."*
- *"One's temperament results primarily from childhood upbringing, and influence of parents and culture."*

Not like me ☐ ☐ ☐ ☐ ☐ A lot like me

Planner Inspector™ • ISTJ

Lead Process (Si)

Introverted Sensing—Compare something to expected details and reliable precedents.

Support Process (Te)

Extraverted Thinking—Create structures, reason by measures and evidence, and implement plans.

Unique Themes

Drawing up plans and being prepared. Take responsibility. Getting work done first. Being active in the community. Loyalty to their roles. Cultivating good qualities. Doing the right thing. Bear life's burdens and overcome adversity. Talented at planning, sequencing, and noticing what's missing. Having to learn so much in hindsight is painful at times.

Protector Supporter™ • ISFJ

Lead Process (Si)

Introverted Sensing—Compare something to expected details and reliable precedents.

Support Process (Fe)

Extraverted Feeling—Connect with people by sharing values and taking on their needs and yours.

Unique Themes

Noticing what's needed and what's valuable. Talent for careful and supportive organization. Know the ins and outs. Enjoy traditions. Work to protect the future. Listening and remembering. Being nice and agreeable. Unselfish willingness to volunteer. Feeling a sense of accomplishment. Exasperated when people ignore rules and don't get along.

Implementor Supervisor™ • ESTJ

Lead Process (Te)

Extraverted Thinking—Create structures, reason by measures and evidence, and implement plans.

Support Process (Si)

Introverted Sensing—Compare something to expected details and reliable precedents.

Unique Themes

Talent for bringing order to chaotic situations. Educating themselves. Industrious, work-hard attitude. Balance work with play. Having a philosophy of life. Having the steps to success. Keeping up traditions. Being well-balanced. Connecting their wealth of life experiences. Often disappointed when perfectionistic standards for economy and quality are not met.

Facilitator Caretaker™ • ESFJ

Lead Process (Fe)

Extraverted Feeling—Connect with people by sharing values and taking on their needs and yours.

Support Process (Si)

Introverted Sensing—Compare something to expected details and reliable precedents.

Unique Themes

Accepting and helping others. Managing people. Hearing people out. Voicing concerns and accommodating needs. Admire the success of others. Remember what's important. Talented at providing others with what they need. Keep things pleasant. Maintaining a sense of continuity. Accounting for the costs. Often disappointed by entrepreneurial projects.

Theorist™ Types

Here are essential qualities of this temperament pattern.

Motivators: Acquiring knowledge, competence, expertise, self-mastery, progress, concepts, and principles.

Primary Contribution: Innovate tools and ideas.

Needs/Values: The core needs are for mastery of concepts, knowledge, and competence. People of this temperament want to understand the operating principles of the universe and to learn or even develop theories for everything. They value expertise, logical consistency, concepts, and ideas and seek progress. They tend toward pragmatic, utilitarian actions with a technology focus. They trust logic above all else. They tend to be skeptical and highly value precision in language. Their learning style is conceptual, and they want to know the underlying principles that generate the details and facts rather than the details alone.

Talents: People of this temperament prefer using their gifts of strategic analysis to approach all situations. They constantly examine the relationship of the means to the overall vision and goal. No strangers to complexity, theories, and models, they like to think of all possible contingencies and develop multiple plans for handling them. They abstractly analyze a situation and consider previously unthought-of possibilities. Researching, analyzing, searching for patterns, and developing hypotheses are quite likely to be their natural modus operandi.

Learning/Adaptation: Integrate, test, and refine conceptual models, strategies, and objective universal principles.

Self-Concept: People who identify with these types often say the following about their personality.

- *"Each cognitive process or personality is a different strategy for engaging situations. What's important is whether we deploy these strategies smartly."*
- *"We can learn to be different ways; each way is a state of mind."*
- *"I have some questions and concerns about the validity of any theory."*
- *"One's personality results from a multitude of interrelated factors and is likely too complex to define."*

Not like me ☐ ☐ ☐ ☐ ☐ A lot like me

Conceptualizer Director™ • INTJ	Designer Theorizer™ • INTP
Lead Process (Ni) ***Introverted Intuiting***—Realize a greater level of awareness to transform yourself. **Support Process (Te)** ***Extraverted Thinking***—Create structures, reason by measures and evidence, and implement plans. **Unique Themes** Maximizing achievements. Drive for self-mastery. Build a vision. Very long-range strategizing. Realizing progress toward goals. Systems thinking. Talent for seeing the reasons behind things. Being on the leading edge. Maintaining independence. Find it difficult to let go in interacting with others.	**Lead Process (Ti)** ***Introverted Thinking***—Analyze a problem using a framework, and find an angle or leverage by which to solve it. **Support Process (Ne)** ***Extraverted Intuiting***—Flow with imaginative potential possibilities as they emerge. **Unique Themes** Becoming an expert. Seeing new patterns and elegant connections. Talent for design and re-design. Crossing the artificial boundaries of thought. Activate the imagination. Clarifying and defining. Making discoveries. Reflect on the process of thinking itself. Detach to analyze. Struggle with attending to the physical world.

Strategist Mobilizer™ • ENTJ	Explorer Inventor™ • ENTP
Lead Process (Te) ***Extraverted Thinking***—Create structures, reason by measures and evidence, and implement plans. **Support Process (Ni)** ***Introverted Intuiting***—Realize a greater level of awareness to transform yourself. **Unique Themes** Being a leader. Maximize talents. Marshal resources toward progress. Intuitive explorations. Forging partnerships. Mentoring and empowering. Talent for coordinating multiple projects. Balance peace and conflict. Demonstrates predictive creativity. Often overwhelmed by managing all the details of time and resources.	**Lead Process (Ne)** ***Extraverted Intuiting***—Flow with imaginative potential possibilities as they emerge. **Supporting Process (Ti)** ***Introverted Thinking***—Analyze a problem using a framework, and find an angle or leverage by which to solve it. **Unique Themes** Being inventive. Talented at building prototypes and getting projects launched. Enjoys lifelong learning. Enjoy the creative process. Share their insights about life's possibilities. Strategically formulate success. An inviting host. Like the drama of the give and take. Trying to be diplomatic. Surprised when their strategizing of relationships becomes problematic.

Catalyst™ Types

Here are essential qualities of this temperament pattern.

Motivators: Questing for authentic interaction, deep significance, a unique identity, personal and human meaning, and ethics.

Primary Contribution: Inspire human potential.

Needs/Values: The core needs are for the meaning and significance that come from having a sense of purpose and working toward some greater good. They need to have a sense of unique identity. They value unity, self-actualization, and authenticity. People of this temperament prefer cooperative interactions with a focus on ethics and morality. They tend to trust their intuition and impressions first and then seek to find the logic and the data to support them. Given their need for empathic relationships, they learn more easily when they can relate to the instructor and the group.

Talents: People of this temperament tend to be gifted at unifying diverse peoples and helping individuals realize their potential. They build bridges between people through empathy and clarification of deeper issues. They use these same skills to help people work through difficulties. Thus, they can make excellent mediators, helping people and companies solve conflicts through mutual cooperation. If working on a global level, they champion a cause. If working on an individual level, they focus on growth and development of the person.

Learning/Adaptation: Find meaning in dramatic stories and themes, and search for authentic human interaction.

Self-Concept: People who identify with these types often say the following about their personality.

- *"I have all the temperaments inside me. What's important is that I and others have unlimited potential to explore and develop."*
- *"I believe everyone has unlimited potential as part of being human."*
- *"I value all the personality types."*
- *"One's identity is more like a story; maybe self-defined with influence from our relationships."*

Not like me ☐ ☐ ☐ ☐ ☐ A lot like me

Foreseer Developer™ • INFJ	Harmonizer Clarifier™ • INFP
Lead Process (Ni) ***Introverted Intuiting***—Realize a greater level of awareness to transform yourself. **Support Process (Fe)** ***Extraverted Feeling***—Connect with people by sharing values and taking on their needs and yours. **Unique Themes** Personal growth. Sustain the vision. Honoring the gifts of others. Taking a creative approach to life. Talent for foreseeing. Exploring issues. Bridging differences and connecting people. Practical problem solving. Living with a sense of purpose. Living an idealistic life often presents them with a great deal of stress and a need to withdraw.	**Lead Process (Fi)** ***Introverted Feeling***—Choose and stick to what you believe is congruent with your personal identity. **Supporting Process (Ne)** ***Extraverted Intuiting***—Flow with imaginative potential possibilities as they emerge. **Unique Themes** Going with the flow. Knowing what is behind what is said. Uncovering mysteries. Exploring moral questions. Talent for facilitative listening. Relate through stories and metaphors. Balancing opposites. Getting re-acquainted with themselves. Have a way of knowing what is believable. Struggling with structure and getting their lives in order.

Envisioner Mentor™ • ENFJ	Discoverer Advocate™ • ENFP
Lead Process (Fe) ***Extraverted Feeling***—Connect with people by sharing values and taking on their needs and yours. **Support Process (Ni)** ***Introverted Intuiting***—Realize a greater level of awareness to transform yourself. **Unique Themes** Communicate and share values. Succeeding at relationships. Realizing dreams—their own and others. Seek opportunities to grow together. Heeding the call to a life work or mission. Enjoying the creative process. Intuitive intellect. Reconcile the past and the future. Talent for seeing potential in others. Often find living in the present difficult.	**Lead Process (Ne)** ***Extraverted Intuiting***—Flow with imaginative potential possibilities as they emerge. **Supporting Process (Fi)** ***Introverted Feeling***—Choose and stick to what you believe is congruent with your personal identity. **Unique Themes** Inspiring and facilitating others. Exploring perceptions. Talent for seeing what's not being said and voicing unspoken meanings. Seek to have ideal relationships. Recognize happiness. Living out stories. Want to authentically live with themselves. Respond to insights in the creative process. Finding the magical situation. Restless hunger for discovering their direction.

Your Best-Fit Type Pattern

Use the worksheet below to integrate your experience over the past few pages. First, write down two or three personality types that resonate as most like you. Be sure to indicate key elements such as temperament. Do that now.

Option #1

Four-Letter Code: ______
Lead Cognitive Process: ________________
Support Cognitive Process: ________________
Temperament: ________________
What resonates most: ________________________
____

Option #2

Four-Letter Code: ______
Lead Cognitive Process: ________________
Support Cognitive Process: ________________
Temperament: ________________
What resonates most: ________________________
____

Option #3

Four-Letter Code: ______
Lead Cognitive Process: ________________
Support Cognitive Process: ________________
Temperament: ________________
What resonates most: ________________________
____

Next, "triangulate" which type—or at least, which cognitive processes—fit best. Triangulating means using reference points to calculate an agreeable result. For example, a hiker might consider data points including stars, landmarks, and compass readings in order to locate her current position in the wilderness. Similarly, types may feel close but uncertain or incompatible. That is normal. Consider multiple options until you locate the type that aligns best: __________

Your choice here is hardly a final opportunity. Many people find this best-fit process useful before they explore the next chapter.

6. Keys to the Psyche

Your head may feel somewhat full as we reach the summit of our metaphorical mountain. This chapter weaves together many of the earlier threads, from brain waves to personality types. In Chapter 1, I promised you a neuroscience of personality. Here it is!

The table on the next page summarizes eight cognitive processes. These are the same processes we scrutinized in the last chapter. This time, however, the focus is on what has come to light vis-a-vis brain activity. Thus, the table does not offer speculation based on theory and anecdote. It presents the boons of hard-won lab hours: studying the neocortical activity of fifty-eight persons of various personality types as they engaged in a variety of tasks for several hours. Thus, the table's tasty morsels are as close as we can come for now to "seeing" the magician (or magicians?) behind the curtain of the psyche.

The table includes the Myers-Briggs four-letter personality type codes. As it turns out, Dr. Carl Jung enjoyed tremendous insight into the psyche; the research mostly confirms what he proposed nearly a century ago. Moreover, while EEG has been essential to understanding the mind and brain, had I not known Jung's framework or the Myers-Briggs types, I would have missed a lot!

After the table are eight sections. Each section delves into a cognitive process with all the neuroscience that's fit to print. As you explore, keep in mind that a person relies on at least two cognitive processes: a dominant, lead process and an auxilliary, support process.

Each section includes two example persons of the relevant personality types. These are case studies of specific individuals and do not represent all or even most persons of those types. Everyone is unique due to his or her background.

Table 6-1: The Eight Jungian Cognitive Processes in the Brain

Extraverted Processes	Introverted Processes
Perceiving—how we access data and focus attention	
Extraverted Sensing (Se) *"Act quickly and smoothly to handle whatever comes up in the moment."* Excited by motion, action, and nature. Adept at physical multitasking with a video game-like mind primed for action. Often in touch with body sensations. Bored when sitting with a mental/rote task. Strong memory for details in context. Use their whole brain to handle crises. May be impatient to finish. Mainly ESFP, ESTP. Also ISFP, ISTP.	**Introverted Sensing (Si)** *"Review and practice in order to specialize and meet group needs."* Constant practice helps their brain specialize. Improve when watching a role-model or example. Often in touch with body sensations. Easily track where they are in a task. Use their whole brain to review the past. Strong memory for kinship and raw details. May over-rely on authority for guidance. Mainly ISTJ, ISFJ. Also ESTJ, ESFJ.
Extraverted Intuiting (Ne) *"Perceive and play with patterns of relationships across contexts."* Think analogically: notice and apply patterns of relationships across contexts. Stimuli are springboards to generate analogies and ideas. Easily guess details. Adept at role-play and mirroring others. Brain activity tends to look chaotic, with many highs and lows at once. May find it hard to stay on-task. Mainly ENTP, ENFP. Also INTP, INFP.	**Introverted Intuiting (Ni)** *"Draw upon the whole brain to realize an answer to a novel problem."* Enter a very brief trance to answer problems. Focus on what will happen. Use their whole brain to foresee the future. Manage their own mental processes and are aware of where they are in an open-ended task. May use a physical action or symbol to focus the mind. May over-rely on the unconscious. Mainly INTJ, INFJ. Also ENTJ, ENFJ.

Table 6-1 Cont.

Extraverted Processes	Introverted Processes
Judging—how we organize and make decisions	
Extraverted Thinking (Te) *"Manage resources efficiently to quickly decide based on the evidence."* Highly efficient use of brain resources. Focus on word content, recall facts and figures, see and manipulate images, and then decide. Adept at giving decisive explanations. Tend to utilize other brain regions only when those regions are truly needed. May display confidence even when wrong. Mainly ESTJ, ENTJ. Also ISTJ, INTJ.	**Introverted Thinking (Ti)** *"Reason multiple ways to objectively and accurately analyze problems."* Rely on interior regions of neocortex. Adept at deductive reasoning, defining and categorizing, weighing odds and risks, and/or navigating spaces. Can shut out senses to think. Tend to back-track to clarify thoughts. Separate body from mind when arguing or analyzing. May quickly stop listening. Mainly ISTP, INTP. Also ESTP, ENTP.
Extraverted Feeling (Fe) *"Evaluate and communicate values to enhance social relationships."* Attend keenly to how others judge them. Quickly adjust behavior for social harmony. Like to use adjectives to convey values. The true degree of their emotional response about morals/ethics is often held back and given only in words or ideas. May be easily coerced or embarrassed. Mainly ESFJ, ENFJ. Also ISFJ, INFJ.	**Introverted Feeling (Fi)** *"Listen with your whole self to locate and support what's important."* Evaluate personal importance along a spectrum from love/like to dislike/hate. Use their whole brain to listen to others. Attentive and curious for what is not said. Focus on word choice and voice tone. Hard to embarrass. Can respond strongly to specific, high-value words. May not utilize feedback Mainly ISFP, INFP. Also ESFP, ENFP.

Extraverted Sensing (Se)

"Act quickly and smoothly to handle whatever comes up in the moment."

Mainly ESTP and ESFP. Also, ISTP and ISFP.

Key Findings

Here are key features of this cognitive process based on the lab research.

The Se types often **show a "tennis hop" brain pattern**. Tennis players tend to lightly hop back and forth when they await the return of the ball from their opponent. This light, rapid hopping **maintains their momentum and helps them respond quickly,** regardless of which way the ball comes back at them. Building up momentum from a still position is more work than simply letting minor motions carry the player into action.

When the tennis hop pattern occurs, all regions of the neocortex are low amplitude and out of synch. That is, each region keeps shifting frequency even though the brain as a whole looks inactive, perhaps even presenting itself on the EEG monitor as a black or nearly-black screen, as if the person is awake but unconscious. **This state is very effective**. A low amplitude requires little energy while the shifting frequencies allow the brain to quickly direct whichever regions are needed for a surprise, incoming task.

The tennis hop shows up when people of all types **play games that involve tactical action**. In the Mario Cart video game, for example, the player directs a race car along a winding, unpredictable urban speedway. A baby carriage, rising bridge, or other obstacle may intrude at any moment, requiring the driver to stay on high alert. Yet this game does not tax the brain. Rather, the brain efficiently uses a "tennis hop" to conserve its resources while maximizing flexibility to take advantage of opportunities and avoid obstacles.

The Se types **easily go "in the zone", a pattern of solid bright blue, when engaging a crisis situation**. A fun role-play scenario can evoke this response. As the situation becomes more dramatic and perilous, the neocortex is ever more likely to zone-in and remain there until the situation resolves. Some time afterward, the person may experience a headache, stomachache or other illness that reflects the crisis' stress, which was deferred. No other types demonstrate this pattern of zoning under duress. By the way, a safe "politically correct" role-play hardly arouses the same excitement as one that is risqué, lightly testing limits or offering something exciting to win or lose.

The Se types **quickly integrate body and sensory information** and are highly capable at physical, concrete tasks, especially tactile and physical multitasking such as juggling even if they have not done a task before. They quickly get in the zone when juggling with another person. This is truest for ESTP and ESFP, the types that have this process in the lead role.

Because their neocortex is often ready for tactical action, the Se types are **frequently bored**. Quietly sitting in a classroom or office doing pencil-paper work is like a tennis player waiting endlessly on a court for a game with no opponent and no ball. It is no surprise they are more engaged when moving. The Se types may easily **show more brain activity while looking out the window or rising to stretch than when doing desk work**. As one lab subject reported, "Standing helps me think."

The Se types **focus on literal or common interpretations** over metaphor, abstraction, and "weird" interpretations. When asked to explain the meaning of the sentence, "she married a rock", they likely give the expected meaning, "She married someone who is stable, or maybe unresponsive and boring." In this case, the literal interpretation is the oddball.

Finally, Se types **favor details that are dramatic or in motion**. They perform the best among all types when tasked to recall the details of an illustration of a dramatic scene they were shown fifteen minutes earlier.

Essential Tips

When working with persons who prefer this cognitive process, consider the following tips.

- They prefer stimulating environments with rich sensory input. Work in a place with windows, enticing views, and interesting decor.
- Provide and encourage movement. Consider ways to take breaks while remaining productive, such as talking while walking through a park.
- Make your ideas meaningful with relevant context, sensory details, and physical tools. Allow them to test the tools by trial and error.
- Don't rely on metaphor. You can use metaphors, just use familiar metaphors and start with and support the metaphors with literal meanings.
- Focus on challenges, and allow for resourceful responses to crises. Hold back from over-defining the experience or making it too safe.
- Let them respond to whatever comes up, and be willing to join them if you wish to earn their friendship and respect.

Ross: He is highly tactical, using deductive logic and gut feeling to pragmatically tackle situations in a hands-on way, with an impulse to take risks for big rewards. He works in finance as an investment counselor and enjoys sports of all kinds including video games and weekly poker. His best-fit personality type is ESTP, which is ~13% of the USA population.

ESTP: Extraverted Sensing (Se) in lead role with Introverted Thinking (Ti) in support role.

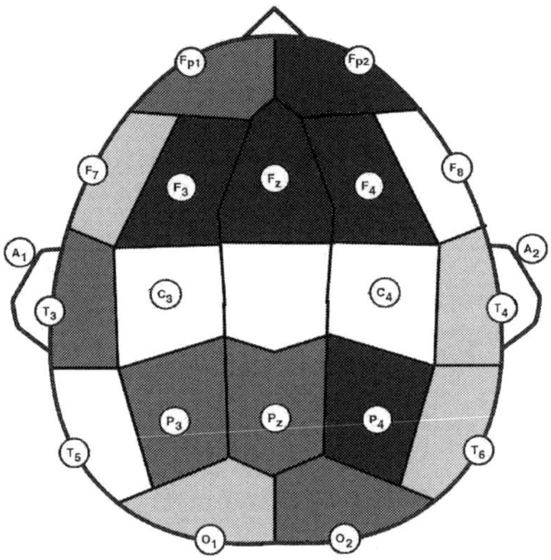

Figure 6-2: Ross's neocortex activity.
Active regions are darker here.

Table 6-2: Ross's Cognitive Skill-Set (based on his EEG results)

Activity	Skill-Set
High	Process Manager (Fp2), Deductive Analyst (F3), Expert Classifier (F4), Strategic Gamer (P4)
High-Mid	Chief Judge (Fp1), Precise Speaker (T3), Tactical Navigator (P3), Abstract Impressionist (O2)
Low-Mid	Imaginative Mimic (F7), Intuitive Listener (T4), Purposeful Futurist (T6), Visual Engineer (O1)
Low	Factual Storekeeper (C3), Flowing Artist (C4), Sensitive Mediator (T5), Grounded Believer (F8)

Cognitive Focus: Ross relies on a mental "tennis hop" to maintain momentum and responds swiftly to challenges as they come up. Also, he may get "in the zone" when engaging a crisis or doing a task with expertise.

Sandy: She is very sociable, with insight into people's motives and issues and an impulse to happily tackle situations in a hands-on way while staying true to her beliefs. She has dabbled in many jobs from waitressing to executive assistant to media event planner. Her best-fit personality type is ESFP, which is ~13% of the USA population.

ESFP: Extraverted Sensing (Se) in lead role with Introverted Feeling (Fi) in support role.

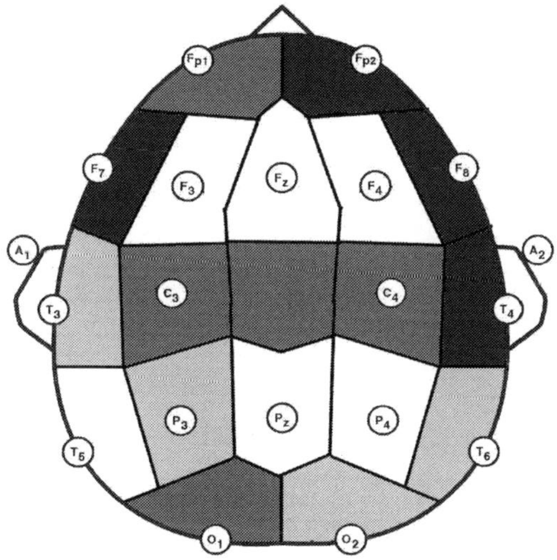

Figure 6-3: Sandy's neocortex activity.
Active regions are darker here.

Table 6-3: Sandy's Cognitive Skill-Set (based on her EEG results)

Activity	Skill-Set
High	Process Manager (Fp2), Imaginative Mimic (F7), Grounded Believer (F8), Intuitive Listener (T4)
High-Mid	Chief Judge (Fp1), Factual Storekeeper (C3), Flowing Artist (C4), Visual Engineer (O1)
Low-Mid	Precise Speaker (T3), Tactical Navigator (P3), Purposeful Futurist (T6), Abstract Impressionist (O2)
Low	Deductive Analyst (F3), Expert Classifier (F4), Strategic Gamer (P4), Sensitive Mediator (T5)

Cognitive Focus: Sandy relies on a mental "tennis hop" to maintain momentum and responds swiftly to challenges as they come up. Also, she may get "in the zone" when engaging a crisis or doing a task with expertise.

Introverted Sensing (Si)

"Review and practice in order to specialize and meet group needs."
Mainly ISTJ and ISFJ. Also, ESTJ and ESFJ.

Key Findings

Here are key features of this cognitive process based on the lab research.

The Si types often show **brain activity that reflects their background, training, and job expertise**. This might show up as surprisingly high activity in a particular brain region, or they might present themselves one way most of the time and then suddenly switch on neocortex regions that normally lie dormant. Either way, the Si types are stimulated by focusing on activities that correspond to their specific experiences and training.

The Si types may **get "in the zone" when reviewing past events**. People of other types show blips of activity in C3 or C4 when recalling. However, ISTJ and ISFJ easily enter an expert flow state while recalling, particularly if they close their eyes and take the time to immerse themselves in the memory, reliving it in rich detail.

The Si types are **specialists**. They can remain focused with skill on a single activity that they have practiced, and they have a propensity for **rote memorization, repetition, and in-depth reviews of daily events—all habits that help them burn new neural pathways**. For the brain to really learn something, exposure to a new idea is not enough. We must practice it through repeated exposure and regular use. Consider tasks such as painting pictures or playing piano. Exceptional skill requires many hours of practice a week, over many years. When the Si types are given appropriate step-by-step instruction, liberal doses of help, and an effective role-model, they develop the regions most relevant to their specialty. Thus, they may easily surprise us, showing a characteristic pattern of brain activity most of the time and then suddenly switching on new regions, often intensively, that are normally quiet.

The Si types are highly capable at **recalling information that has little or no context**, such as lists of random words, and they are by far the most adept at **recalling kinship data** such as listing birthdays and other familiar details. How do they do this? One trick: as they take in a word list, they rapidly **repeat back to themselves** what they have heard so far, to better impress the words into memory. Of course, if the words are given too rapidly or they are distracted then the trick won't work as well. The Si types draw upon tricks like this which they have figured out or been taught.

All Si types show high activity in region T5, which helps us **attend to social feedback**. When we receive negative input from others such as frowns, this region evokes a feeling such as embarrassment, guilt, or shame that prompts us to adjust our behavior. The feedback triggers the feelings; it doesn't matter whether we have actually acted inappropriately. The Si types are among the most responsive to these feelings.

The Si types also show moderate to high activity in region T6, which helps us **consider the future**. It gets active when we say the word "will", as in "I will go to the store tomorrow". This region is not about wishful thinking or imagination; rather it helps us plan actions ahead of time.

The Si types show other patterns. ISTJ and ISFJ are both **visual**, showing high activity in regions O1 and/or O2. In general, the back half of the brain is more active for them, and they show relatively more activity in region Fp2 than in Fp1. Region Fp2 helps us **manage processes, such as monitoring which step we are on during a task**, what we have already done, and what comes next. In contrast, the more extraverted ESTJ and ESFJ types show the opposite: more activity in the neocortex's front half and more activity in Fp1 than Fp2, making them more focused on executive decision-making.

Essential Tips

When working with persons who prefer this cognitive process, consider the following tips.

- They prefer low-distraction environments and need time to review experiences in order to ground new learnings.
- Utilize step-by-step methods to help them develop skills, and provide a road map for them to track their progress.
- Provide a skillful role-model for them to observe and copy, and schedule follow-up time, review sheets, etc. to practice with correction.
- Recognize they may want to focus on one path or goal longer than you might, or may simply keep working to please you or until you say "stop".
- Stay alert for a surprising skill they might have that doesn't fit their usual pattern. They may not mention the skill unless asked about it.
- Take care with your feedback. They are adjusting their behavior in light of your input including nonverbal clues such as facial expressions.

Stan: He is diligent, loyal, steady, and occasionally quite funny. His friends and family know him as an honest man of conviction and a hard worker who contributes to his community. He works as a computer programmer, has played football since college, and keeps up a small radio comedy show. His best-fit personality type is ISTJ, which is ~5% of the USA population.

ISTJ: Introverted Sensing (Si) in lead role with Extraverted Thinking (Te) in support role.

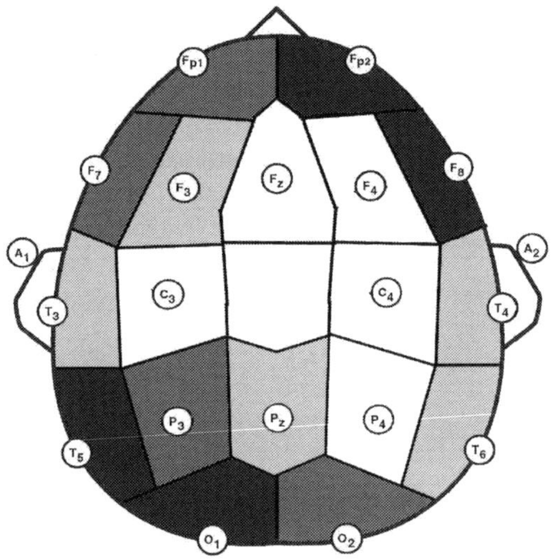

Figure 6-4: Stan's neocortex activity.
Active regions are darker here.

Table 6-4: Stan's Cognitive Skill-Set (based on his EEG results)

Activity	Skill-Set
High	Process Manager (Fp2), Grounded Believer (F8), Sensitive Mediator (T5), Visual Engineer (O1)
High-Mid	Chief Judge (Fp1), Imaginative Mimic (F7), Tactical Navigator (P3), Abstract Impressionist (O2)
Low-Mid	Deductive Analyst (F3), Precise Speaker (T3), Intuitive Listener (T4), Purposeful Futurist (T6)
Low	Expert Classifier (F4), Factual Storekeeper (C3), Flowing Artist (C4), Strategic Gamer (P4)

Cognitive Focus: Stan relies on rote memorization and practice to burn new neural pathways and become highly specialized. Also, he may get "in the zone" when reviewing past experiences or doing a task with expertise.

Heather: She is modest, hard-working, and sensitive. Her friends and family know her as a sincere, patient, and supportive friend, daughter, sister, wife, and mother. She keeps her life tidy. She studied painting and ballet for many years and now enjoys the life of a choreographer. Her best-fit personality type is ISFJ, which is ~5% of the USA population.

ISFJ: Introverted Sensing (Si) in lead role with Extraverted Feeling (Fe) in support role.

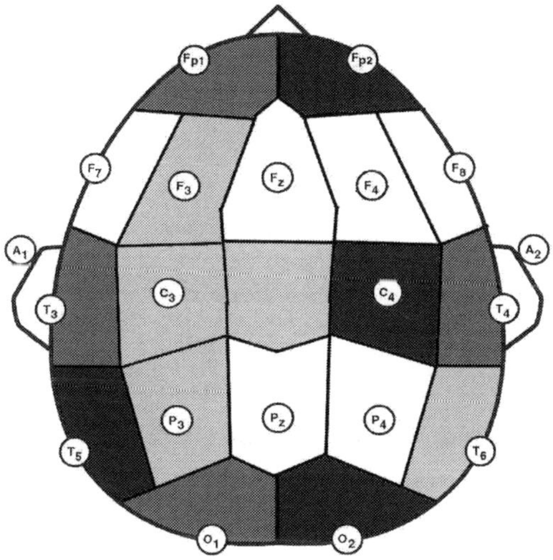

Figure 6-5: Heather's neocortex activity.
Active regions are darker here.

Table 6-5: Heather's Cognitive Skill-Set (based on her EEG results)

Activity	Skill-Set
High	Process Manager (Fp2), Flowing Artist (C4), Sensitive Mediator (T5), Abstract Impressionist (O2)
High-Mid	Chief Judge (Fp1), Precise Speaker (T3), Intuitive Listener (T4), Visual Engineer (O1)
Low-Mid	Deductive Analyst (F3), Factual Storekeeper (C3), Tactical Navigator (P3), Purposeful Futurist (T6)
Low	Imaginative Mimic (F7), Expert Classifier (F4), Grounded Believer (F8), Strategic Gamer (P4)

Cognitive Focus: Heather relies on rote memorization and practice to burn new neural pathways and become highly specialized. Also, she may get "in the zone" when reviewing past experiences or doing a task with expertise.

Extraverted Intuiting (Ne)

"Perceive and play with patterns of relationships across contexts."

Mainly ENTP and ENFP. Also, INTP and INFP.

Key Findings

Here are key features of this cognitive process based on the lab research.

The Ne types **often show a "Christmas tree" pattern**. Imagine a holiday tree decked with a myriad of flashing lights of various colors, each light a different brain region, and each color a different level of activity therein. In this state, the neocortex is active all over, and each region is of high amplitude and out-of-synch with the others. The regions are all busy doing their own thing and possibly generating a surprise result.

What's going on? Cognitively, this pattern is called **trans-contextual thinking**. Regardless of what kind of stimulus enters the brain—be it a sight, sound, smell, sensation, or so forth—the brain **responds by rapidly processing that stimulus in multiple regions, including regions seemingly not applicable** to the stimulus. For example, for most people, hearing the words "dog" and "cat" will evoke auditory regions like T3 and perhaps some visual or memory regions like O1 or C3. Perhaps we recall a beloved childhood pet. However, the Ne types get busy using all regions to **tap relationships across situations**, perhaps suddenly imagining a story about two brothers, one of whom is faithful and sociable (like a dog) while the other is independent and quiet (like a cat). They might wonder about dog and cat writing styles too!

The Ne types often experience **creative highs**. The Christmas tree pattern is a creative engine. If region F7 is about thinking in context, including imagining fantasy locales or mimicking others, then this pattern thinks across contexts. For example, chocolate is to romance as beer is to what? Or, the antidote for falling down a pit of despair is... discovering a ladder that allows us to climb up into hope. The Ne types provide **fast, creative responses**. **Sometimes the responses are too creative**, resulting in baloney raining from the sky. However, with a few parameters, Ne types can produce captivating, out-of-the-box results, zooming from "microwave oven" to "philosophy oven". We can stimulate or imitate the Christmas tree pattern by introducing word games, what-if questions, ambiguous meanings, and quixotic analogies.

With highs come **creative hangovers.** The Christmas tree pattern is very energy intensive. The brain uses a lot of energy already; even more so when we activate every region for any input. Imagine a large company. An incoming payment might normally head to the accounting department. But for Ne types, every employee from janitors to executives starts exploring the meanings and possibilities of the payment. Naturally, squabbling and contradictions may occur, and routine work is delayed. Thus, **Ne types may feel off-task, contradict themselves,** or pursue possibilities that hinder each other.

Of all personalities, the Ne types might seem least likely to find a solid blue, zen-like state of flow, when every region is in synch and working together efficiently. Yet the Ne types **can find zen, but only after practicing and internalizing an activity over weeks, months, or years**. An ENFP actor finds zen when performing his honed part in a play, while an ENFP musician finds zen while playing guitar and singing his favorite song, and the ENFP ballet dancer of fifteen years finds zen just by visualizing herself performing a favorite ballet piece. The irony is that Ne types, who have some of the shortest attention spans, require laborious practice in order to find inner peace.

The Ne types are more than flashing lights. They **use regions that support imagination**. In particular, ENFPs are usually good at acting as-if and mimicking others while ENTPs are adept at weighing multiple pros and cons at once in a strategic way, as masterful game players.

Essential Tips

When working with persons who prefer this cognitive process, consider the following tips.

- They prefer diverse inputs for brainstorming. Allow sensory distractions with television, radio, friends, and so forth all present at once.
- Allow their goals and meanings to coalesce from various inputs, mental processes, and side treks rather than pushing a linear process.
- Focus on meanings and relationships *between* ideas, starting perhaps with metaphors and analogies. Make sure the analogies work well!
- They may need help taking abstract and associational ideas into literal communications that will be effective with others.
- Encourage role-play, acting as-if, and ad-hoc problem solving. Feel free to propose fanciful or vague scenarios that afford improvising and imagining.
- Use some humor, word-play, and similar cognitive games. If people are laughing together, there is a good chance they are using this process.

Andrea: She loves books, meeting new people, and talking about ideas. She is close to her friends and family, who know her as outgoing, dramatic, and smart as a whip. She works as a lead video game designer, enjoys nonlinear plots, and likes exploring lots of options for visual effects and music. Her best-fit personality type is ENTP, which is ~3% of the USA population.

ENTP: Extraverted Intuiting (Ne) in lead role with Introverted Thinking (Ti) in support role.

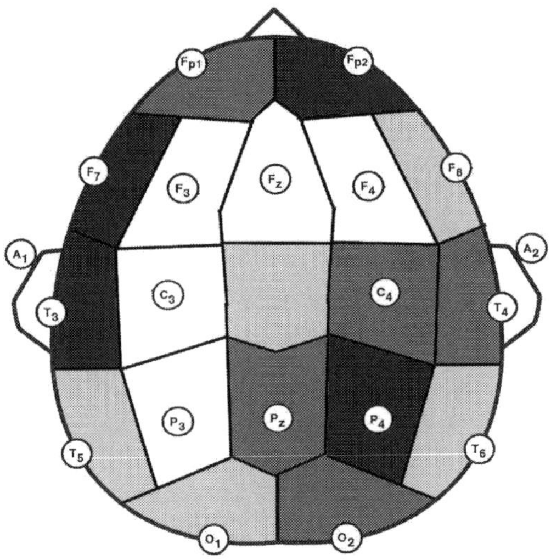

Figure 6-6: Andrea's neocortex activity.
Active regions are darker here.

Table 6-6: Andrea's Cognitive Skill-Set (based on her EEG results)

Activity	Skill-Set
High	Process Manager (Fp2), Imaginative Mimic (F7), Precise Speaker (T3), Strategic Gamer (P4)
High-Mid	Chief Judge (Fp1), Flowing Artist (C4), Intuitive Listener (T4), Abstract Impressionist (O2)
Low-Mid	Grounded Believer (F8), Sensitive Mediator (T5), Purposeful Futurist (T6), Visual Engineer (O1)
Low	Deductive Analyst (F3), Expert Classifier (F4), Factual Storekeeper (C3), Tactical Navigator (P3)

Cognitive Focus: Andrea relies on a "Christmas tree" pattern to feed all brain regions and quickly tap relationships across contexts. Also, she may get "in the zone" doing a rehearsed activity or doing a task with expertise.

Phineas: He is energetic, imaginative, random, adventurous, inspiring, and highly observant of people, able to size up someone's psychology in an instant. His closest friends know him as loyal. He is an actor, though he has sampled many life experiences from martial artist to bartender to poet. His best-fit personality type is ENFP, which is ~5% of the USA population.

ENFP: Extraverted Intuiting (Ne) in lead role with Introverted Feeling (Fi) in support role.

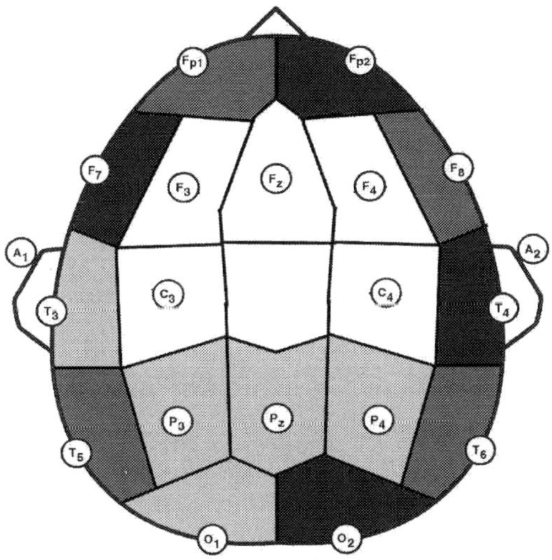

Figure 6-7: Phineas's neocortex activity.
Active regions are darker here.

Table 6-7: Phineas's Cognitive Skill-Set (based on his EEG results)

Activity	Skill-Set
High	Process Manager (Fp2), Imaginative Mimic (F7), Intuitive Listener (T4), Abstract Impressionist (O2)
High-Mid	Chief Judge (Fp1), Grounded Believer (F8), Sensitive Mediator (T5), Purposeful Futurist (T6)
Low-Mid	Precise Speaker (T3), Tactical Navigator (P3), Strategic Gamer (P4), Visual Engineer (O1)
Low	Deductive Analyst (F3), Expert Classifier (F4), Factual Storekeeper (C3), Flowing Artist (C4)

Cognitive Focus: Phineas relies on a "Christmas tree" pattern to feed all brain regions and quickly tap relationships across contexts. Also, he may get "in the zone" doing a rehearsed activity or doing a task with expertise.

Introverted Intuiting (Ni)

"Draw upon the whole brain to realize an answer to a novel problem."

Mainly INTJ and INFJ. Also ENTJ and ENFJ.

Key Findings

Here are key features of this cognitive process based on the lab research.

The Ni types often **show a whole-brain, zen-like pattern**. This pattern occurs when all regions of the neocortex are in synch and dominated by brain waves that are medium-low frequency and very high-amplitude. This pattern is typical of someone whose mind is awake yet relaxed. It shows as a solid, bright blue on the EEG monitor and occurs for all personality types when they engage in their specific area of expertise. Yet Ni types also show this pattern whenever they are tasked with the opposite: to **tackle unfamiliar, novel problems**.

What is this zen state like? When presented with a problem, the Ni types seek to **harness all neocortex regions in order to "realize" an answer**. Imagine a troop of blind men trying to identify a secret object by touch. One man feels a trunk and says, "tree"; another detects four legs and says "table"; a third feels tusks and says "boar". Like the blind men, each region offers a different perspective, and a zen-like synchronous state allows the person to reconcile various perspectives to arrive at a best-fit answer (an elephant).

This zen state might occur in a jiffy or hold for the duration of a task, or it might manifest later when the person returns to the problem, more informed with knowledge and life experiences and/or free from competing distractions. Sometimes, when the brain's regions offer highly divergent answers, no amount of triangulation can synthesize an answer.

This zen state **works best when focusing on a single question, without distractions** that might cause the various regions to fall out of synch. The person might think, "Be quiet world, I just need to stop and think!" When an answer does pop to mind, it **might seem like an expert's work** with flourishes of novelty or even an unusual approach to a task. After all, other types show this state when acting as experts. Or the result might be incomprehensible, far from what people understand, even if it works well.

The Ni types may easily **show a zen state when tasked to envision the future**. "Close your eyes and imagine your life ten years from now in as much detail as possible, focusing on what will occur." When tasked with this question, people of all types may show activity in region T6, which weighs what will occur, or sometimes in regions that reflect wishful thinking, odds-assessment, and so forth. Ni types show activity in T6 but may easily enter the zen state instead. The future: what could be more novel and unfamiliar!

The INTJ and INFJ types show other patterns. Both have **strong visual thinking** (regions O1 and/or O2) with **openness to novelty and attention to process** (region Fp2). For this reason, they may be slow to arrive at decisions or struggle to provide explanations. Moreover, INFJs tend to show activity in region F7 for empathizing with people while INTJs tend to have more efficient brain activity overall, like other Te types.

Types with this process in a support role, ENTJ and ENFJ, **usually benefit from a physical or sensory focus**—an exercise or mnemonic—to get to the zen state. Appeals to **metaphysical questions** such as expounding on the meaning of a life after death can also provoke this state. These two types also show relatively less interest in brainstorming and asking what-if questions.

Besides holistic problem-solving, the Ni types **respond to tasks in a serious and predictable manner**, though they lack an appetite for rote practice, which is key to burning new neural pathways to enjoy specialization. Thus, Ni types are **generalists**, not specialists. They are slow to commit to permanently hard-wiring their brain around a particular task.

Essential Tips

When working with persons who prefer this cognitive process, consider the following tips.

- They prefer time away from external stimulation and mundane demands in order to access their rich internal processes.
- They benefit from a physical or sensory focus (e.g. using a finger while reading) to stay focused while gathering information (reading, etc.).
- Help them verbally or visually communicate the hazy multitude of factors they consider as they arrive at a holistic solution to a problem.
- Provide techniques for them to turn to when their introspective intuiting process isn't working and they need to act fast.
- Carve out time for them to explore the future and visions of what will be. Also work with them to develop specifics to actualize these visions.
- Encourage rich experiences that feed different brain regions, so when they search within themselves, their brain has something to offer them.

Tom: He is quiet, hard-working, analytical, and usually busy at his computer completing various creative technical projects. Inside his mind, anything can be conjured up when a creative formula is applied. He is trained as an aeronautical engineer but transitioned to become a science fiction writer. His best-fit personality type is INTJ, which is ~1% of the USA population.

INTJ: Introverted Intuiting (Ni) in lead role with Extraverted Thinking (Te) in support role.

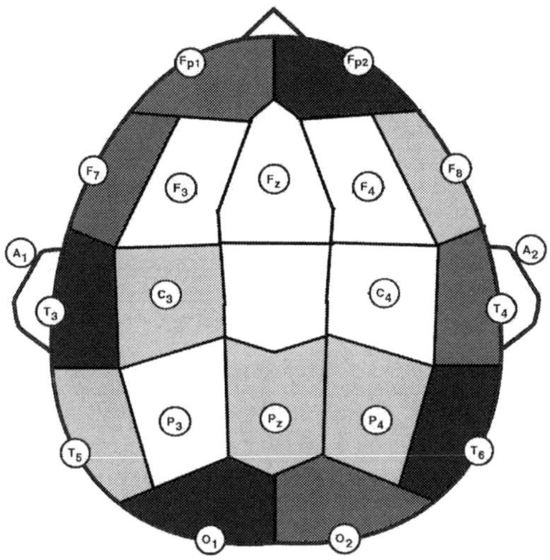

Figure 6-8: Tom's neocortex activity.
Active regions are darker here.

Table 6-8: Tom's Cognitive Skill-Set (based on his EEG results)

Activity	Skill-Set
High	Process Manager (Fp2), Precise Speaker (T3), Purposeful Futurist (T6), Visual Engineer (O1)
High-Mid	Chief Judge (Fp1), Imaginative Mimic (F7), Intuitive Listener (T4), Abstract Impressionist (O2)
Low-Mid	Grounded Believer (F8), Factual Storekeeper (C3), Sensitive Mediator (T5), Strategic Gamer (P4)
Low	Deductive Analyst (F3), Expert Classifier (F4), Tactical Navigator (P3), Flowing Artist (C4)

Cognitive Focus: Tom relies on getting "in the zone" to solve novel or highly complex problems, to allow his brain to triangulate an answer. Also, he may get "in the zone" when doing a task with expertise.

Melissa: She has several sides: usually friendly and occasionally critical, often driven and then exhausted, very sensitive and sometimes wildly enthusiastic. She has a wide circle of friends and is involved in many projects including technical editing, stage plays, and couples counseling after earning a social work degree. Her best-fit personality type is INFJ, which is ~1% of the USA population.

INFJ: Introverted Intuiting (Ni) in lead role with Extraverted Feeling (Fe) in support role.

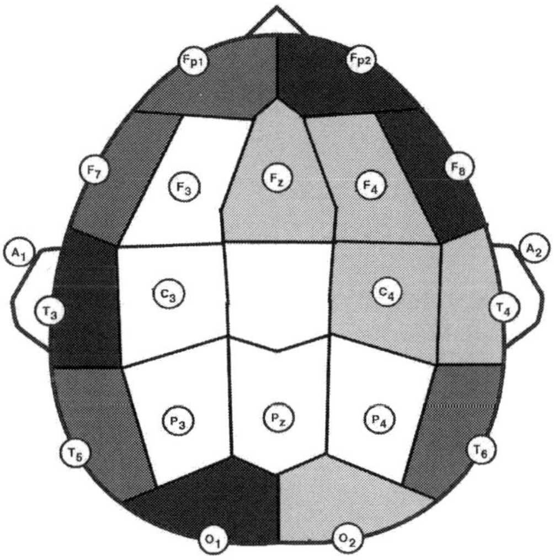

Figure 6-9: Melissa's neocortex activity.
Active regions are darker here.

Table 6-9: Melissa's Cognitive Skill-Set (based on her EEG results)

Activity	Skill-Set
High	Process Manager (Fp2), Grounded Believer (F8), Precise Speaker (T3), Visual Engineer (O1)
High-Mid	Chief Judge (Fp1), Imaginative Mimic (F7), Sensitive Mediator (T5), Purposeful Futurist (T6)
Low-Mid	Expert Classifier (F4), Flowing Artist (C4), Intuitive Listener (T4), Abstract Impressionist (O2)
Low	Deductive Analyst (F3), Factual Storekeeper (C3), Tactical Navigator (P3), Strategic Gamer (P4)

Cognitive Focus: Melissa relies on getting "in the zone" to solve novel or highly complex problems, to allow her brain to triangulate an answer. Also, she may get "in the zone" when doing a task with expertise.

Extraverted Thinking (Te)

"Manage resources efficiently to quickly decide based on the evidence."
Mainly ESTJ and ENTJ. Also ISTJ and INTJ.

Key Findings

Here are key features of this cognitive process based on the lab research.

The Te types often **show efficient use of mental energy as they rely on evidence-based decision-making**. Consider, the brain is the body's hungriest organ. Intense thinking uses up a lot of calories and can leave us fatigued, perhaps exhausted, even after sitting most of the day. With fatigue, come mistakes. Yet individuals who are leaders must often be on-the-go for many hours, providing plausible explanations that others accept and making decisions that are effective, at least for the time being. The Te types often excel as executives because their brains are well-suited to meet this challenge.

The Te types rely on **four key regions**. They show activity in **left-brain regions for hearing, seeing, recalling, and deciding** (regions T3, O1, C3 and Fp1, respectively). Beyond these key regions, the rest of the lights may be shut off in the metaphorical mansion that is the neocortex. Even when prompted to use other regions, the Te types may choose to simply rely on region Fp1 to quickly work up a response that is doable and sufficient.

The four key regions all work to promote evidence-based thinking. The Te types **rely on measurable sensory information**. They exercise good hand-eye coordination, gravitate to factual and numeric detail, speak clearly and grammatically with few vague "whatchamacallits", and tend to arrange information spatially, using charts, tables, and diagrams. They may notice, but are usually not swayed by, tone of voice or aesthetics or such, though they may decide to so do for expedience or when they notice measurable results.

The Te types **focus on goals and are stimulated by task completion and error correction**. Besides explaining and deciding, region Fp1 notes errors in the environment and filters out unwanted information, including negative feedback from others. Thus, Te types tend to brush off negatives or distractions and point out errors. This region also helps suppress emotional responses from deeper brain layers in favor of cognitive responses. Finally, though goal driven in general, ESTJs and ENTJs are **less excited about the minutia of implementing goals** and prefer to direct others to do so.

For Te types, **actionable comes before accurate or what-if**. An ENTJ may speed through a math problem set and self-report that his answers are accurate; however, inspection reveals mistakes. Or an ESTJ manager may do a great presentation, speaking with energy and confidence with solid statistics and a neat flow chart; yet, she is passed over for promotion because she was "predictable" or didn't draw upon other brain regions to round-out things. Thus, **quick efficiency may sometimes become a pitfall**.

All Te types show high activity in region F8, which handles **deeply felt personal values, often expressed in a negative way**. For example, the region alights when they say "stupid" or "immoral" rather than when they say "smart" or "moral", which they may take for granted as necessary. This, along with error detection using Fp1, means they are acutely aware of failures to live up to standards, moral or otherwise.

There are variations. **Female Te types tend to show more diverse brain activity and respond more to social feedback**. ISTJs and INTJs are more visual, more attentive to voice tone, and focus on implementing ideas over quick decision-making. ESTJs attend more to details, are more open to brainstorming, and tend to listen intently to authority figures. Finally, ENTJs can enter a creative mode (similar to INTJs) and rely on cortical circuits (page 45) that link key brain regions for hyper-fast thinking.

Essential Tips

When working with persons who prefer this cognitive process, consider the following tips.

- They use their brain in an energy-efficient way, relying chiefly on seeing measurable elements, hearing words, and making decisions.
- They use and respond to facts and figures, preferably using visual/spatial formats like charts, diagrams, and grids.
- They attend to the specific words they and others use, such that the choice of one word over another can alter the bigger picture for them.
- Brainstorming, especially when it is off-task, is a non-preferred activity. That said, they may get creative for leisure or in quiet moments.
- Help them invest in defining their areas of strength. Important: Do not mistake their confidence and speed for competence.
- They can do rapid decision-making and/or explaining for many hours. Encourage them to take time to consider their responses more thoroughly.

Jocelyn: She is a paragon of leadership with an iron will. She works tirelessly as a diplomat while also fulfilling duties at home with family, including caring for her aging parents. She reads, tracks news, and talks with others constantly to grow her storehouse of facts, treaties, laws, customs, and procedures. Her best-fit personality type is ESTJ, which is ~18% of the USA population.

ESTJ: Extraverted Thinking (Te) in lead role with Introverted Sensing (Si) in support role.

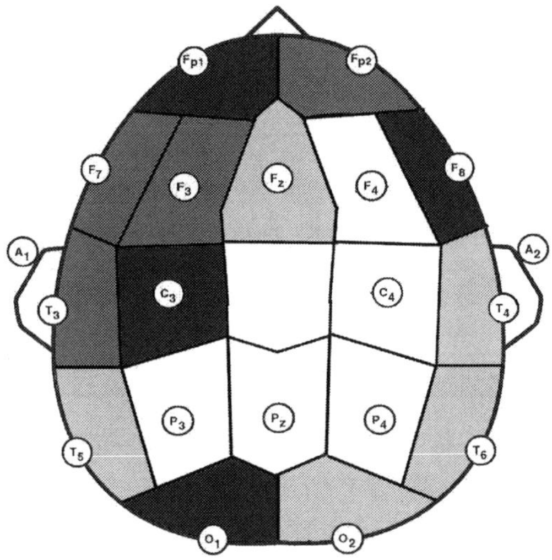

Figure 6-10: Jocelyn's neocortex activity.
Active regions are darker here.

Table 6-10: Jocelyn's Cognitive Skill-Set (based on her EEG results)

Activity	Skill-Set
High	Chief Judge (Fp1), Grounded Believer (F8), Factual Storekeeper (C3), Visual Engineer (O1),
High-Mid	Process Manager (Fp2), Imaginative Mimic (F7), Precise Speaker (T3), Deductive Analyst (F3)
Low-Mid	Intuitive Listener (T4), Sensitive Mediator (T5), Purposeful Futurist (T6), Abstract Impressionist (O2)
Low	Expert Classifier (F4), Tactical Navigator (P3), Strategic Gamer (P4), Flowing Artist (C4)

Cognitive Focus: Jocelyn relies on efficient activity—seeing, hearing, steps, and facts with the analytical left brain—to confidently make rapid, evidence-based decisions. Also, she may get "in the zone" doing a task with expertise.

Scott: He is confident, energetic, efficient, and highly focused on manifesting his career dreams. His life as an entrepreneur in biotechnology demands that he constantly self-educate, manage others' gifts and pitfalls, and stay tuned to bottom-line results in order to maximize his opportunities. His best-fit personality type is ENTJ, which is ~3% of the USA population.

ENTJ: Extraverted Thinking (Te) in lead role with Introverted Intuiting (Ni) in support role.

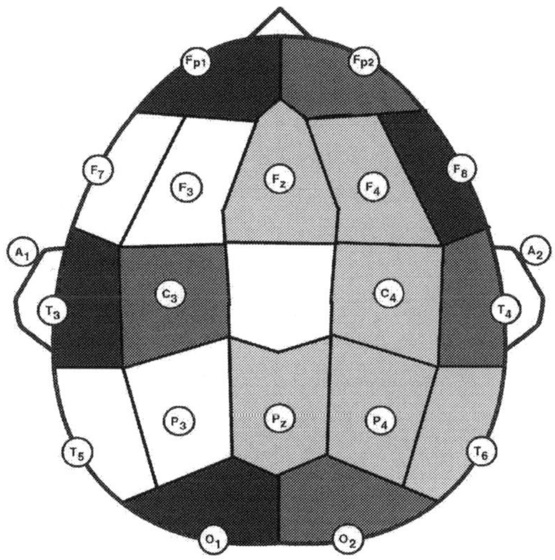

Figure 6-11: Scott's neocortex activity.
Active regions are darker here.

Table 6-11: Scott's Cognitive Skill-Set (based on his EEG results)

Activity	Skill-Set
High	Chief Judge (Fp1), Grounded Believer (F8), Precise Speaker (T3), Visual Engineer (O1)
High-Mid	Process Manager (Fp2), Factual Storekeeper (C3), Intuitive Listener (T4), Abstract Impressionist (O2),
Low-Mid	Expert Classifier (F4), Flowing Artist (C4), Strategic Gamer (P4), Purposeful Futurist (T6)
Low	Imaginative Mimic (F7), Sensitive Mediator (T5), Deductive Analyst (F3), Tactical Navigator (P3),

Cognitive Focus: Scott relies on efficient activity—seeing, hearing, steps, and facts with the analytical left brain—to confidently make quick, evidence-based decisions. Also, he may get "in the zone" doing a task with expertise.

Introverted Thinking (Ti)

"Reason multiple ways to objectively and accurately analyze problems."

Mainly ISTP and INTP. Also, ESTP and ENTP.

Key Findings

Here are key features of this cognitive process based on the lab research.

The Ti types show **high use of four regions that afford complex logical reasoning** (regions F3, F4, P3, and P4). While everyone shows *some* use of these regions, every Ti type shows ongoing, strong activity in at least one of the four, with moderate activity in the others that is either ongoing or occurs during problem solving situations. Comparatively, Ti types dedicate themselves to using brain resources that other people tend to neglect.

Region F3 helps Ti types **linearly derive solutions** using verbal/symbolic reasoning. For example, if A=B, and B=C, then logically A=C. Using this region is like moving (and perhaps backtracking) along the branches of a tree. ESTPs use this region above the other four Ti types, followed by INTPs.

Region F4 helps Ti types **categorize and define concepts** in a holistic way using a best-fit process. For example, it helps us determine whether a dolphin better fits in the mammal or fish category as it sorts many categories simultaneously. INTPs use this region above the other four, followed by ESTP.

Region P3 helps Ti types **integrate visual-kinesthetic data**. It aids object identification, motor skills such as aim, and mathematical calculating using a grid. It also helps us determine where we end and the rest of the world begins. ISTPs use this region above the other four, followed by ENTP.

Finally, region P4 helps Ti types **holistically weigh numerous pros and cons of many uncertain or risky factors or options** at once to arrive at a single result. For example, how are the odds when you play a particular betting game? ENTPs use this region the most, followed by ISTP.

These four regions are nestled inside the neocortex, away from direct contact with the outside world. Thus, these types can think even when there are visual, auditory, and kinesthetic distractions. This gives their decision-making a **"deep" or "detached" quality** which fits their self-reported tendency to withdraw from the world in order to think thoroughly and clearly.

The Ti types are more likely than others to show a disassociated brain state. That is, the EEG monitor shows the neocortex as a solid green (theta waves). The Ti types often show this pattern when meeting a new person or starting a new activity, or when arguing an idea with someone. **In a dissociated state, their neocortex shuts out raw emotions in order to enjoy objectivity**. In interpersonal situations, this green "shield" may easily come up and remain for several minutes while they assess the new person or task. In addition to a disassociated state, they may sometimes show a tennis-hop pattern (ISTP and ESTP) or a Christmas tree pattern (INTP and ENTP).

Of all types, Ti types show **the least interest in listening**. They show low to no activity in regions T3 and T4, which are typically active for other people. Male Ti types in particular are likely to listen for only a second or two when someone starts speaking; then, activity in T3 and T4 vanishes as their attention moves elsewhere unless they force themselves to focus on listening. When they stop listening, they can't report back accurately what was said. Female Ti types are somewhat more attentive listeners, though with effort.

When Ti types discuss contentious or complex ideas, such as one-on-one debates about politics or philosophy, they may quickly engage all four regions plus executive regions Fp1 and Fp2. These regions alight bright red on the EEG monitor, indicating maximal attention to **examining a topic from multiple angles**—each angle from a different brain region—while **integrating the angles into a coherent way** as part of an explanation or decision.

Essential Tips

When working with persons who prefer this cognitive process, consider the following tips.

- They tend to rely on sophisticated, complex reasoning using multiple reasoning methods including deducing, categorizing, weighing odds, etc.
- Their thought processes are not directly linked to sensory inputs, so their decision-making tends to be "deep" and "detached".
- Set aside time for them to clarify—to make and correct mistakes and inconsistencies—as they strive for high accuracy before implementing.
- They are adept at navigating conceptual terrain, and possibly physical terrain, so provide space for them to shift course or backtrack.
- Provide techniques—besides putting up a "brick wall"—to deal with excessive social and emotional data, which may overwhelm them.
- They may quickly stop listening as they assess the relevance of what others are saying. Consider asking them to repeat back what they've heard.

Natalie: She is self-contained, keenly observant, and analytical. She enjoys animals, the beautiful vistas of the outdoors, and computer graphics. No one says she is emotional or rash as she weighs odds and abstains from opinions until she informs herself. She is a professional musician and mainly plays drums. Her best-fit personality type is ISTP, which is ~4% of the USA population.

ISTP: Introverted Thinking (Ti) in lead role with Extraverted Sensing (Se) in support role.

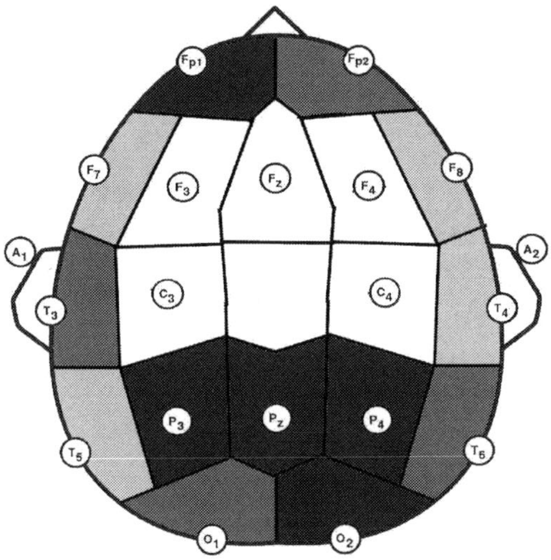

Figure 6-12: Natalie's neocortex activity.
Active regions are darker here.

Table 6-12: Natalie's Cognitive Skill-Set

Activity	Skill-Set
High	Chief Judge (Fp1), Tactical Navigator (P3), Abstract Impressionist (O2), Strategic Gamer (P4)
High-Mid	Process Manager (Fp2), Precise Speaker (T3), Purposeful Futurist (T6), Visual Engineer (O1)
Low-Mid	Imaginative Mimic (F7), Grounded Believer (F8), Intuitive Listener (T4), Sensitive Mediator (T5)
Low	Deductive Analyst (F3), Expert Classifier (F4), Factual Storekeeper (C3), Flowing Artist (C4)

Cognitive Focus: Natalie relies on four interior brain regions that focus on complex reasoning including deduction, categorization, odds-assessment, and spatial navigation. Also, she may get "in the zone" doing a task with expertise.

John: He is quiet and analytical with an arm-chair love of wordplay, philosophy, and history. He is warm with his family but not with strangers, and he collaborates with dozens of peers around the world. He is trained as a chemist and now shepherds a team of younger scientists on complex research projects. His best-fit personality type is INTP, which is ~1% of the USA population.

INTP: Introverted Thinking (Ti) in lead role with Extraverted Intuiting (Ne) in support role.

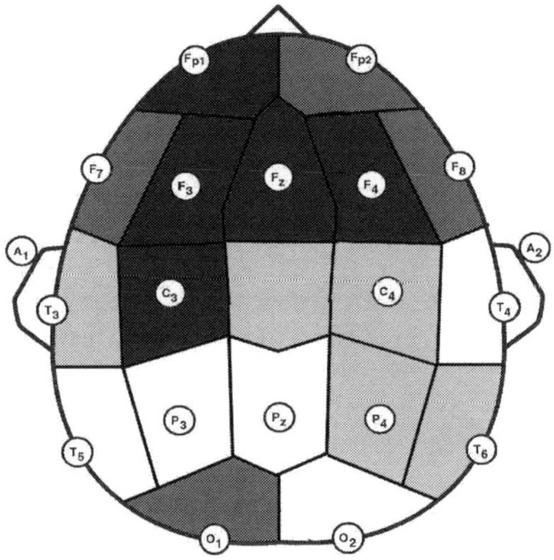

Figure 6-13: John's neocortex activity.
Active regions are darker here.

Table 6-13: John's Cognitive Skill-Set (based on his EEG results)

Activity	Skill-Set
High	Chief Judge (Fp1), Deductive Analyst (F3), Expert Classifier (F4), Factual Storekeeper (C3)
High-Mid	Process Manager (Fp2), Imaginative Mimic (F7), Grounded Believer (F8), Visual Engineer (O1)
Low-Mid	Precise Speaker (T3), Flowing Artist (C4), Strategic Gamer (P4), Purposeful Futurist (T6),
Low	Intuitive Listener (T4), Tactical Navigator (P3), Sensitive Mediator (T5), Abstract Impressionist (O2)

Cognitive Focus: John relies on four interior brain regions that focus on complex reasoning including deduction, categorization, odds-assessment, and spatial navigation. Also, he may get "in the zone" doing a task with expertise.

Extraverted Feeling (Fe)

"Evaluate and communicate values to enhance social relationships."

Mainly ESFJ and ENFJ. Also, ISFJ and INFJ.

Key Findings

Here are key features of this cognitive process based on the lab research.

The Fe types often show brain activity that reflects their **focus on social responsibility**. They use neocortex regions that help them communicate, evaluate others' behavior, plan for the future, and analyze complex problems. That said, regardless of which regions are in use, Fe types are masters of explaining and deciding, with a focus on values, ethics, and social action.

The Fe types show a lot of activity in region Fp1, particularly as they talk. They focus on people-related issues and goals, and are **stimulated by communicating their explanations and decisions**, often using and responding to highly **value-laden language** and issues of social and **ethical responsibility**. Besides explaining and deciding, region Fp1 notes errors in the environment and filters out unwanted information such as others' negative feedback. Thus, Fe types notice others' problems and seek to work past negatives or distractions.

Region Fp1 also helps **suppress emotional impulses from deep in the brain in favor of sophisticated cognitive responses**. For example, an ENFJ heard about a drunk driver whose behavior ended up killing someone. When asked how she felt, she avoided a "simplistic emotional response" and launched into a larger discussion of human beings' ethical responsibilities, with a lot of activity in Fp1. Similarly, when an ESFJ heard the same story, she stated she was "outraged" but spoke in a calm tone atypical of other types. She too showed high activity in region Fp1 as she explained her response, with a focus on rules for social responsibility. Fe types show lower activity in region Fp2, which helps us introspect and apply disruptive information at the cost of feeling depressed. When Fp2 fails, we get hostile. This may explain why Fe types **may sometimes suddenly switch from highly composed to very angry**.

All Fe types show high activity in region T5, which helps us **adjust to social feedback**. When we receive negative input from others such as frowns, this region hits us with feelings of embarrassment, and possibly guilt or shame, to prompt us to adjust our behavior. The Fe types are highly responsive to these feelings. Of all personality types, ISFJ shows the most activity in this region.

Male Fe types tend to show more activity in T5 than their female counterparts. Studies suggest that, in general, males use T5 more than females to disambiguate faces; and in fact, like male Fi types, male Fe types focus on values over logic and attend a lot to people, which may explain the extra activity.

Both ENFJ and ESFJ also show very high activity in region T3, which helps handle diction, grammar, and other **analytical aspects of speech**. At the same time, both types show the least activity of all personality types in visual regions O1 and O2. Only an introduction to a new person ignites these regions.

ENFJ and ESFJ show **high activity in one or maybe two reasoning regions** (F4, F4, P3 or P4) while showing no activity in the others. Thus, along with a highly active Fp1 region, they can sometimes look highly logical.

ESFJs are more left-brained, showing high activity in C3 and F7, regions that relate to recalling facts, following steps, and using imagination to copy others' behaviors. ESFJs may also show activity in region F3 or P3, which help them make linear deductions and navigate the environment.

ENFJs are more right-brained, showing high activity in C4 and T4, regions that relate to whole-body motion and assessing intentions. ENFJs may also show activity in region F4 or P4, which help them classify, define, and weigh odds. ENFJs also rely on cortical circuits (page 45) that link key brain regions for hyper-fast thinking. Overall, this gives them an "intuitive" feel.

Essential Tips

When working with persons who prefer this cognitive process, consider the following tips.

- They attend to you, your words, and how you may be evaluating them, though they may show few outward physical signs of doing so.
- Give them room to discuss considerations of justice and injustice. Ethics of people's choices and failings are highly salient to them.
- While they often stay sociable and may self-disclose in order to build a relationship, be cautious about implying that you fully understand them.
- They use and respond to value-laden language. They focus on word choice more than tone of voice, which may be steady even when upset.
- They are more verbal than visual, and may look and sound highly logical sometimes, for certain tasks, while eschewing logic in general.
- Some of them are more visionary and planful for the future while others are more playful and willing to consider what-if.

Suravi: She is cheerful, planful, energetic, friendly, and talkative. She has a huge circle of family and friends. She works at a large company where she helps people turn their work into audio-visual presentations with charts, timelines, and such. She likes the people more than the work, though she says she has learned a lot. Her best-fit personality type is ESFJ, which is ~18% of the USA population.

ESFJ: Extraverted Feeling (Fe) in lead role with Introverted Sensing (Si) in support role.

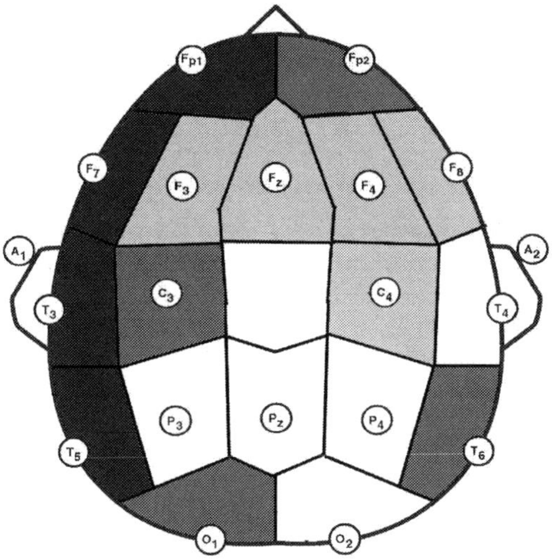

Figure 6-14: Suravi's neocortex activity.
Active regions are darker here.

Table 6-14: Suravi's Cognitive Skill-Set

Activity	Skill-Set
High	Chief Judge (Fp1), Imaginative Mimic (F7), Sensitive Mediator (T5), Precise Speaker (T3)
High-Mid	Process Manager (Fp2), Factual Storekeeper (C3), Purposeful Futurist (T6), Visual Engineer (O1)
Low-Mid	Deductive Analyst (F3), Expert Classifier (F4), Flowing Artist (C4), Grounded Believer (F8)
Low	Intuitive Listener (T4), Tactical Navigator (P3), Strategic Gamer (P4), Abstract Impressionist (O2)

Cognitive Focus: Suravi relies on key brain regions for speech, decision-making, and social behavior in order to communicate with and manage people. Also, she may get "in the zone" doing a task with expertise.

Jerome: He is sociable, business-like, smart, and meticulous. He is a hospital administrator. He loves the people he works with and he cares deeply about health, though slow progress and institutional fear of change frustrate him. He enjoys beach trips with his family, quiet time at his piano, and nights dancing with his wife. His best-fit personality type is ENFJ, which is ~5% of the USA population.

ENFJ: Extraverted Feeling (Fe) in lead role with Introverted Intuiting (Ni) in support role.

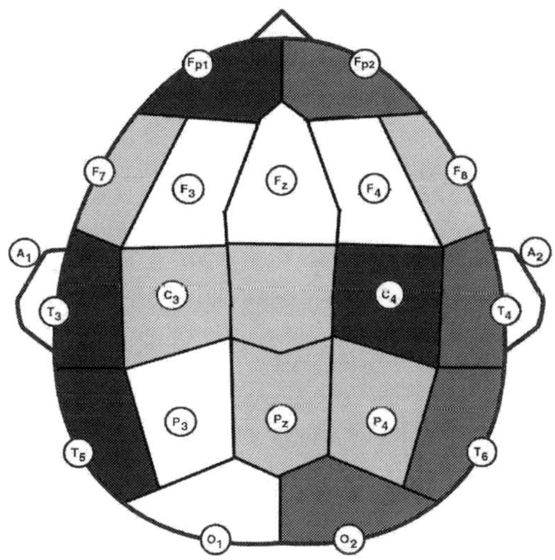

Figure 6-15: Jerome's neocortex activity.
Active regions are darker here.

Table 6-15: Jerome's Cognitive Skill-Set (based on his EEG results)

Activity	Skill-Set
High	Chief Judge (Fp1), Precise Speaker (T3), Flowing Artist (C4), Sensitive Mediator (T5)
High-Mid	Process Manager (Fp2), Intuitive Listener (T4), Purposeful Futurist (T6), Abstract Impressionist (O2)
Low-Mid	Imaginative Mimic (F7), Grounded Believer (F8), Factual Storekeeper (C3), Strategic Gamer (P4)
Low	Deductive Analyst (F3), Expert Classifier (F4), Tactical Navigator (P3), Visual Engineer (O1)

Cognitive Focus: Jerome relies on key brain regions for speech, decision-making, and social behavior in order to communicate with and manage people. Also, he may get "in the zone" doing a task with expertise.

Introverted Feeling (Fi)

"Listen with your whole self to locate and support what's important."
Mainly ISFP and INFP. Also, ESFP and ENFP.

Key Findings

Here are key features of this cognitive process based on the lab research.

The Fi types often enter a special listening mode. They are **consummate listeners**. They thoroughly engage all brain regions that process voice, words, and sounds; moreover, they may easily enter a unique whole-brain state when listening to other people, whoever those people might be.

The Fi types can **listen in a holistic way** that recruits all regions of the neocortex. When someone starts talking, they enter this state, which shows on the EEG monitor as a solid bright blue. All regions are alert and yet relaxed and open to input; also, all regions are in synch rather than jumping around. The whole brain acts as a metaphorical still pond that allows a speaker to project herself and be heard. In the midst of a contentious debate, most people jump to formulate a response even before others have finished their turn. Yet the Fi types can really wait patiently and keep listening.

INFPs and ISFPs differ in how they listen. INFPs are more likely to enter the listening mode and stay with it longer. They can hold this state for ten minutes or more as they truly, actively listen. In contrast, **ISFPs listen briefly for a quick assessment and then move to action**. Both styles have merit.

INFPs may really get to the core of a person's psychology by listening for so long. The flip side: INFPs are less likely to defend their own views or take action, though when they stop listening, region Fp1 usually gets very active as they make a strong (and perhaps final) decision. INFPs may also show the highly-creative Christmas tree brain pattern typical of Ne types.

ISFPs are **attentive when others withhold information**. They show high activity in region T5 when they are curious about someone's thinking. This region normally prompts us to adjust to social feedback. Conversely, region T5 is active for ISFPs only when they *haven't* received feedback; and after they get it, T5 goes quiet and they don't adjust their behavior. ISFPs sometimes show the tennis-hop pattern typical of Se types, helping them adapt quickly to the moment. Taken together, they are good at talking with others to find practical solutions.

All Fi types show **high activity in regions T3 and T4, which handle**

language including diction, grammar, and voice tone. The Fi types hear with precision and insight, and also **carefully compose their own speech, attending to both content and delivery**, for the desired impact. Region T4 also helps weigh motivation and intent, and gets active when they feel wronged. ISFP and ESFP, in particular, rely heavily on voice tone to hear other people's intentions when evaluating a person's authenticity or the morality of a situation.

The Fi types show high activity in region F8. These types are **stimulated by ranking of importance**, or what is more or less worthwhile. All people show activity here when expressing what's important to them, such as a musician saying "my music" or an idealist saying "my values" or when someone ranks their friends and family members from most to least likeable.

The Fi types show the **least activity in interior regions that aid logic** such as deducing, classifying, and defining. However, they use some logic to help evaluate people. The Fi types also show moderate activity in visual and kinesthetic regions (O1, O2, C3, and C4). Finally, they **rely on left-brain decision-making** (Fp1) more than attention to process (Fp2). That is, for all their listening and open-ended style, they can be quite definitive about decisions.

There are some variations. INFPs show activity in region F7, which helps them exercise a rich imagination. In contrast, ISFPs show more activity in T6, which helps them predict what will come next in the future.

Essential Tips

When working with persons who prefer this cognitive process, consider the following tips.

- They are listening intently to you, especially for tone of voice, motivations, words that link to your values, and what's left unsaid.
- Speak thoughtfully, take your time, and don't rush; because when they are done listening, they may seem surprisingly definitive about decisions.
- Speak to their values, especially positively-felt values, to get their attention. At the same time, remain true to yourself to avoid phony affect.
- They experience strong gradations of importance from like to dislike but may only verbalize circumstantial reasons for their evaluations.
- When trying to persuade them, know that their deep values and moral assessments tend to resist pragmatic arguments or contextual factors.
- Withholding feedback arouses their attention. Otherwise they are hard to faze and may not adjust their behavior to fit social expectations.

Bryan: He is full of contradictions: serious, fun-loving, academic, athletic, accommodating, rebellious—whatever his mood and the situation beckon. He is emotional, a keen listener and observer, and very independent. He travels a lot as an anthropologist, has built his own home, and rides a motorcycle. His best-fit personality type is ISFP, which is ~4% of the USA population.

ISFP: Introverted Feeling (Fi) in lead role with Extraverted Sensing (Se) in support role.

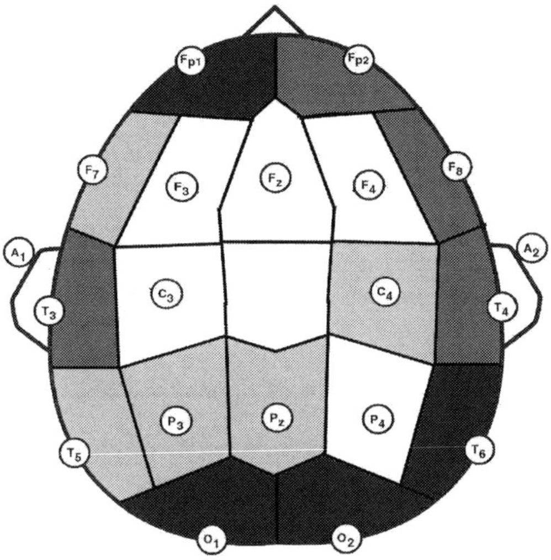

Figure 6-16: Bryan's neocortex activity.
Active regions are darker here.

Table 6-16: Bryan's Cognitive Skill-Set (based on his EEG results)

Activity	Skill-Set
High	Chief Judge (Fp1), Visual Engineer (O1), Abstract Impressionist (O2), Purposeful Futurist (T6)
High-Mid	Process Manager (Fp2), Precise Speaker (T3), Intuitive Listener (T4), Grounded Believer (F8)
Low-Mid	Imaginative Mimic (F7), Tactical Navigator (P3), Flowing Artist (C4), Sensitive Mediator (T5)
Low	Deductive Analyst (F3), Expert Classifier (F4), Factual Storekeeper (C3), Strategic Gamer (P4)

Cognitive Focus: Bryan relies on speech centers and can easily get "in the zone" while listening to others in order to "hear" with his whole brain. Also, he may get "in the zone" when doing a task with expertise.

Maria: She relies on her deeply felt personal identity and conscience to make decisions; and she is a patient, nuanced listener with a rich, playful imagination. She meets many "selves" as a psychologist and has written and illustrated a few books that use humorous stories to help people. Her best-fit personality type is INFP, which is ~1% of the USA population.

INFP: Introverted Feeling (Fi) in lead role with Extraverted Intuiting (Ne) in support role.

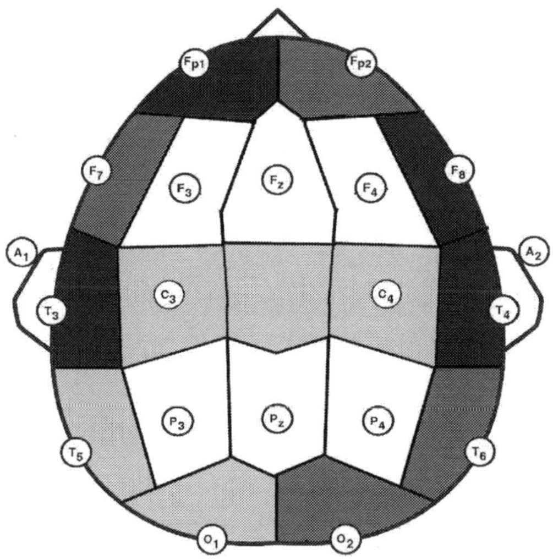

Figure 6-17: Maria's neocortex activity.
Active regions are darker here.

Table 6-17: Maria's Cognitive Skill-Set (based on her EEG results)

Activity	Skill-Set
High	Chief Judge (Fp1), Grounded Believer (F8), Precise Speaker (T3), Intuitive Listener (T4)
High-Mid	Process Manager (Fp2), Imaginative Mimic (F7), Purposeful Futurist (T6), Abstract Impressionist (O2)
Low-Mid	Sensitive Mediator (T5), Factual Storekeeper (C3), Flowing Artist (C4), Visual Engineer (O1)
Low	Deductive Analyst (F3), Expert Classifier (F4), Tactical Navigator (P3), Strategic Gamer (P4)

Cognitive Focus: Maria relies on speech centers and can easily get "in the zone" while listening to others in order to "hear" with her whole brain. Also, she may get "in the zone" when doing a task with expertise.

Table 6-2: Cognitive Processes Used by You and People You Know

Extraverted Processes	Introverted Processes
Perceiving—how we access data and focus attention	
Extraverted Sensing (Se) *"Act quickly and smoothly to handle whatever comes up in the moment."* a) People who use this process: b) Benefits of using this process: Mainly ESFP, ESTP. Also ISFP, ISTP.	**Introverted Sensing (Si)** *"Review and practice in order to specialize and meet group needs."* a) People who use this process: b) Benefits of using this process: Mainly ISTJ, ISFJ. Also ESTJ, ESFJ.
Extraverted Intuiting (Ne) *"Perceive and play with patterns of relationships across contexts."* a) People who use this process: b) Benefits of using this process: Mainly ENTP, ENFP. Also INTP, INFP.	**Introverted Intuiting (Ni)** *"Draw upon the whole brain to realize an answer to a novel problem."* a) People who use this process: b) Benefits of using this process: Mainly INTJ, INFJ. Also ENTJ, ENFJ.

Table 6-2 Cont.

Extraverted Processes	Introverted Processes
Judging—how we organize and make decisions	
Extraverted Thinking (Te) *"Manage resources efficiently to quickly decide based on the evidence."* a) People who use this process: b) Benefits of using this process: Mainly ESTJ, ENTJ. Also ISTJ, INTJ.	**Introverted Thinking (Ti)** *"Reason multiple ways to objectively and accurately analyze problems."* a) People who use this process: b) Benefits of using this process: Mainly ISTP, INTP. Also ESTP, ENTP.
Extraverted Feeling (Fe) *"Evaluate and communicate values to enhance social relationships."* a) People who use this process: b) Benefits of using this process: Mainly ESFJ, ENFJ. Also ISFJ, INFJ.	**Introverted Feeling (Fi)** *"Listen with your whole self to locate and support what's important."* a) People who use this process: b) Benefits of using this process: Mainly ISFP, INFP. Also ESFP, ENFP.

General Observations To-Date

In light of data, what is the neurological basis of Jung's theory and Myers' work?

1. Every individual is unique, a blend of personality type and life background.
2. There are clear correlations to the Jungian framework. These correlations take time to observe in the lab (several hours, not minutes).
3. Each of the eight Jungian cognitive processes can be defined as a pattern of holistic neurological tendencies, with various regions tapped when needed.
4. Statistical summation of activity over time reveals one's preferred regions and thus one's possible personality type. However, qualitative features like whole-brain states are truly key and not captured by an aggregate statistic.
5. The eight cognitive processes relate to how the neocortex works as a whole. For example, the Extraverted Thinking process doesn't just help us use resources efficiently. It shows up as efficient use of brain resources!
6. Personality shows up in multiple ways, including 1) Threshold of activation (how much stimulus is needed to get a region going), 2) A synergy of motivation and competence, 3) Speed of response time to various tasks, and 4) Whole-brain patterns such as what sends us into a state of flow.
7. There are whole-brain states, one of which reflects "flow" (creative expertise). A person's specific expertise can be related to his or her personality type pattern and/or background and training (dance, music, etc).
8. Besides one's lead cognitive process, there are multiple supporting processes. For example, ISFP has Fi as a lead process, and it appears that Se is second, Ni as third, etc. In contrast, ISFPs don't use much of Ti and Ne.
9. Post-experiment self-reflective questions, and both introverted and extraverted activities in controlled and free environments, are necessary to truly understand the full scope of what's going on in the brain.
10. Neuroscience is not like pencil-paper assessments such as the MBTI® assessment or the PTI® or ISCA™. It delivers raw data rather than inferred data. Thus, a study of five dozen people is valid and illuminating.
11. Posterior regions are more active for people who prefer introverting. People who prefer Sensing show more alpha activity (8.0 - 14.0 Hz). For people with a lead perceiving process (Se, Ne, Si, Ni), Fp2 is more active than Fp1.
12. Sex matters somewhat and culture matters for learned tasks like math. As for age, I've done no longitudinal research and limited myself to young adults.
13. Watching a brain in action is a profound experience!

7. Natalie: A Case Study

Say Hello to Natalie

What's brain mapping like? It is tremendously illuminating and humbling to watch people's brain activity in real time as they do various tasks. Here's a taste from a 3-hour session with one subject, a female ISTP whom I'll refer to as "Natalie" for her privacy. Natalie previously completed a ten-week seminar on personality and neurolinguistic programming, and we were both comfortable with ISTP as her best-fit type. She was only the second ISTP of my many subjects, so I was really curious. This is the same Natalie described on page 112.

What does ISTP mean? Here's a quick reminder. The 4-letter code points to an underlying pattern of eight mental functions described by Jung. One function is dominant while a second plays a support role, like this for ISTP:

- **Lead Process is Introverted Thinking (Ti)**: Decide based on theories, models, definitions, and principles.
- **Support Process is Extraverted Sensing (Se):** Focus on first-hand experience and enjoy sensory data.

Natalie was present with her boyfriend "Grant" (INFP) and my assistant, Yasha (ESTP). The lab occurred in a smallish, plain room in the early evening. I described to Natalie what to expect while Yasha and I linked her to the EEG machine. She had short hair so the red, elf-like EEG cap fit snugly! We injected gel between the cap's pickups and her scalp. The gel allows the machine to reliably read electromagnetic activity in the neocortex, that outer layer of the brain that is quintessentially human.

I normally run subjects through thirty minutes of individual tasks, thirty minutes of social tasks, and thirty minutes of open-ended tasks that fit their interests. That day I went much longer.

Meditating

Natalie started with three meditation exercises to try to reduce brain activity to solid black (inactive) as a baseline. The first exercise was progressive relaxation, eyes closed, with instructions to "clear your mind". As she "relaxed", I saw lots of brain activity, mainly in her visual and kinesthetic regions. Not so inactive! The next two exercises—staring at a fixed point and repetitively drawing a circle—quieted her brain. Since ISTPs prefer the Sensing and Thinking functions, and focus on a rich inner life, I was not surprised to see lots of kinesthetic and visual activity with eyes closed.

Signing Her Name

Next, Natalie signed her name with her preferred hand and with her non-preferred hand, and then signed backward with her non-preferred hand. A reasonable hypothesis is that signing with her nonpreferred hand should take more brainpower. After all, doing something unusual should take more work than doing something familiar, right? Not necessarily. The hypothesis holds true for Intuitors. Sensors consistently show the opposite result. As Yasha (ESTP) offered, and Natalie agreed, "The real way is more important than this fun idea task." This reminded me that brain activity links to both competence and motivation, and our type preferences influence what motivates us.

Solving Math Problems

Natalie completed math problems that started easy and got harder. A reasonable hypothesis is that harder problems beg more brainpower. But again, type showed its hand. Natalie's brain remained really quiet from start to finish, but she took longer to do the harder problems. She was working slowly and steadily, a tortoise rather than a hare, as theorized for folks who prefer Introversion and Sensing.

Moreover, she showed big bursts of activity between problems (after finishing one and before starting another) rather than during the problems. What was going on? As she explained afterward, she would break a problem into parts, work it, and then check her answer afterward. Checking spurred the extra activity. This reminded me how types with Introverted Thinking (INTP, ISTP) like to work problems following a known model or technique and then review afterward to improve and clarify their work. Her technique was natural and easy to her, and her energy went into checking.

The last and hardest problem did get her brain active. There was even a beautiful flash of pre-frontal "executive" activity when she said, "gave values to different variables" while explaining how she solved the problems. The pre-frontal regions are responsible for integrating and monitoring the rest of the brain as well as explaining and making decisions. For an ISTP, Introverted Thinking is dominant. Introverted Thinking is much about weighing different variables and perspectives. It's no surprise that her brain's executive regions got active around such a task.

General Observations

At this point, we were twenty minutes into a three-hour session. We took a short break. As I reviewed my notes about her brain activity in general, I noticed four major patterns:

Disassociated State: I saw frequent periods of solid green over the entire neocortex. I often see this pattern when subjects solve problems, argue, lose a game, or don't like someone. Solid green indicates a "disassociated" state. Natalie often started tasks with this pattern. For example, during a speed dating exercise, her brain spent several minutes here before she "warmed up" to the guy she was speed dating. It's as if Natalie raises a shield of objectivity and lets it down when she gets comfortable.

Sensory Immersion: Natalie frequently showed bright yellow splotches, especially when we got to musical activities. Yellow has the opposite meaning of green. It shows when people win a game, like someone, listen to music with eyes closed, or feel connected in their body. It's an associated state. Natalie is an avid musician and drummer. Her EEG was often solid yellow when she listened to her favorite music. Consider that ISTPs and ISFPs are known to immerse themselves in physical hobbies like surfing, music, dance or such. And in general, I find Sensors show more yellow in their pattern than Intuitors.

Concrete Reasoning: P3 was the most active region. P3 lies toward the back-left quadrant of the brain. This was Natalie's most active region over the whole lab. P3 is usually active in ST types, particularly STPs. It relates to motor activity. It lights up when people handle objects while blindfolded, or when they use a kinesthetic method to solve a math problem. Conversely, it is one of three least-active regions for NFJ types! Also, P3 doesn't directly link to any sensory regions. Natalie can think clearly and logically even in sensory-rich environments that might distract other types. No surprise for ISTP!

Effortful Listening: She showed low amplitude red in auditory regions. Introverted Thinking types (INTP, ISTP) tend to show low to no auditory activity—particularly among males. These types are quick to stop listening to others, perhaps when they determine low relevance or interest. This is the opposite of INFPs, who listen a lot, and listen actively with their whole brain. The amount of red indicated that when she did listen, doing so was a lot of work.

Figure 7-1 at right summarizes the average amplitude of activity in various regions for Natalie over the whole session. The pattern was fairly clear after twenty minutes and did not change substantially even as we tried various activities, though she did show some whole-brain "blue zone" activity while drumming later.

In the figure, region P3 is very high. It is responsible for integrating visual, spatial, and kinesthetic information. It also regulates one's sense of boundaries between oneself and the world. Pre-frontal and visual regions (Fp1, Fp2, O1, and O2) were also highly active. In contrast, regions for social conformity, factual recall, and abstract categorizing (T5, C3, C4, and F4) were dim. F4 is active for INTPs, a similar type; yet P3 helps identify objects, a concrete categorizing process. And the central regions? They handle motion as well as memory. Her lab time involved relatively little body movement, so we cannot say for sure what her preference might be in everyday life.

Mental Rotation

I gave Natalie a diagram of two geometric objects, one flat and one 3-D, which she mentally rotated to match up. This evoked activity in visual regions (O1 and O2), executive regions (Fp1 and Fp2), and a mental modeling region (F7). However, region F8 was the most active. This F8 activity was unusual for her. In general, F8 is most active for subjects who prefer Introverted Sensing or Introverted Feeling. It lights up when people work with visual details such as recalling features of an image or when they verbalize their likes and dislikes, such as stating which friends they like more than others. It is a favorite region for ISTJ and INFP. For Natalie, we might link F8 to the task's visual nature.

There's an interesting, second hypothesis. Many people with autism do visual tasks much better than the average person, and this region is highly active for them compared to other people. Type research has linked mild autism with Introverted Thinking, or at least introversion and Thinking in general.

Whatever the link, Natalie explained that she folded the flat object in her head and broke it into parts to match. She did not comment on liking the task.

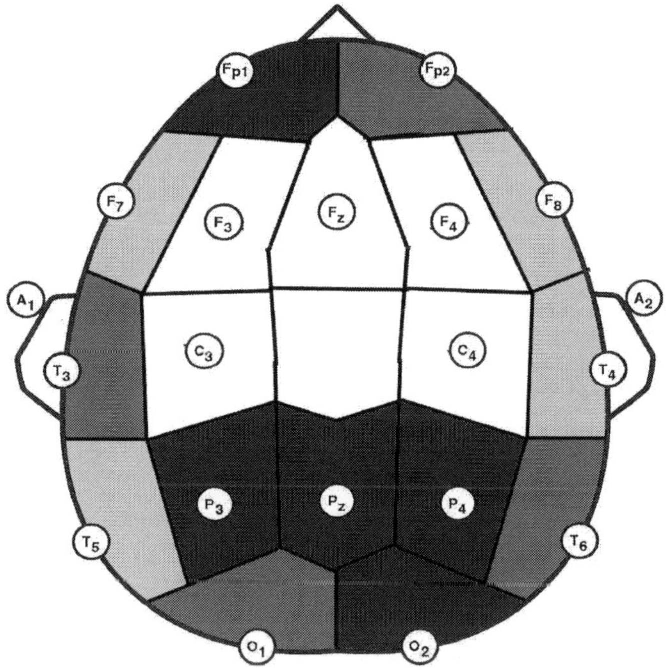

Figure 7-1: Natalie showed high activity in regions Fp1, Fp2, P3, P4, and O2.

Table 7-1: Natalie's Cognitive Skill-Set

Activity	Skill-Set
High	Chief Judge (Fp1), Tactical Navigator (P3), Abstract Impressionist (O2), Strategic Gamer (P4)
High-Mid	Process Manager (Fp2), Precise Speaker (T3), Purposeful Futurist (T6), Visual Engineer (O1)
Low-Mid	Imaginative Mimic (F7), Grounded Believer (F8), Intuitive Listener (T4), Sensitive Mediator (T5)
Low	Deductive Analyst (F3), Expert Classifier (F4), Factual Storekeeper (C3), Flowing Artist (C4)

Visual Analysis and Recall

We delved further into visuals and their meanings. I presented Natalie with a still life drawing of two people that is used in psychological "projective" tests. The drawing depicts ambiguous and dramatic elements, such as a furtive older woman in a black veil behind a youth of ambiguous gender. I asked, "What comes to mind?" Natalie offered literal associations. The people were from the 1800s, the old woman was maybe the boy's grandmother, and so on. This differed from the abstract and fanciful psych-drama descriptions offered by some types. I also noticed unusual "dark red" activity in P3, which was her most active region overall, though it usually showed yellow or green, not red. A mystery lingers!

Ball Toss

Subjects who really prefer Extraverted Sensing (ESTP and ESFP) do this activity very well, quickly showing a solid blue state of flow as they juggle or toss one, two or more balls, though if their partner can't keep up, the pattern isn't as solid. In contrast, prior ISTP and ISFP subjects have shown less instant skill and more sporadic flow, and Natalie fit the pattern. Yasha (ESTP) acted as her toss partner. He was fluid at it, so any missteps were hers to make.

Dating Game

I often do two dating experiments: one with photographs and a second with live people. For the first game, Natalie started with $100 of play money and then looked, one at a time, at sixteen photos of collegiate young adults. The photos alternated female and male and presented various ethnicities and clothing styles. For each photo, I asked three questions:

1. How much money, if any, do you spend on this person?
2. Rate the person's attractiveness from one to ten where one is low attractiveness and ten is high attractiveness.
3. In a few words, what comes to mind?

Like other female subjects, Natalie spent money on herself upfront ($25) and rarely spent money on her dates. She offered $10 for three males, whom she rated above average in attractiveness, and no others. Regarding "what comes to mind?" she quickly offered terms to characterize each person's persona such as "jock" or "guitar hippy" or "full of himself" or "MySpace denizen". Four times she offered either "reserved but friendly" or "extraverted but friendly", suggesting an underlying mental model that links these qualities. She told me later that the task was generally easy and explained how she determined labels based on details in the photo, starting with a person's face, focusing on his or her eyes in particular, and then dress. The brain's executive regions (Fp1 and Fp2) were very active as she explained how she considered their character.

By the way, the third question allows a person to take a flight of fancy, and she stuck to "on task" literal interpretations.

The results point to a Sensing preference. That said, the details of the brain activity were unique. Unlike many other subjects, particularly an ISFP I assessed earlier, her brain did not betray whom she liked most. Rather, her brain got active, with bright red, yellow or green when she "couldn't read the person's face" due to a hat or glasses or lighting or when she had "no idea" after studying the image. Her brain puts on a good "poker face" when she's evaluating people.

The experiment concluded by asking her to select one photo from her top-three picks for a date. Auditory regions (T3 and T4) suddenly got very active, which was unusual for her, as she stated her decision. Like all female subjects before her, she settled on the friendly-looking "all American" male in the football jersey.

Speed Date

Natalie did one face-to-face speed date with my lab assistant, Yasha. I usually present three or four dates for comparison. Although she had brief interaction with him in the lab, they were unacquainted. All the while, her real-life boyfriend Grant was observing from about eight feet away.

Natalie started "solid green" and remained there for the first few minutes. This pattern indicates a disassociated state linked to losing, disliking or arguing, although she spoke cordially. The EEG suddenly shifted to solid black, when Yasha touched on his plans for the future, and then shifted to blue and a mix of colors with extra activity in the executive regions (Fp1 and Fp2) as the conversation loosened up with a more natural give and take. Interestingly, her favorite P3 region lit up considerably when he and she both said a particular phrase, "not anymore", regarding some sports activities. This suggests she was mapping his experience onto her own experience, a form of empathy.

Future Visualization

"Please relax, close your eyes, and imagine your life ten years from now. Imagine in as much detail as possible, as if you are there." For many people, this activity provokes region T6, which also lights up when people utter the word "will," as in, "that will happen for me." For Natalie, I noted a lot of yellow in visual regions O1 and O2, and generally much yellow in P3, P4 and especially T6. O1 and O2 are visualization regions, and the yellow suggests she was visualizing in the first-person, through her own eyes as if she were there. She confirmed that was the case. I asked her how she "decided" on the images. She explained they were 50% what she wanted to happen and 50% images that came to her "creatively on their own". The latter half sounded like Introverted Intuiting, which is receptive to unbidden dream-like outputs from the unconscious mind.

In a later task, Natalie engaged in a brief creative brainstorming activity. Brainstorming is often linked to the Extraverted Intuiting function. Subjects who prefer this process (ENFP and ENTP) show a "Christmas tree" pattern where every region of the brain is out of synch with every other region, and all regions have high amplitude. In contrast, Natalie showed solid blue while brainstorming just like INTJ or INFJ, who prefer Introverted Intuiting. This suggested to me that Natalie was again using Intuiting in an introverted way; clearing her mind and allowing ideas to just come her as if out of nowhere.

Creative Word Play

"You will be presented with two-word phrases such as "dog leash" or "microwave oven". Please use each phrase in a sensible sentence as best you can. For example, "I took my dog for a walk using his dog leash." This is one of several verbal exercises that evaluates transcontextual thinking, since unbeknowst to Natalie, she would also need to work with phrases like "fish leash" and "philosophy oven". The experiment alternates familiar and fanciful phrases.

Natalie showed a "tide" pattern, with more activity and longer time to respond for the fancial phrases. She explained later that she "didn't know how to anticipate" the fanciful phrases, though she "noticed a pattern" that they alternated.

A second verbal activity offered a series of grammatically correct sentences that sound unusual when heard (but not read). For example, "she turned to handle the door" or "he was open to the window"; both twist familiar word pairings. Normally we open a window rather than being open *to* the window!

She tended to give more literal answers. Regions P3 and P4 were very active, as was region T6. All three neighbor the visual regions. She explained later that she tried to visualize the sentences. Perhaps more interestingly, immediately after she heard each sentence, her map turned solid blue. This is where the visualizing truly came in. I suspect this global pattern was the same one she used for visualizing the future.

Drumming

I often ask subjects to visualize or perform their hobbies. For example, one time, a student who is a professional guitar player and singer gave various performances, and a ballet dancer for fifteen years closed her eyes and focused on simulating ballet. What I hope to see is a sustained pattern of "solid bright blue". This pattern means the person is "in the zone" or "in flow" with all neocortex regions in synch. Blue normally indicates a relaxed or receptive state, and a bright blue indicates high engagement. The professional guitar player sustained a state of flow for over two minutes as he played and sang his own original music!

Natalie's hobby is Hindu drumming. She couldn't bring her drums into the lab but she mentally simulated drumming. The mental drumming evoked a lot of activity in visual regions (O1 and O2). Then she performed with hand slaps on the wooden lab tabletop, which evoked "solid blue" for the entire first piece she played. She knew that piece very well. Her second piece, which was less complex and less rehearsed, evoked more green, indicating more energetic and analytical brain activity. Finally, the third piece evoked a "tennis hop" pattern, which is a myriad of very low-level brain activity that is typical of types with Extraverted Sensing (the SP types) and with all subjects while playing video games that call on quick reflexes and tactical thinking to respond to surprises.

Her results reminded me of an ENFP theater student who acted various scenes during his EEG. He did cold-reading, highly rehearsed reading, and improvisational reading. The highly rehearsed reading showed the same "solid blue" pattern as Natalie's first drumming piece, which was also highly rehearsed.

Response to a News Article

I'll close with a noteworthy illustration of opposite types. This wasn't the last activity but it yielded an amazing result. I read aloud a news article about a teenage boy who was killed by a drunk driver on Christmas Eve. After reading it, I asked, "Please use one or two words to describe how you feel right now." People invariably said they are sad, depressed, angry, or outraged. Only two subjects of five-dozen have ever differed.

The first exception was a female ENFJ. Her brain got very busy when I asked this question. She talked about the event's philosophical implications for us as human beings. Her brain went into a "solid blue" pattern. This pattern indicates creative flow. Every type is brought here differently. After listening to the ENFJ's fascinating response, I asked her, again, to reply using one or two emotions. She replied, "No, that would be too easy. Just naming emotions is simplistic."

In contrast, when I asked Natalie, "What do you feel?" she sat quietly for a long moment with little brain activity and replied, "I feel nothing." She explained, "I wasn't there", "it's not related to me", and "I was attending to the details of the story and didn't process it emotionally". She then accurately reported the article's details such as times, names, places, and order of events. By the way, Natalie showed a similar reaction when asked to debate another student about the war in Iraq. Unlike most students, who happily opine, she replied, "I haven't researched the topic so I don't have an opinion on it."

The focus on details and objectivity is a hallmark of Sensing and Thinking. In terms of brain activity, Natalie showed generally low activity while listening to the news story except when I read the word "killed", which evoked a big spike. Also, ISTP has a "chart the course" interaction style. What if I had instructed her at the start to focus on emotions instead?

Self-Leadership

Natalie's cognitive profile suggests her strengths, pitfalls, and growth areas. For example, she will enjoy a better learning experience using a visual-spatial approach rather than an auditory approach or visuals without movement. Even her drumming was more kinesthetic than auditory! Learning by doing through physical activity will also prove effective. What else have we learned? She is self-contained and shows less activity in social regions than most people, though she is hardly oblivious. She is disinterested in hosting strong beliefs and not as quick as some to make use of fanciful ideas. She will likely fill her roles, and respond to others' overtures, by appeals to independence, objectivity, and concrete data. Finally, she has an intuitive and strategic side that may surprise others.

8. Insights In Action

We can draw upon brain insights to improve our lives with others. Doing so requires good leading and coaching. People define these terms in various ways. I like the following short definitions:

- **Leading**: Influencing people toward a common desired outcome.
- **Coaching**: Helping people identify and develop their capabilities.

These definitions are deceptively simple and imply numerous elements, such as how to identify people's capabilities, how to influence others, and how to target mutually satisfying outcomes. Effective leading and coaching rely on some fundamental principles, and a marriage of brain research with those principles can produce amazingly easy results.

Leading and coaching often go together. When you are helping one person, there is a larger system to consider such as the organization and culture. Similarly, when you are leading, you will sometimes end up attending to individuals. What varies is what's in the foreground or background!

This chapter helps you take stock of your current situation and leads you through ten essential principles. Some principles will feel easier and more appealing to you at the start, and with practice you may stretch to master all ten, drawing upon them as the need arises. As you read, pick a person or group of people to keep in mind as your target.

A Person or Group: ____________________________________

After each principle, reflect on how you can apply it to yourself and your target. If you are unsure about a principle, you can return to it at any time as you tackle your situation.

1. Evaluate The Relationship

Respect and trust are essential to enjoy a satisfying relationship. In fact, without these, life with others is tremendously more difficult.

Use the scales below to rate your current situation with a person or group. A lower score indicates less satisfaction than a higher score, with five in the middle. If you are unsure how to rate the relationship, compare it to past satisfying and unsatisfying experiences. Also jot down observable clues (behaviors, events, etc.) that inform your rating.

1. Do you respect the person or group?

⟵ 1 — 2 — 3 — 4 —— 5 —— 6 — 7 — 8 — 9 — 10 ⟶

Contempt ... Respect

Observable Clues: ______________________________

2. Does the person or group respect you?

⟵ 1 — 2 — 3 — 4 —— 5 —— 6 — 7 — 8 — 9 — 10 ⟶

Contempt ... Respect

Observable Clues: ______________________________

3. Do you trust the person or group?

⟵ 1 — 2 — 3 — 4 —— 5 —— 6 — 7 — 8 — 9 — 10 ⟶

Fear ... Trust

Observable Clues: ______________________________

4. Does the person or group trust you?

⟵ 1 — 2 — 3 — 4 —— 5 —— 6 — 7 — 8 — 9 — 10 ⟶

Fear ... Trust

Observable Clues: ______________________________

If you provided any ratings below 5, the relationship needs attention. Even if you gave high ratings, regularly re-visit the relationship to head off surprises. Sometimes, you can heal a relationship by applying the principles in this chapter. Other times, repeated harm has burned into the brain negative associations that are challenging to overcome, and you need to think and act carefully as you continue.

2. Attend to Sensory Feedback

Rapport means adjusting how you interact with someone to mirror his or her experience and perspectives. As you establish rapport, the person grows comfortable and starts moving with you. Some people seem like natural pros at rapport building—likely, the neocortex's F7 region is very active for these natural mimics. That said, everyone can practice and improve at rapport.

Basic rapport means attention to sensory feedback. When talking with a person, notice where does her body or gaze turn? When does she smile or nod yes to agree or no to disagree? While most of us vaguely notice these nonverbal messages, we may be unsure how to respond, or we may respond in an unproductive way. Let's explore what to notice and ways to respond.

People rely on and often think in terms of their senses: sight, sound, and sensation. Neuroscience suggests we need to go a step beyond the senses and appeal to both hemispheres of the brain. We have two eyes, two ears, two hands and two feet, each of which links to the right or left hemisphere. The chart below briefly summarizes six sensory modes.

Sense	Left Brain ("analytical")	Right brain ("holistic")
Auditory	Word choice/content	Tone of voice/intention
Kinesthetic	Precise, step-wise motion	Free-style, whole-body motion
Visual	Chart or diagram	Painting or photograph

People have sensory preferences that mix senses and hemispheres. For example, a client might be comfortable with charts, diagrams, and precise word choice (all in the left brain) yet also be more at home with free-form, whole-body motion (in the right brain) than following steps.

These sensory modes suggest how to gauge others' responses. Does a client get animated when you show her a set of photographs while her eyes glaze over when presented with diagrams? You can present sensory options one at a time or several at once to elicit the person's preferences and level of engagement. Attend to facial clues, posture, eye motion, and other physical clues as well as people's verbal feedback about what captures their attention.

Provide a multi-sensory experience when you are unsure what a person will like or when you are appealing to a group. While presenting a new idea, show the idea visually, link key words to it, and provide motion. A visual might be a photograph or diagram. Consider what words best define the idea in a pithy way. Also allow people to stand up or otherwise do something that helps make the idea come alive. For example, when giving a speech, you might mingle to engage the audience rather than stand rigidly behind a podium.

Beyond attending to sensory modes, you can mirror a person's interests, values, context, and ways of thinking. These skills require practice and knowledge that we will explore in the coming pages and chapters.

What happens when a person doesn't attend to sensory feedback? You may have encountered such a person before. Whether the person is acting as a leader or a teammate, he or she is often out-of-step with others. The person's work may be solid, but there is a distinct lack of social coordination. For example, he or she might keep talking even as everyone else has zoned out.

Keeping up with sensory feedback is a balancing act. Studies suggest that moderate mirroring greatly aids rapport while too little leaves others feeling disengaged and too much projects phoniness. Some people rely on a metaphor: you engage in a dance that compliments others' style while quietly mentioning the values you share. You are welcome to develop your own metaphor.

What are your sensory preferences? ______________________________

____

____

3. Focus on a Positive Shared Goal/Ideal

In addition to attending to sensory feedback, consider where you wish to go. A shared goal or ideal acts as a destination.

Some people crave goals. A goal is a specific desired outcome, often measurable in some way. You can list clues that suggest you are meeting a goal, such as milestones reached or dollars earned. Sometimes it is best to hold a general goal such as "grow our business" with a set of specific sub-goals such as "double our customer base" and/or "double our profits". This allows you to meet the general goal by several routes. Other times, it is more effective to hold up a single specific goal, akin to a political candidate winning office. Either way, have a back-up plan or two in order to cope smoothly if the goal falls out of sight.

In contrast, some people refer to ideals. An ideal usually taps a strongly held value or principle. You move *with* an ideal. When you do so, you trust that specific outcomes will occur so long as you stay true. An ideal might be, "let's be inclusive and egalitarian," or "let's hold people accountable for their choices".

Principles can be pithy: "survival of the fittest" or "the platinum rule". Whenever a person comes to us or a situation demands our attention, we reference the ideal and then creatively (and perhaps doggedly) apply it. At times, ideals may conflict with each other, or we feel torn between flexibility and consistency.

Usually, it's best to address both goals and ideals. People will prefer one or the other and benefit from both. Holding just one in mind may not, by itself, produce desirable results, and each acts as a check against the other. While pursuing an ideal, we stumble against hidden rocks, the bottom-line or the facts on the ground. While reaching a goal, we may forget our purpose. When ideals promote a specific, mutually-beneficial goal, and the goal is congruent with everyone's shared ideal, then you know you are likely in as good a shape as you can be.

You may wonder, "How can I speak to everyone's goals and ideals?" When you walk into a room, ask yourself, "What is a need or value that everyone here holds in common?" The answer might be simple and pragmatic, such as making money. More often, people will gravitate to specific outcomes that likely sit at different levels of priority, and may even conflict. Is a set of trainees in a class mostly there to learn a new skill, qualify for a promotion, take a fun break from work, or engage in self-help? Differing priorities are the source of friction and storms. To minimize friction, build in roles and activities that feed each priority in some way, no matter how small. If you don't, people will seek ways to fulfill those for themselves, often with disruptive results.

Focus on positive commonalities. Likely, all those trainees have a goal to stay employed! Prodding others through threats can seem effective, briefly. But when people receive negative input, they tend to close themselves to new information and reduce higher-level decision-making as their emotions jostle to the front. Literally, region Fp1 first gets active to block out the negative input and then, when the input passes the person's threshold of tolerance, Fp1 shuts down higher reasoning altogether as the fight or flight response takes over.

A shared goal or ideal can really help transcend breakdowns in rapport and other missteps. Often, it looks like we are all communicating effectively when in fact its the goals and ideals that act as glue. Each day, consider creative ways to keep everyone reading on the same page from the same book.

What are your goals and ideals? ______________________________

____

____

4. Clarify Roles and Boundaries

What roles do you play? You may be an instructor, student, consultant, parent, researcher, artist, coach, or manager. You likely play multiple roles. Roles may be situational and are often tacit agreements.

In your environment, are people stepping on each others' toes, frustrated that they can't do what they do best? If so, you can create harmony by matching up people with roles that suit their interests, capabilities, and maturity. The table below describes key qualities of the four temperaments that are relevant to roles and boundaries. Let's explore some key lessons in that table.

First, when there is a mismatch between a person's personality and his or her roles, the person steps out-of-role. A Catalyst who is assigned to work alone on an impersonal project will grope for personal meaning in it and look to inspire human potential, even if that means creating drama and delaying or changing the project to fit a unique creative meaning.

Second, people harbor unspoken ideas about how to relate. A Stabilizer manager will be uncomfortable stepping outside his official role and will evaluate others' performance in terms of their roles. This may easily clash with an Improviser's penchant to view people as teammates. When a crisis arises, an Improviser will look for quick solutions and want action regardless of what role officially defines him or others.

Third, people's brain activity in various regions informs what roles they gravitate to or avoid. The table on page 49 names sixteen distinct brain regions according to a role: Chief Judge, Imaginative Mimic, Deductive Analyst, and so forth. When a brain region has a low activation threshold, outside input easily triggers that region. The person cannot help but respond. For example, a person with a low threshold for region F3, the Deductive Analyst, will automatically start analyzing what she hears or reads for logical consistency. The reverse

Table 8-1: Contributions of the Four Temperaments

Catalyst (NFs, page 84)	Stabilizer (SJs, page 80)
Inspire human potential.	Support day-to-day continuity.
View people as unique individuals.	View people as filling various roles.
Theorist (NTs, page 82)	**Improviser (SPs, page 78)**
Innovate tools and ideas.	Handle crisis situations.
View people as offering competencies.	View people as teammates.

is true for high threshold regions, where the person simply cannot get started in that role; and when he does, he may grossly over do it and likely do it poorly.

A great away around these challenges is to work with people to officially designate additional roles that meet their personality and cognitive abilities. Let the Stabilizer who rates high as a Deductive Analyst add her needs, values, and contributions to her list of roles.

Don't assume people can self-manage. The brain provides resources, mainly region T5 (the Sensitive Mediator), that help us notice and adjust to others' feedback. When there is too little activity in T5, a person is under-responsive regarding boundary and role problems: "Don't know, don't care!" Conversely, when there is too much activity, a person may feel like a puppet without boundaries, constantly placating others. Try to gauge a person's activity in this region to help know how much supervision is necessary.

Finally, when we cross boundaries, we may create negative associations: we link a place, or object or person, to a memory, and then the memory returns whenever we re-encounter the trigger. For example, constant arguing around the water cooler make it synonymous with unhappiness. Do not underestimate the power of associations. Once formed, they are very hard to undo. So look for ways to create positive associations or at least seek to diffuse negativity.

What roles do you like to play? ______________________________

____

____

5. Ask Questions to Encourage Flexibility

When people feel stuck with a problem, you can help them become more flexible—notice, consider, and try out more options—by asking a few questions. The table on the next two pages offers numerous questions and groups them by the eight cognitive processes.

To encourage flexibility, start by asking questions linked to the person's personality type. These are cognitive processes they prefer most. If you know the person's type code, you know where to start. Otherwise, chat with the person for a few minutes to assess which questions evoke an animated frustration. The questions that go with the person's type won't help solve the problem—if so, the person would already be care-free! Rather, the questions build rapport, clarify the problem, and suggest that new thinking is needed.

Table 8-2: Facilitative Questions to Encourage Flexibility

Extraverted Processes	Introverted Processes
Perceiving—how we access data and focus attention	
Extraverted Sensing (Se) *"Immersing in the present context."* • What are you seeing, hearing, and/or feeling right now? • What do your gut instincts tell you? If unsure, consider how your body feels as you consider various options). • What actions can you take right now? Briefly set aside any possible consequences and focus on options for action right now. • What are some possible rewards for taking one or more small risks? • What can you get away with? Mainly ESFP, ESTP. Also ISFP, ISTP.	**Introverted Sensing (Si)** *"Stabilizing with a predictable standard."* • What have you become accustomed to? • Has a similar situation happened before? Let's review in detail how the previous situations and this one compare. • What's typical or expected in this kind of situation? If anything, what is culturally expected? • What has typically stabilized the situation in the past; or consider, what might stabilize it now? • How can you invest for the future? Mainly ISTJ, ISFJ. Also ESTJ, ESFJ.
Extraverted Intuiting (Ne) *"Exploring the emerging patterns."* • What if you could change just one small thing about the situation? What might that be? • Is something like this happening now elsewhere in your life? • Could you use a metaphor or analogy to describe what's going on? • How does that analogy or metaphor [from the previous question] suggest a way to shift the situation? • What if someone new came into your life? Mainly ENTP, ENFP. Also INTP, INFP.	**Introverted Intuiting (Ni)** *"Transforming with a meta-perspective."* • What do you see yourself doing in the future? • Clear your mind; then ask yourself for an insight. What enters your mind's eye? • Try sleeping on the problem and let's discuss it in the morning. • The realization you mentioned, how has that impacted the situation? • Who is someone who could handle this situation? Now imagine yourself as that person. Mainly INTJ, INFJ. Also ENTJ, ENFJ.

Table 8-2 Cont.

Extraverted Processes	Introverted Processes
Judging—how we organize and make decisions	
Extraverted Thinking (Te) *"Measuring and constructing for progress."* • What factual evidence can you list or show to support what you are saying? • How has the situation changed over time? Can you calculate what comes next? • Consider various casual factors. Have two or more of those factors varied together? • Say you decide on an action; what are three things that could happen next? • Consider a goal. Now work backwards to figure out what steps are needed to reach that goal. Mainly ESTJ, ENTJ. Also ISTJ, INTJ.	**Introverted Thinking (Ti)** *"Gaining leverage using a framework."* • Could you define or classify this situation? • The word that you just used, could you perhaps define that for me? • What theory or principle fits this situation? • What is something minor that you could say or do that might tip the situation in a new direction? • If you were an impartial observer, a scientist of sorts, what would you observe? Mainly ISTP, INTP. Also ESTP, ENTP.
Extraverted Feeling (Fe) *"Nurturing trust through giving relationships."* • What do the other people involved in this situation need and value? And in what ways are you helping to meet those needs? • What are ways to help meet others' needs? • Do you feel trusted and respected? • How much do you trust and respect others? • What is something you can share about yourself to build trust with someone else in this situation? Mainly ESFJ, ENFJ. Also ISFJ, INFJ.	**Introverted Feeling (Fi)** *"Staying true to who you really are."* • What's really important to you personally? What's important in this situation and also in general for you? • What do you feel is the "good" thing to do, regardless of what others think or say? • Do you believe you can handle the situation? • If you were to do a certain action, what would your conscience say? • What is a typical human reaction to this situation? Mainly ISFP, INFP. Also ESFP, ENFP.

Next, ask questions linked to other cognitive processes, preferably ones related to the person's opposite personality type code. Just exploring these questions will help the person feel less stuck and notice there are more options, including perhaps a great way to make a new choice.

For example, an INFJ client is dissatisfied with her job. Start by asking a question listed under Introverted Intuiting, which is INFJ's lead cognitive process. You might ask, "What do you see yourself doing in the future?" No doubt she has asked and answered this question for herself. Perhaps she lacks a clear vision of the future or is encountering obstacles. Next move to Extraverted Feeling, which is INFJ's support process. You might ask, "Do you feel trusted and respected?" Perhaps she explains that she spends so much time helping others realize their goals that she has little energy left for her own dreams, despite the trust and respect she has earned. From here, go to her opposite type, ESTP. Ask questions under Extraverted Sensing and Introverted Thinking. You may eventually ask, "What is something minor that you could say or do that might tip the situation in a new direction?" This asks her to identify leverage points, to consider something small yet impactful that she can do now rather than feel overwhelmed.

Now it's your turn to practice. Answer the question below and then use the table on the next page to help yourself gain more flexibility in your life.

What questions can you ask about a current issue? ______________

____

____

6. Nurture Creative Moments

The brain shows various holistic brain states, one of which is creative flow. When the EEG monitor turns a solid bright blue, the person is doing something for which they are really adept. The question then becomes, how can we activate these peek moments and keep nurturing them?

We get in the zone one of two ways. Often, expertise comes from training. A professional musician gets in the zone while playing his songs. When we are really adept, closing our eyes and imagining doing the activity is enough to trigger us into the zone. Other times, peek moments relate to a person's personality type, from reviewing the past to active listening, managing crises, or imagining the future. Essentially, the person is an expert at listening, foreseeing, or so forth. Either way, being in the zone often provides us with an avalanche of nearly flawless creative output.

You likely have no means to read a person's brain activity. Fortunately, you can pay attention to a person's favorite activities and personality type in order to pinpoint what's likely and thus how to get the best results possible. Pay attention when people do tasks, and ask these questions:

- Do they get absorbed in the moment like a child with a favorite toy?
- Do they produce results that are ready to deploy right from the get-go without much, if any, revision?
- Do they report the task is easy and natural, perhaps downplaying results?
- Does their mind wander back to the task at every opportunity?

If the answer is yes to most of these questions, then you have likely identified where the person will shine creatively.

There is more than being in the zone. Our initial creative "Ah ha!" moments show in the brain, usually with a surge of incredibly high activity across the entire brain as the EEG monitor turns a solid red (beta waves). This surge may last just a moment, but it's key: multiple brain regions feed into each other to produce the insight, and simultaneously, the insight is sent out to every brain region as important new information, a fresh set of operating instructions.

All too often, we don't adequately nurture insights. That is, your brain will forget an insight unless you try it out. Fortunately, people are motivated to try out their own insights; and when we try them, we quickly learn whether they are true or false. True insights start working for us, practically solving a problem. False insights feel right but don't lead to actual improvement. We say, "It seemed like a good idea at the time but didn't work out". Practice the true insights. As we practice, we carve out neural connections that turn a flash of activity into lasting circuits.

The upshot? Attend to creative "Ah ha!" moments. Capture and run with insights, and encourage self-direction to let people generate their own answers, to create their own solutions. Even if a particular insight feels likely to prove false, consider how to try it out in a limited way. Allow the person who thought of the idea to help test it or implement it in order to internalize the insight. The insights we internalize take us into the zone.

What are your recent insights and how might you try them? ________

____

____

7. Boost Competence and Motivation

As described in Chapter 3: Overview of the Neocortex, your brain activity rises when you engage in tasks for which you are competent and motivated.

Engaged = competent + motivated

This principle is so important that it bears repeating! As the graph below illustrates, brain activity increases progressively as motivation and challenge to your competence increase. However, when a task's difficulty surpasses your competence and/or motivation, brain activity drops, suddenly and drastically, as you give up.

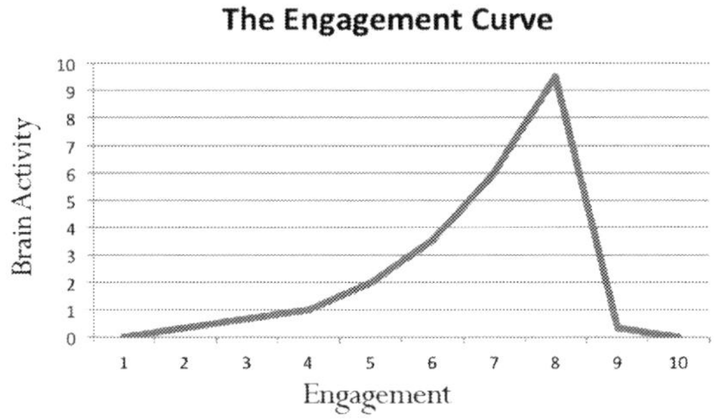

Figure 8-1: More engaging tasks evoke more brain activity, up to a point.

Your first step to leverage your engagement curve is to identify what goes where on the curve, as suggested in Table 8-3 below. Besides your favorite activities, you have unused talents, undeveloped areas, and activities you avoid. Take a moment to brainstorm where life's various activities fit within the table. For example, how might you classify the following activities: mathematics, health/fitness, socializing, financial acumen, and artistic endeavors?

Table 8-3: The Engagement Matrix

	High Motivation	**Low Motivation**
High Competence	Favorite Activities Perform with ease and value as useful and necessary.	Unused Talents Perform well but take for granted and quickly bored.
Low Competence	Unfortunate Failings Wish to develop and excel but far from skillful.	Avoidant Areas Lack skill and perhaps devalue the skill.

Table 8-4: Learning Needs of the Four Temperaments

Catalyst (NFs, page 84)	Stabilizer (SJs, page 80)
The activity fits your identity? Find meaning in dramatic stories and themes, and search for authentic human interaction.	The activity fits your role? Memorize, practice, practice more, and look to authority for guidance and proper form.
Theorist (NTs, page 82)	**Improviser (SPs, page 78)**
The activity fits your strategy? Integrate, test, and refine conceptual models, strategies, and objective universal principles.	The activity fits your context? Use trial-and-error, variation on a theme, and hands-on tools to "find a fit".

Next, consult Table 8-4 above to identify what is worth developing and the key means to build competence, boost motivation, or both. For example, if you are skilled at sports but have no interest, then that's an unused talent. Why is your interest low? The answer depends on your temperament, as Table 8-4 suggests. For an Improviser, the activity must fit the context; for a Theorist, the activity must fit some larger strategy; and so forth. If the activity doesn't fit, then you don't feel motivated. Conversely, we often crave activities that fit our temperament needs but do not come easily to us. You might wish to develop your financial acumen but prior efforts have fallen flat. Has it been you, your instructors, or what? When we learn in a way that fits our temperament, then learning becomes a lot easier. An Improviser who takes a trial-and-error approach with hands-on tools will learn a lot faster than trying a Theorist method, which likely involves book learning with a focus on conceptual models and abstract strategies. Moreover, learning usually comes even easier when you adopt a role-model of the same temperament as yourself who already has the competence or motivation you are looking for. An hour with such a person, using a temperament-specific method, can convey years worth of learning.

Finally, it's worthwhile to start small, perhaps even trivial. What's 2 + 2? Then start increasing the level of challenge. What's 17 + 34 - 19? And so on. Be sure as you continue that you keep meeting your temperament needs.

What activity might you develop? ______________________________

____

____

8. Attend to Emotions

We are emotional creatures. Deeply ingrained neural circuits swirl in the amygdala and other regions of the primal deep brain, equally informing us with useful gut-reactions and misleading us with destructive impulses. In contrast, the neocortex is a relatively dispassionate and lifeless Mr. Spock.

By age twenty-five or so, we finish developing the circuitry that links the deep brain and neocortex so that we can listen to and channel our instincts to get by in everyday life. In order to balance our emotions, the neocortex engages in a continuous, ever-changing dance that allows us to keep our equilibrium. Knowing the possibilities of the dance is key to understanding the emotional side of one's personality.

Every region of the neocortex plays a role in our emotional life. Each region mediates feelings and behavior, with attendant benefits and limitations. Pages 166 and 167 describe seven particularly important regions that play a role in our emotional intelligence. Which of these regions are active for you?

- ☐ **Fp1**: Ignore or deny bad news in order to enjoy happiness.
- ☐ **Fp2**: Dwell on bad news, introspecting and experiencing sadness.
- ☐ **T4**: Notice others' motives, perhaps getting angry and acting out.
- ☐ **T5**: Are sensitive to others' feedback and try to please them.
- ☐ **P3**: Are acutely aware of and protect our personal boundaries.
- ☐ **F7**: Imagine others' experiences and maybe feel as they do.
- ☐ **F8**: Harbor strong likes (or dislikes) and feel devoted to them.

How can we manage all these regions? Some psychologists describe four essential skill-sets to effectively manage our own and others' emotional life, as summarized in Table 8-5 above-right.

Feel free to use the table to rate your aptitude with each skill-set. Rating yourself accurately requires the self-awareness skill-set! Thus, it is useful to get feedback from others regarding your capabilities and limits. Honing self-awareness is a first step even as people of various personality types like to start with skills suited to their type. Likely, the brain-savvy insights you've gained in this book have already boosted your understanding yourself and others and provided you with ideas about how to better manage your emotional life.

What are your typical emotional responses? ____________________

____

____

Table 8-5: Four Skill-Sets for Emotional Aptitude

Self-Awareness (Step 1)	Social Awareness (Step 2b)
• Name what you are feeling. • Assess your capabilities and limits. • Evaluate what aids or stresses you. • Recognize inner conflicts. Not me ☐ ☐ ☐ ☐ ☐ A lot me	• Name what others are feeling. • Assess others' capabilities and limits. • Recognize ways to support others. • Recognize others' conflict points. Not me ☐ ☐ ☐ ☐ ☐ A lot me
Self-Management (Step 2a)	**Relationship Management (Step 3)**
• Comfortably share feelings with others. • Decide based on your capabilities. • Adjust your own emotional responses. • Resolve/balance inner conflicts. Not me ☐ ☐ ☐ ☐ ☐ A lot me	• Help people process their feelings. • Deploy and mentor others' capabilities. • Catalyze and inspire others to action. • Resolve/balance others' conflicts. Not me ☐ ☐ ☐ ☐ ☐ A lot me

9. Foresee the Wider Impact

People exist within larger systems. Our words and actions have repercussions, which in turn have a broader impact that may boomerang back to us. For example, when someone pushes us physically, socially, or otherwise—we feel abused, threatened, or negated. While we often consider how our choices may impact the immediate people involved, we may forget to consider how others are linked to and influence each other, perhaps when we are not around.

Whenever you consider an action to take, fill out a matrix like this one:

Person	#1 ________	#2 ________	#3 ________
#1 ________			
#2 ________			
#3 ________			

In the matrix, at each intersection of two persons, use a numeric value to characterize their relationship. Use -1 to indicate a poor relationship, +1 to indicate a good relationship, and 0 to indicate a neutral relationship. After filling the matrix, consider each -1 and +1, tracing how people in your life may likely respond to your potential decision. Whatever your choice, you will at least have a better idea of how people will react, including their interactions with each other. Often, it is not our initial choice, but how we respond to the unintended consequences, that drives a situation in a more positive or negative direction.

What are the broader consequences of your behavior? ____________
____
____

10. Beware Pitfalls

According to Dr. Sue Cooper, there are two unpleasant syndromes that plague all our relationships: BLM and BLT. I add two more, for four total:

- **"Be Like Me" (BLM)**: We evaluate others based on how well they match us, or at least how we like to imagine ourselves.
- **"Be Like Them" (BLT)**: We alter our behavior and perhaps even kid ourselves in order to conform to others' wishes.
- **"It's My Brain" (IMB)**: We excuse our behavior as caused by our brain or personality type rather than take responsibility.
- **"Master of All" (MOA)**: We rate ourselves as good at everything, at least in theory, and thus better than other people.

These syndromes often travel with their best friends, the admonitions "must" and "should" (aka "mustn't" and "shouldn't"). They also show up when we complain and evaluate ourselves and others by highlighting character flaws as the cause of difficulties rather than circumstances. Finally, these syndromes erupt when we wonder why other people do not perceive what we perceive or use the same brain regions we do, often without appreciating how much we ourselves may be missing. Of course, we might be quite right at times! The challenge is to keep these syndromes in check, to ensure we aren't doing BLM, BLT, or whatnot when we interact with others.

With knowledge comes power, and thus responsibility. I hope you enjoy and use the brain-savvy insights within these pages. I also hope that you use these tools wisely. Fortunately, there is a fail-safe in the brain: when we start using new tools unethically, we tend to forget them.

What are your "should's" and which ones are you ready to let go? _____
____
____

Chapter 9: In-Depth Exploration

Are we more nature or nurture? What percentage of our brain activity is decided by personality type versus context and upbringing? Jung elaborated on more than eight distinct cognitive processes. He offered a dynamic framework with psyche at the intersection of nature and nurture. Do his ideas hold up?

First, Jung proposed that extraversion (E) versus introversion (I) was the most significant personality difference. Since then, numerous studies have confirmed this dimension as a lasting characteristic in people, with strong evidence in the brain. This dimension also shined in my research.

Beyond "E" and "I", Jung proposed that people sort into "dominant judgers" versus "dominant perceivers". In fact, these two types decisively differ by whether they prefer left pre-frontal activity (region Fp1) or right pre-frontal activity (region Fp2). These two regions act as important executives. They mediate activity from all over the brain. Like any organization, rule by two executives may cause conflict. Thus, we each prefer one executive over the other.

Jung also described dynamics. We each prefer two cognitive processes over others. One process serves us in a lead role while a second serves us in a support role. The result: sixteen distinct personality patterns. But what about the other processes? Can we access all of them? If so, can we predict when and how? Since Jung, theorists have offered specifics. The EEG data suggests there are sixteen patterns; beyond that, we are—each and all—unique in our use of brain resources, though there is a tendency to step into our opposite type.

As we explore, I promise to keep the statistics simple. That said, fluency with prior chapters is useful to follow this one. Now, let's get under the hood!

Past Research

There are several published studies and recorded seminars by Martha Alcock and John Newman; Peter Gram and Bruce Dunn; and Laposky, Wilson, and Languis. These studies focused on the four static dimensions of the MBTI® questionnaire rather than Jung's underlying dynamic theory. Thus, while these researchers enjoyed some results, they did not uncover the big trove: brain activity relates most to the eight cognitive processes, with each process linked to a unique whole-brain pattern. Appendix: Resources lists these works.

Cognitive Profiles

The Interstrength Cognitive Assessment™ is an on-line questionnaire to help people assess their use of the eight cognitive processes. My lab students completed the ISCA™, received feedback, and engaged in a self-discovery process that included self-rating of the eight processes, plus on-line or at-home reading using *16 Personality Types: Descriptions for Self-Discovery*. Every attempt was made over the ten-week lab course to arrive at a best-fit type and clarify cognitive preferences.

Figure 9-1 below is a sample ISCA™ cognitive portrait. It presents one person's use of each cognitive process along a scale from 0 to 50. The assessment also reports three of sixteen likely best-fit personality types such as INTJ, ENTJ, and ISFP. Statistical analysis of ISCA™ data confirms the assessment evaluates eight distinct categories. Please contact me for the ISCA™ white paper.

Some people are possibly mis-typed, though studies suggest mis-typing

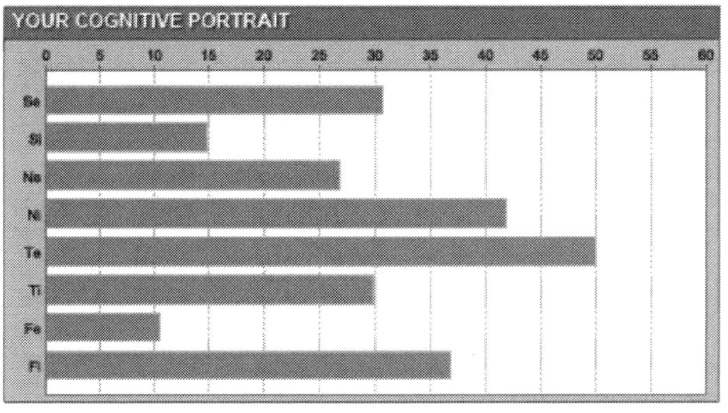

Figure 9-1: Example profile using the Interstrength Cognitive Assessment™.

after even a brief self-discovery process amounts to a maximum of a 25% error rate (one out of four code letters, such as ENTP for INTP, or ISTJ for INTJ). Since we took many weeks to verify type, I am confident of accuracy.

The EEG results are based on a study of fifty-eight people following the experimental process outlined in Chapter 2. The table below breaks down subjects by their preferred cognitive processes. The table's left column indicates the cognitive processes. The middle column counts persons who have the relevant process in a lead role. The right column is more generous and counts persons who have the relevant process in either a lead or support role. This generosity affords sixteen types, where each type represents use of two processes so that a person can effectively perceive and decide in the inner and outer world.

I sought diversity but not all types are equally represented. Even though I did not end up with even numbers, it was helpful to see a half-dozen instances of particular types (namely, INFP and ISTJ) to gauge individual variations.

Table 9-1: Lab Subjects by Jungian Cognitive Process

Jungian Cognitive Process	No. of Subjects (Who Have Process as Lead Role)	No. of Subjects (Process is Lead or Supporting Role)
Se	4	9
Si	8	14
Ne	10	19
Ni	8	14
Te	8	19
Ti	6	12
Fe	4	9
Fi	8	16

The Five Factor Model and the MBTI®

Why did I use the ISCA™ instead of the Five Factor Model or the MBTI® questionnaire? Jung's underlying framework is not a behavioral model with measurable static traits like the "Big Five". Nor is it about preference dimensions like the MBTI®. Rather, the Jungian framework offers explanatory power by proposing cognitive dynamics. These dynamics afford complex, flexible behaviors that vary by background and context, with room for development.

Brain Activity Across Types

What happens when we randomly compare any two persons in the population? For example, how might a person who identifies as ISTJ compare to an INFP, ESTP, or so forth? Does a lot of the neocortex activity match, or not?

Figure 9-2 below shows the similiarity and difference between randomly selected people. The graph is all over the place. The result: there is a good chance that two randomly selected persons from my lab will share very little. When we look at the EEG monitor, the neocortex activity will mostly differ. We might look at two people and perhaps see only a 5% overlap! Overall, randomly selected persons shared 33% of their neocortex activity. There were enough people in the study to make this a meaningful result.

Who differs from whom? We might think that people contrast significantly with people of the "opposite" personality type. That is, INFPs and ESTJs would show very different brain activity. Sounds reasonable. But the answer is "no" and the truth is often the other way around. For example, INTJ and ISFP subjects relied on very similar brain regions. Ultimately, all we can say is that persons of the same personality type tend to be similar to each other.

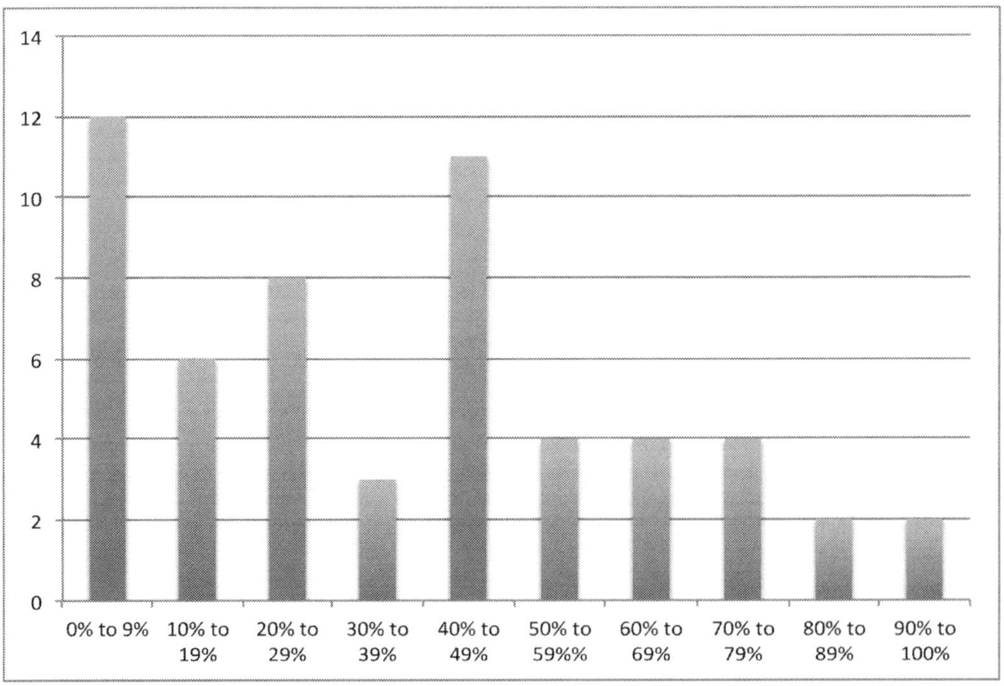

Figure 9-2: Number of people versus percentage of shared neocortical activity for people of different personality types.

Brain Activity Within Type

A model of personality types is neurologically valid if persons of the same type have relatively similar brain activity. How similar are two ISTJs? Chapter 6 describes how persons who prefer the same cognitive processes show similar *holistic* brain states. But what about use of individual brain regions?

Figure 9-3 is arranged like Figure 9-2 but compares persons of the same type. It states that half of the lab subjects shared from 70% to 90% of their brain activity with other people of the same type. That is, for a slim majority of people, when we look at the EEG monitor, 70% to 90% of what we see is the same for them and others of their type. The other half of subjects skew to the middle of the graph and are likely to have moderately similar brain activity. This result held true regardless of how many subjects there were of a type. Clearly, knowing someone's personality type code can likely tell us a lot about them!

About 20% of the time, a person's activity will be pretty atypical of his type. This might be due to context, gender, physiology, training, upbringing, and other factors, possibly including influence from deeper brain regions. The results remind us that people are more than their personality type.

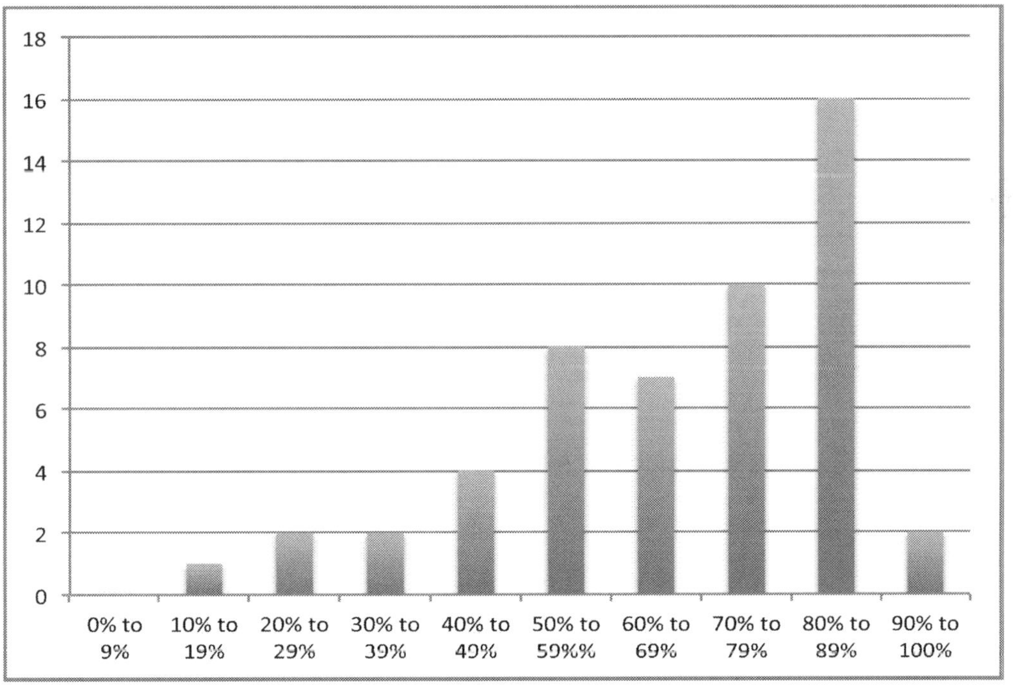

Figure 9-3: Number of people versus percentage of shared neocortical activity for people of the same personality type.

Statistical Analysis

A statistical method called factor analysis sorts data into groups. Another method called Pearson provides linear correlations between data sets. Statistical methods like these show us how various persons and personality types compare.

Extraversion/Introversion

Sorting the EEG data into two factors reveals extraversion-introversion as a meaningful preference, a result that fits Jung's framework and mirrors other neuroscience studies. Generally, extraverts tend to show more activity in the anterior (front half) of the neocortex while introverts tend to show more activity in the posterior (back half) of the neocortex.

However, when we dig deeper, people of all personality types display high activity in executive regions Fp1 and Fp2. Moreover, there is no clear dividing line between front and back. For example, introverted types such as INFP and ISTJ rely heavily on region F8, which lies in the brain's front half. Similarly, INTP is highly active in region F4, also in the front, while ENTP is most active in region P4, in the back. Moreover, while introverts are more visual, showing more activity in regions O1 and/or O2, extraverts show more activity in regions P3 and P4, regions that also lie in the back of the brain. Thus, talking about "front" versus "back" is about as useful as talking about left versus right brain types.

Other research studies show that introverts are "stimulus enhancing" while extraverts are "stimulus reducing". That is, what an introvert considers very noisy, busy, sweet, or painful might strike an extravert as normal, or even boring. Sadly, I did not explore this dimension and cannot report on it.

Lead Process: Judging or Perceiving?

Beyond extraversion-introversion, Jung focused on two subgroups: people who prefer to take in and process information versus people who prefer to organize and make decisions. The first group has Sensing or Intuiting as a lead process while the second group has Thinking or Feeling as a lead process.

Table 9-2 at top-right displays the sixteen types and their use of the left and right pre-frontal regions. For example, the first entry is ISFP. Persons of this type had 68% of their pre-frontal activity on the left side, in region Fp1, with the remaining 32% on the right side, in Fp2.

The eight types that show more Fp1 activity have Thinking or Feeling as a lead process, while the eight types with more Fp2 activity have Sensing or Intuiting as a lead process. This supports Jung's framework!

Table 9-2: Pre-Frontal Cortex Activity

Type	Fp1/Fp2	Type	Fp1/Fp2
ISFP	68% / 32%	INFJ	49% / 51%
ENFJ	63% / 37%	ENTP	48% / 52%
ENTJ	63% / 37%	ENFP	48% / 52%
ISTP	59% / 41%	INTJ	48% / 52%
INFP	52% / 48%	ESFP	48% / 52%
ESFJ	52% / 48%	ISTJ	47% / 53%
ESTJ	52% / 48%	ESTP	46% / 54%
INTP	51% / 49%	ISFJ	45% / 55%

There is a hint of a deeper correlation that is not statistically significant but worth future investigation. The types in Table 9-2 clump into subgroups: ISP with ENJ, then INP with ESJ; next, INJ with ENP, and finally, ESP with ISJ. Moreover, each of eight pairings is a "complementary type": ISFP and ENFJ, ENTJ and ISTP, and so forth. This may be coincidence. Or maybe not!

The differences between Fp1 and Fp2 activity are generally small and there is an overall basis toward Fp1 in the left hemisphere in any case, which we expect because right-handed persons are generally left-hemisphere dominant.

The Four Functions

There were statistically significant results when looking at the four functions that are highlighted by the MBTI® questionnaire. These results are statistical.

Sensing—Intuiting: People with a Sensing preference show more yellow (alpha waves) activity compared to Intuiting types. They also show more activity in the left hemisphere, especially regions F3, C3, and P3. Conversely, Intuiting types show more activity in the right hemisphere, especially regions F4, C4, and P4.

Thinking—Feeling: People with a Thinking preference show more null-band activity (a black EEG) with frequency below five Hertz. Aside from this dearth of activity, they show more activity than persons with a Feeling preference in reasoning regions F3, F4, P3, and P4. Also, Thinking types show more activity in region C3 while Feeling types show more activity in region C4.

These correlations are statistical, hide a lot of useful information, and are not indicative of particular personality types, much less individuals.

Detour: Cognitive Quartets

Studies that utilize MBTI® data often analyze results in groups of four, each group containing four types. Let's call these groups quartets. Anecdotally, some quartets lend themselves well to particular applications such as communication, education, leadership, or so forth.

The list below names typical applications and indicates quartets according to which type code letters they share. For example, researchers often look at communication style by grouping the ET types (ESTP, ESTJ, ENTJ, ENTP) and comparing them against three other groupings including EF types (ESTP, ESFJ, ENFJ, ENFP) and IT types and IF types. I explored the following quartets:

Career choice	ST, SF, NT, NF
Communication style	ET, EF, IT, IF
Decision-making style	TJ, FJ, TP, FP
Information access	SP, SJ, NP, NJ
Learning style	ES, IS, EN, IN
Needs and values	SP, SJ, NT, NF
Work style	IP, EP, IJ, EJ

All the quartets performed better than chance. Variation between any two types in the same quartet is fairly low, averaging around 17%. That is, when we look at two personality types (types, not persons) in the same quartet, the activity in a particular region will vary between those two types by an average of 17%. In fact, the variation will run no lower than 12% and no higher than 22%. Moreover, no quartet performed better or worse than any other quartet.

Recall Figure 9-2, which illustrates what happens when we compare any two random persons from the population. While many people are sure to have little in common, there is a big spike in the data set. There is a decent chance that randomly-selected people will share 40% to 50% of their brain activity in common. Why is that? The spike may occur because those people share something key even though they are not the same type. Perhaps such people are members of the some quartet! For example, ISFP and INTP share a similar work style (both have an "I" and "P" in their code) and both are dominant judging types.

Overall, the results suggest there are more than personality type "boxes". Rather, there is an underlying set of dynamics. When people share a dynamic, they share brain activity that helps them get along.

A Hierarchy of Preferences?

Since Jung's original work, theorists have proposed a "hierarchy" of cognitive processes. For each type, in addition to two preferred processes, perhaps the other six unfold in a typical or best manner. What does the data say?

Chapter 6 describes eight holistic EEG patterns that correlate to the eight cognitive processes. When a person shows a holistic pattern, that pattern usually matches the cognitive process that serves the person in a lead role, as predicted by his or her personality type. For example, ESFPs have Extraverted Sensing as their lead process and they usually show the "tennis hop" EEG pattern.

Other times, the EEG pattern matches the cognitive process that serves the person in a support role, as predicted by his or her personality type. When an ESFP's holistic pattern isn't the tennis hop, it is an active listening mode, which is typical of Introverted Feeling. This secondary pattern shows up in narrower circumstances than the lead process. For example, an ESFP male subject did active listening with females but not with other males. Similarly, an INFP showed a "Christmas tree" pattern typical of his extraverted counterpart ENFP, but only when engaging in imaginative word games and brainstorming.

Rarely, a person shows a different pattern in narrow circumstances or when prompted in a specific way. For example, an ESTJ subject showed the active listening mode but only with authority figures. Somewhat similarly, most people show a "tennis hop" pattern when they play tactical video games. This suggests that people can use all eight cognitive processes in limited situations.

Before we go beyond these general observations, consider some caveats. First, brain activity does not equal behavior. For example, most people who join a brainstorming activity do not show the holistic Christmas tree pattern typical of personality types (ENTP, ENFP, INTP, and INFP) that shine at trans-contextual thinking. Also, we can't assign cognitive processes to certain regions. For example, region F7 handles several related functions including making inferences based on context, mimicking others' behavior, and imagining what-if scenarios. All these activities sound like traditional definitions of Extraverted Intuiting. Most people show some activity in this region. That fact does *not* mean most people use Extraverted Intuiting. Yes, thinking in-context aids use of Extraverted Intuiting; and yes, we might harness region F7 to ploddingly switch between contexts one at a time, but doing so differs from thinking across many different contexts and brain regions at once.

Table 9-3: The Eight Cognitive Processes

Dominant Judging (region Fp1 more active)	**Dominant Perceiving** (region Fp2 more active)
Expedite Decision-making	**Catalyze the Process**
Te: Use brain regions that promote evidence-based decision-making. (ESTJ and ENTJ)	**Se**: Rely on a low-energy mode that affords rapid responses to crises. (ESTP and ESFP)
Fe: Use brain regions that promote social/interpersonal cohesion. (ESFJ and ENFJ)	**Ne**: Rely on a high-energy mode that bridges across contexts and ideas. (ENTP and ENFP)
Refine Decision-making	**Track the Process**
Ti: Use brain regions that promote complex/subtle logical reasoning. (ISTP and INTP)	**Si**: Rely on high specialization from practice to fulfill specific group tasks. (ISTJ and ISFJ)
Fi: Use brain regions that promote listening around identity and values. (ISFP and INFP)	**Ni**: Rely on low specialization with a holistic zen state to do novel tasks. (INTJ and INFJ)

We have a toe in our opposite type. We tend to use brain regions that help us do some of what a person of our opposite type does. For example, ISFP prefers Introverted Feeling in a lead role and Extraverted Sensing in a support role. ISFP shows a listening mode and tennis-hop mode typical of these cognitive processes. Besides regions that support listening and such, ISFP also uses some regions typical of ENTJ and INTJ, which prefer Extraverted Thinking and Introverted Intuiting. For example, ISFPs often use region T6, which helps us project what will occur in the future. ISFPs also gravitate to some evidence-based thinking by tapping sensory regions in the left hemisphere such as T3 and O1. Moreover, ISFPs may even show a holistic pattern typical of INTJ or ENTJ.

Such use occurs at highly selective times. One ISFP subject briefly got "in the zone" when imagining her future, as INTJs do. In contrast, ISFPs do not show the Christmas tree pattern typical of Extraverted Intuiting, nor do they engage in transcontextual thinking, as typical of ENFP or ENTP. Similarly, they eschew Introverted Thinking, Introverted Sensing, and so forth. When we measure the statistical distance between ISFP and other types, its closest match is INTJ.

This toe-hold into our opposite type holds across all sixteen types. ENTJs are also like ISFPs in some ways. For example, both show high activity in region F8, which helps handle identity. Similarly, the Extraverted Feeling types (ENFJ and ESFJ) tend to tap one region of several related to logic (F3, F4, P3 or P4) that is normally favored by their opposite types (ISTP and INTP). ESFJ's closest statistical match is ENTP; ENFP's closest match is ESTJ, and so forth.

Overall, it is as if our opposite type is "built in" to our type. The three case studies in the next section demonstrate how these individual differences play out.

Other Brain Models

People often ask how my work fits with other brain-based models including the Benziger model and the Herrmann model.

The Benziger model was developed by Katherine Benziger. According to an advertising website, her "model and assessment systems are instead based on the measurement of brain function and energy consumption in the brain". She describes four specialized quadrants, each handling a different brain function, and proposes that a person is generally adept in only one quadrant. Benziger also champions the ethical use of assessments. Her work appears to be based on reading and other second-hand sources; most unfortunately, the brain is not organized in the way her model describes.

The Herrmann brain dominance instrument was developed by William Herrmann. It describes four thinking styles based upon generalized notions of brain lateralization. Specifically, he links analytical and sequential styles with the left brain and interpersonal and imaginative styles with the right brain. He proposes that we tend to prefer one brain region and style, and can develop our creative potential by using our whole brain. However, the brain is not so broadly organized, and personality type strongly influences one's whole-brain states.

While these models, and the support systems developed around them, are grounded in good intentions, the brain is not a barber-shop quartet. It is a subtle and complex symphonic orchestra that dizzies the imagination.

Case Studies—Three ISFPs

This section explores the neocortex activity of three real people who identify with the same type: ISFP. The graph on the next page summarizes their brain activity. All three—Ian, Brett, and Katie—share commonalities, including a holistic "listening" mode and a holistic "tennis hop" mode. They rely upon some similar brain regions and also use different brain regions. Let's take a look.

ISFP Case Study #1: Ian

Ian is an "A" college student and also an improvisational stage performer skilled with acting, magic tricks, music, poetry, and singing. He is serious about his career aspirations and performs professionally.

Throughout his session, he showed high activity in region Fp1 (explaining/deciding) and O2 (abstract visualization). Oppositely, he showed almost no activity in region F4 (categorizing and defining) or C3 (factual memory and step-wise action). Region F4 is typically most active for Introverted Thinking types such as INTP. In fact, none of the three ISFPs showed activity in F4.

Ian demonstrated active listening. He often entered a solid blue listening mode, though he did not maintain this mode for long. Auditory regions T3 and T4 were moderately active, particularly when he composed a story based on a prompt of a half-dozen, picturesque tarot cards. Composing evoked mostly left-brain analytical activity as he analyzed what story options were reasonable.

Ian got "in the zone" with a solid blue EEG several times around his expertise as a stage performer, remaining in the zone for several minutes each time when he did improvisational acting, evaluated a poem, performed a magic trick, and sang.

Overall, his EEG showed a lot of yellow (alpha waves) including periods of solid yellow over the whole neocortex, which is typical of people with a Sensing preference. That is, he spent a lot of time in an associated state, allowing his body and emotions to inform his cognition. He showed a solid yellow EEG when he imagined an embarrassing situation, truly feeling the embarrassment rather than just considering it abstractly. Interestingly, his EEG was solid green (theta waves) when he laughed or otherwise felt humored. This might be odd, except his career requires humor, so perhaps he processes humor objectively?

Ian showed back-and-forth activity between regions T6 and P4 (future

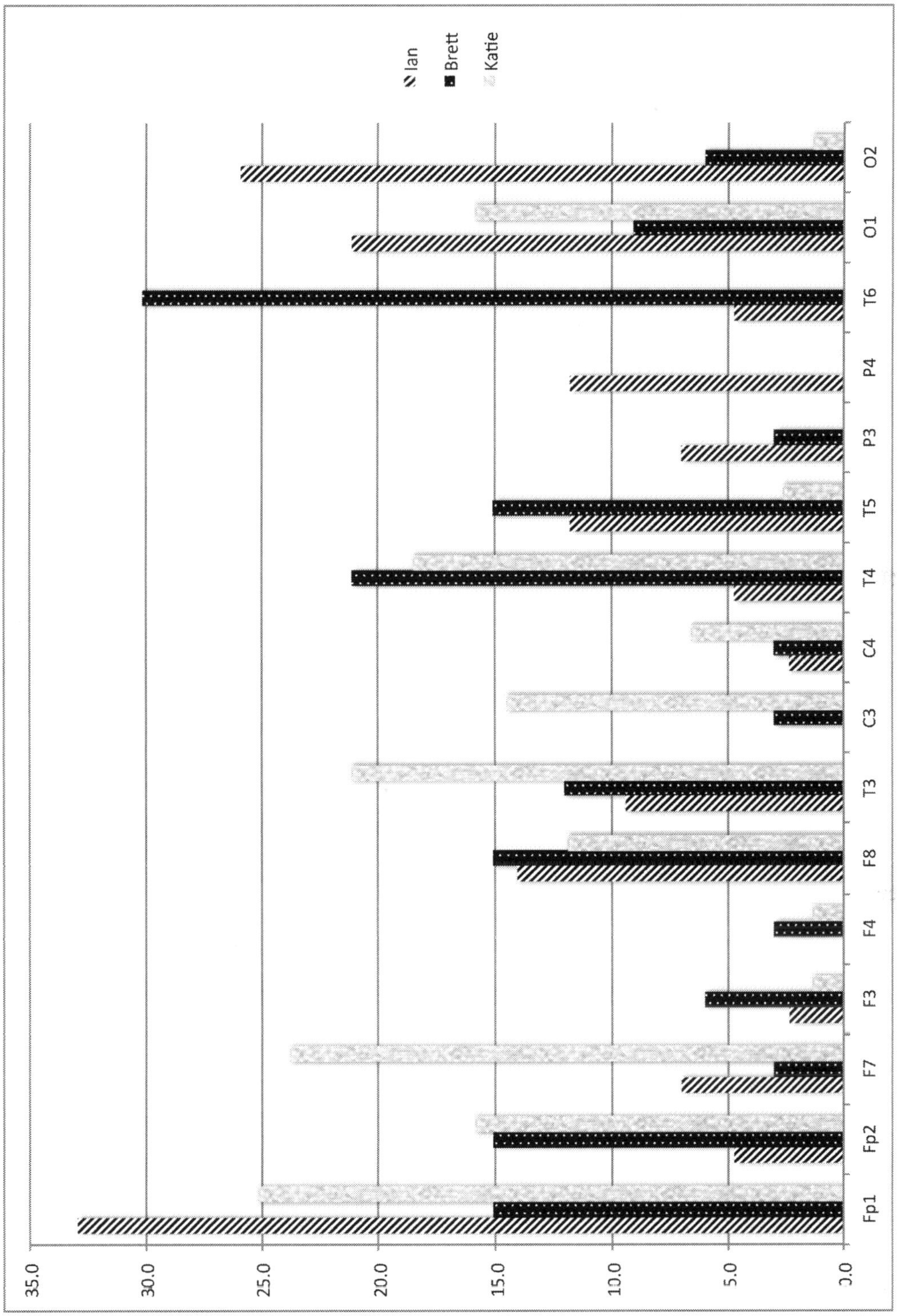

Figure 9-4: Comparison of aggregate neocortex activity of three ISFPs.

projection followed by weighing of odds) as if he were considering various futures to select a best one. He was the only ISFP to show activity in P4, which is most active for Introverted Thinking types. This circuit could be really useful for someone who does improvisation. It allows him to rapidly play out ahead of time several scenarios in his mind and then select the most promising one.

Finally, like all ISFPs, Ian focused on his values. Region F8 (considering values and recalling details) was fairly active. It activated most when expressing values in a negative way, such as describing a strained relationship with his dad. This focus on negatives is typical of ISFP and its opposite type, ENTJ.

ISFP Case Study #2: Brett

Brett is an "A" college student. His interests include travel, school, motorcycles, guitar, snowboarding, and the beach, with a self-described fondness for "thrill seeking, anthropology, video games, and anything out of the ordinary".

Brett took the MBTI® questionnaire in addition to the ISCA™. He scored INFJ on the former and ISFP on the latter. He ultimately settled on ISFP as his best-fit personality type. His EEG results shed light on why he scored and settled like he did.

Throughout his session, Brett showed high activity in region F8 (consider values and recall details) as well as region T4 (notice tone of voice and moral intention), region T5 (social sensitivity) and region T6 (future projection). According to the personality literature, the latter two regions sound typical of INFJ, which has Introverted Intuiting as a lead cognitive process.

Region T5 was most active when Brett talked about other people, such as recent activities with his friends; when he commented on his lack of ability, such as his mediocre drawings; and when we waited patiently between tasks, wondering what I was thinking about him. Like Ian, the other male ISFP, Brett's heightened T5 activity was typical of males with a Feeling preference. Perhaps male Feeling types, as a minority among men, are more self-conscious about social feedback and/or hyper-attentive to interpersonal interactions.

Region T6 was Brett's most active region, surpassing even region F8. It lit up with specific utterances such as, "I'm planning to...", "I'm kind of worried about...", "Glad that's never happened to me", "One choice seemed it would be bad", "They think they're going to be stars", and finally, "Should they be obvious lies?" when I asked him to provide me with lies. All of these utterances involved choices along time lines: what will happen, what didn't happen, what might happen, or what should happen.

Brett was a good listener when talking with a group or focusing on an important speaker. He showed a solid blue listening mode while on the phone with a friend and while listening to everyone in the room at once. He displayed strong activity in regions T3 and T4 when reading aloud or listening to me, but not to other students individually. Perhaps he decided I was more important than his peers, at least during the lab session!

Brett also got "in the zone" with a solid blue EEG while exploring and classifying objects while blindfolded and while following through on a task to artistically arrange a random assortment of grab-bag items in a way that conveys high emotional impact. This links to the compositional talents of ISFPs.

Region F8 activated around people, activities, and beliefs important to Brett, whatever he liked or respected, such as when mentioning a favorite band, his best-friend, and "what's worth doing in life". Region F8 also lit when he said, "Nobody should be paid that much money!" regarding celebrity performers, indicating some should-not's along with positively expressed values.

Brett's EEG often lit up between tasks as he looked out the window to enjoy the beautiful view of a park. This is typical of Extraverted Sensing types, who easily tire of desk work and are stimulated by movement and the outdoors. Also typical of a Sensing type in general, Brett showed a lot of yellow (alpha waves) throughout his session, especially when meditating; and he provided concrete, literal interpretations (as opposed to fictive interpretations) when asked to brainstorm meanings of a dramatically illustrated scene. In fact, both Fp1 and Fp2 were at maximum amplitude as he brainstormed one interpretation after another. This differs substantially from ENFP or ENTP subjects who would show a holistic Christmas tree pattern.

Finally, when I read to him a sad news story that involved the death of a innocent teenager due to a drunk driver, he showed a strong circuit pattern that cycled from F3 (linear deductive reasoning) to T4 (weigh voice tone and moral intention), then across to T3 (word content), then Fp2 (process management and self-reflection), and finally back to F3. Clearly he was engaging in some kind of assessment process that included logical deduction and perhaps also applying some of the implications to himself. Whatever the details, a high speed circuit pattern across the brain is typical of ISFP's opposite type, ENTJ.

ISFP Case Study #3: Katie

Katie is an "A" college student. Her interests include dance, fashion, music, psychology, and travel. She enjoys composition, design, and crafts. She presents herself as highly sociable and friendly.

Katie's self-assessment score differed from her final best-fit type. She scored as ENFP on both the MBTI® questionnaire and ISCA™ but settled on ISFP. Her EEG results shed light on why she scored and settled like she did.

Throughout her session, Katie showed a lot of activity like other ISFPs in region Fp1 (decision making), region F8 (weigh importance and recall details), and region T4 (notice voice tone and moral intention). However, she also showed tremendous activity in region F7, which helps us make inferences based on context, mimic others' behavior, and imagine what-if scenarios, all of which sound a lot like an ENFP, which has Extraverted Intuiting as a lead cognitive process. Yet Katie showed no Christmas tree pattern typical of ENFPs. Considering the MBTI® and ISCA™ questionnaires tend to tap skills or behaviors, and not brain activity, it is no wonder Katie scored as ENFP.

Katie's F7 activity showed across numerous tasks including signing her name, solving math problems, handling a 3-D geometric object, mimicking others' facial expressions, interpreting a dramatic image, and so on. Simultaneously, regions T3, T4, and O1 were also active as she spoke about her choices on these tasks, interpreted intentions, and visualized what she was thinking.

Different Means, Similar Results

Compared to the male ISFPs, Katie addressed people skills and body motion in a different way. The male ISFPs showed low activity in region F7 but high activity in region T5 (social sensitivity), which is typical of male Feeling types. Regions F7 and T5 are both home to "mirror neurons". These neurons help us understand others and smooth social interactions. Region F7 is more about mimicking others while T5 is more about adjusting to social feedback. Similarly, the male ISFPs both showed moderate activity in region P3 (integrate motion with vision, and identify objects), while Katie showed a lot more activity in regions C3 and C4 (factual recall and whole-body sensation). Thus, the male ISFPs handled motor activity in a more analytical, visual way while Katie handled motor activity by mimicking others' body language.

Like other ISFPs, Katie showed high activity in auditory regions T3 and T4, illustrating aptitude and interest around both verbal content and intention. T4 was very high, indicating an intuitive approach to listening where she notices others' motivations by their tone of voice.

Overall, like Ian and Brett, Katie showed a fair amount of yellow (alpha waves) throughout the session, as typical of a Sensing preference. She showed the most yellow while drawing, making a decision, making a comparison, or talking about those decisions or comparisons. She thinks kinesthetically, trusting her instincts. Later, when given ambiguous sentences, she gave literal or typical interpretations at first, also typical of a Sensing preference. However, half way through the task, she showed a flash of intense red (beta waves) across the whole EEG and exclaimed, "Oh, I get it now!" Thereafter, she quickly and easily provided both fanciful and literal interpretations. Similarly, during a geometry task, after I hinted that she might break the problem into parts, her EEG flashed bright red again as she tried my suggestion. Sudden flashes of red are associated with ""Ah ha!"" experiences, which are associated with Introverted Intuiting.

Unlike Ian and Brett, Katie showed little activity in region T6 (future projection). However, she tapped Introverted Intuiting in other ways. For example, like an ENTJ and ENFJ, she used her finger to hold her place while solving math problems and when reading.

Katie showed the tennis hop typical of Extraverted Sensing when she listened to dance club music with her eyes shut, visualized playing soccer (her sport), and imagined her future. Then the EEG showed solid blue when she explained her future. This reminded me of INTJ and INFJ types, who show this pattern when imagining the future, and suggested another instance of Introverted Intuiting.

Finally, region F8 was fairly active around positively and negatively expressed values. For example, F8 lit up when she referred to getting an "education" but it did not light up about her school, UCLA. Saying the word "hypocrisy" lit region F8. She explained she had a hard time thinking of a person without getting to know them because, "I have to have justified my opinion". In contrast, the EEG showed solid green (theta waves) when she exclaimed, "I don't hate people!" when asked to talk about what she disliked or hated. Regions F7 and F8 were highly active when she explained how someone was "not a happy human being and projected that on her students". Katie showed the most cognitive activity here when she talked about what brings her happiness in life.

We Are Dynamic Systems

How do the neocortex's many regions interact with each other and the outside world? The diagram at right illustrates cognitive pathways and exemplifies how we are dynamic systems.

The diagram shows nodes and arrows. That nodes stand for sensory inputs or cognitive operations while the arrows indicate flow between the nodes. For example, the "voice input" node represents when we hear words. It flows to a "listen to word content" node, which flows to the "analyze semantic meaning" node. And so on. The nodes are highly specific and represent more than discrete regions. The nodes just mentioned all relate to region T3.

The brain often follows multiple pathways at once. For example, the "analyze meaning" node flows into three other nodes: "attempt logical deduction", "determine context", and "detect social feedback". These represent typical activity in regions F3, F7, and T5, respectively. Which pathways we emphasize depends on context and each node's "thresholds to activation". A node with a low threshold will easily activate and remain busy, while a node with a high threshold will only blip momentarily or even opt-out of contributing. Thus, there are few straight paths. In fact, pathways often loop back on each other. After we analyze the meaning of words we hear, we might attempt a logical deduction, which feeds into detecting errors and inconsistencies, which further feeds into explaining or making a decision that involves composing a sentence and speaking words. Hopefully, we hear ourselves speak and consider whether we meant what we said or said what we meant!

I implemented and explored the network using an Excel spreadsheet. Specifically, I implemented the network as a "fuzzy cognitive map", which is a type of mind-mimicking method first developed by USC professor Bart Kosko. The program allowed me to enter starting values for the various nodes and then repeatedly "iterate" the network to mimic the flow of mental activity. To no surprise, the network behaved in a seesaw manner. Regardless of starting values, the network vacillated between only two behaviors—two dichotomous polarities—as typical of many dynamic systems. A metaphor is a sink. We can pour water into the sink from any direction, yet the water always swirls down only one (or two) drains. Each of these behaviors or drains is called an "attractor".

The network isn't neurologically accurate. I am refining the network and hope to create a more complete and accurate simulation in the future.

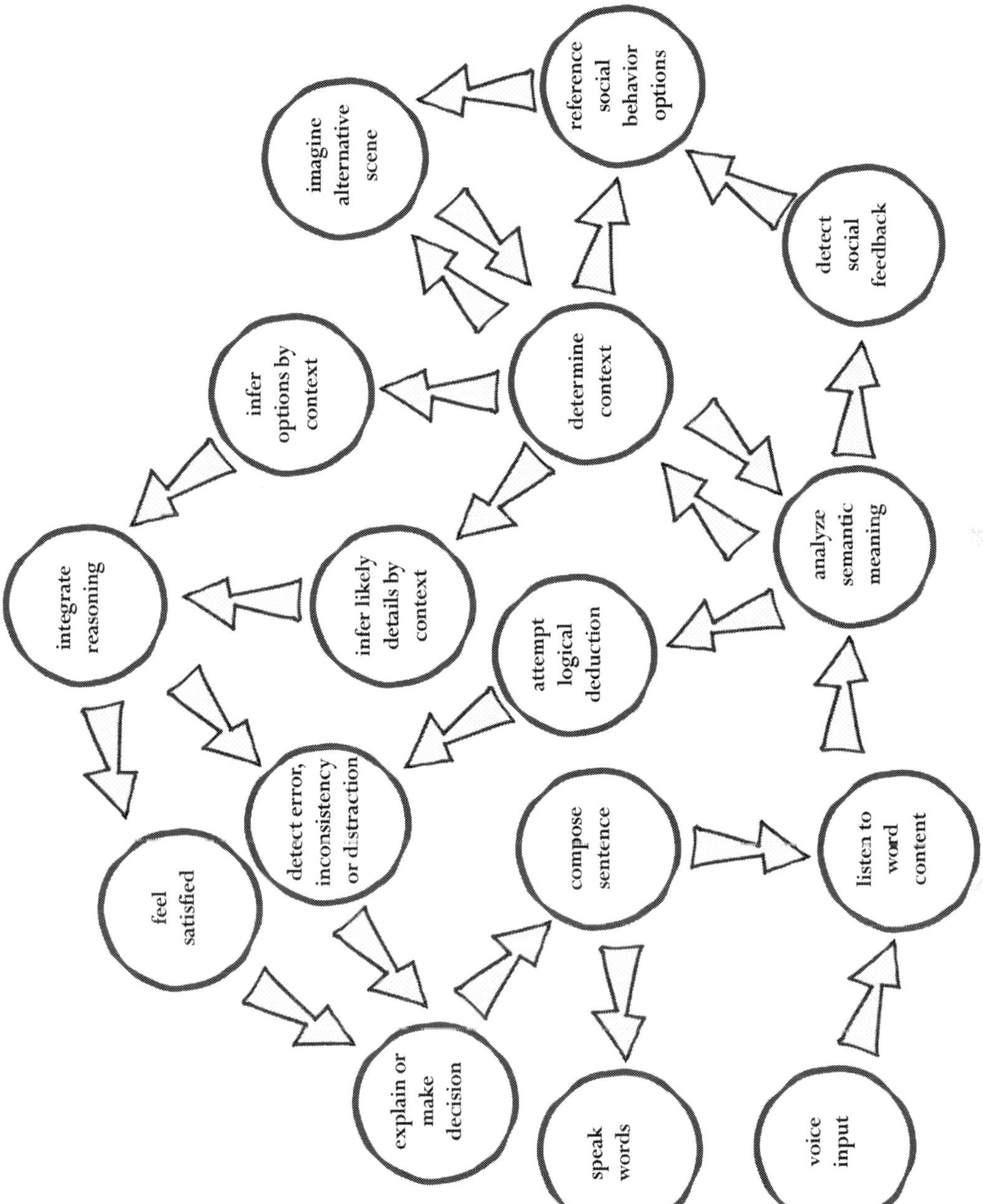

Figure 9-5: A network of interactions results in dynamic behavior.

Minds At Play

Does having fun take brain power? What happens when we play cards, try brain teasers, immerse ourselves in video games, act a part in a theater scene, read a story, or watch television? Results varied from essentially no brain activity to the maximum possible activity captured by the EEG machine.

Watching Television/Movies: Watching television evoked the least brain activity of all tasks. Notably, several students participated in a formally structured experiment where they watched a mix of video clips that mixed humor and violence. Studies suggest that television and movies are passive media that evoke little to no EEG activity. Sometimes, regions Fp1 and Fp2 are active when people watch emotionally-charged scenes. Specifically, Fp1 correlates to positive emotions while Fp2 correlates with negative emotions. I and student researcher Nanae Kido mostly replicated these results. Our video clips rarely evoked any brain activity, and female subjects showed heightened Fp2 activity in response to violence. There were a few exceptions. Ironically, the video clip from the film *Memento* evoked activity. The *Memento* clip is fairly challenging to understand as the film follows a brain-damaged man who experiences events out of order in a confusing way as he tries to solve the homicide of his wife.

Arcade/Shooter Video Games: Many lab students used a hand-held console to play tactical video games like Mario Cart that require a quick reaction time in order to respond to surprise events while rapidly navigating a rich, moving environment. Regardless of personality type, Mario Cart and similar games evoked a "tennis hop" pattern normally only seen among Extraverted Sensing types. While this brain activity is varied and continuously engages the brain, it is less conducive in school or sedentary work life. All in all, these games evoked more activity than watching television.

Reading Fiction: The students read a short (800 word) fantasy story. Reading the story evoked a tide-like pattern where spikes of very high neocortex activity punctuated long stretches of low activity, typically reflecting the reader's process of taking in information and then stopping to process that information every few paragraphs. Two subjects (ENTJ and ENFJ) used an index finger as a running guide while reading. While doing so, the entire EEG monitor except for region P3 stayed in a solid bright blue (delta waves). Removing or adding back the finger motion confirmed the student used region P3 as a visual-kinesthetic guide to achieve focus. Overall, these results match the results of studies that show reading evokes more activity than watching television or movies.

Playing Card Games: The lab students played tactical cards with each other rather than against the computer. Learning a new card game's rules often evoked a solid red EEG (beta waves) while dealing or slapping cards evoked solid blue, and winning or losing evoked solid yellow (alpha waves) or green (theta waves). In general, playing card games with other people evoked more activity than watching television or reading.

Brain-teaser Software Games: A few students tried the handheld Nintendo gaming system, which offers activities like Brain Age that purportedly stimulate activity in pre-frontal regions. In fact, these games did clearly stimulate activity in regions Fp1 and Fp2. The Brain Age game worked as advertised!

Strategic/World-building Games: A few students tried Mahjong or the game Civilization. These are not quick games and require strategy over tactics. Similar to reading, these games evoked brief periods of intense activity followed by severe lulls as the player searched for solutions.

Stage Acting/Dramatic Reading: Two theater students (ENFP and ENTJ) wished to learn how their brains worked while acting. Does the brain show a special state while acting or does it show activity as if one were really doing the acted behavior. The results varied based on amount of preparation.

1. A cold reading of a new script activated regions like T3 related to reading and speaking.
2. Performing a highly rehearsed scene evoked a solid bright blue (delta waves) typical of expert performance.
3. Extemporaneous role-play evoked regions we might expect had the scene occurred in real life.

Other students, mainly ESFP types, tried the extemporaneous role-play. At first, they showed the same results as #3 above. However, they showed the solid blue result of #2 as the situation became more realistic and intense.

Burning Man Festival: In August 2008, I took the EEG equipment to the Burning Man art festival, an annual event held in the Nevada desert that spans five-square miles for a week. It offers an intense, multi-sensory environment of music, lights, fire, and fun for fifty-thousand people. Three subjects—one sober, one inebriated, and one in-between—all showed an EEG at maximum frequency and amplitude for their entire sessions, with only occasional blips of *less* activity in regions needed to complete particular tasks.

Emotional Dynamics

We are inherently emotional creatures. Every region of the neocortex plays a role in our emotional life. Each region mediates our emotions and behavior, with attendant benefits and limitations. Here are descriptions of seven regions that play major roles.

Region Fp1 (Denial+Happiness): This region filters out distracting information, including negative input about oneself, resulting in lowered awareness and also happiness. It gives meat to the adage, "Ignorance is bliss". We entirely forget about bad news or let it sit quietly at the threshold of awareness. People with high activity here can ignore a lot of bad news. Conversely, people with low activity here are not as robust; they take in information and let other brain regions handle situations.

Region Fp2 (Introspection+Sadness): This region is open to new information, which we normally find distracting because what is new does not fit easily with what we know, wish to know, or find relevant. This region also admits and helps manage negative input, encouraging us to introspect. The result is self-awareness with attendant sadness or depression. People with high activity here can admit and reflect calmly on a lot of bad news. Conversely, people with low activity here are less introspective and let other brain regions handle situations.

Region T4 (Anger+Action): This region promotes anger when we receive negative or distracting information. This region also notices tone of voice and intention. People with high activity here are easily agitated and even hostile, either because other regions fail to handle situations or because acute perceptions of others' voice tone and intentions—particularly sanctimony, phoniness, or such—stimulate action. People with low activity here let other regions handle situations; they are slow to anger, rarely act on anger, and likely don't notice or respond to a false tone as much as other people do.

Region T5 (Sensitivity+Appeasement): This region focuses on feedback from others and promotes feelings like embarrassment and guilt that push us to modify our behavior in order to get friendlier feedback. People with high activity here are sensitive to others' perceptions of them and quickly respond by trying more socially acceptable behavior, diplomatically smoothing over interactions, staying quiet with resignation, or leaving the situation. People with low activity here tend to be oblivious to others' social signals and thus don't modify their behavior. They need to see or explicitly hear feedback as they let other regions handle situations.

Region P3 (Aloofness+Independence): This region helps us integrate visual and kinesthetic input; it also defines for us where we end and the rest of the world begins. People with high activity here tend to have an acute sense of self, with strong personal boundaries and an independent streak. In contrast, people with low activity here may view everyone as linked to everyone else, with a sense of interconnectedness that may encourage them to be overly intrusive into others' business, easily crossing boundaries. We can gauge a person's brain activity here just by considering how they hold themselves, whether they use their arms in a self-protective manner or a warm-welcoming manner.

Region F7 (Acting+Empathy): This region helps us mimic others and think in terms of context. In practice, it helps us act as-if, to take on the clothing of an emotion even if that emotion is not our own, and perhaps walk in another person's shoes. It's like our own mental stage upon which we can act. When this region works well and feeds results to neighboring regions like T3, we may engage in mind reading—we "hear" our inner actor on our mental stage. Thus, people who show a lot of activity here tend to demonstrate insight into others' behavior. In contrast, people with low activity here tend to behave in an non-empathic manner and find it hard to predict others' behavior.

Region F8 (Liking+Devotion): This region helps us think without considering the context. In practice, it helps us recall exact details (rather than inferring details), and it acts as a home for the people, places, objects, and events that we believe are really important and worthwhile to us across all situations. Importance shows up along a scale from love and like at one end to dislike and hate at the other. A person's voice tone tends to betray where they place importance by emphasizing keywords. People with high activity here tend to harbor strong beliefs and react strongly to violations of those beliefs. People with low activity here tend to react less strongly, including being less devoted.

While we can consider each region discretely, the regions work together to produce a complex, ever-changing dance. The regions we prefer tend to take the lead in this dance while the other regions follow. And when a move becomes too difficult for a region, it passes, steps out of the dance, and hands over activity to another region. Thus, a person can sometimes shift quickly from happiness to anger, sensitivity to aloofness, and so on.

Remember, the deep brain is the true fount of emotions. The neocortex mediates those emotions to ensure composure for adult behavior.

Mathematics Education

How can we best help students learn? In particular, is there an effective way to teach mathematics? As someone who finds math fairly easy, I am often perplexed why other people exclaim math is hard. School systems have struggled back and forth for decades, often swinging between step-by-step fundamentals versus a "whole math" approach that mixes concepts and allegedly affords students a chance to discover principles on their own.

Before their EEG lab session, my students reported where they were schooled. Then, after solving a math problem, they reported how they solved the problem. For example, did they visualize the numbers, speak the numbers to themselves, experience a sensation or feeling, simply recall memorized answers, or what? Later, while under the EEG, they tackled math problems that started easy and grew harder, like so:

- $2 + 2 = ?$
- $17 + 11 - 3 = ?$
- $17 \times 11 = ?$
- $55 / 4 + 11.2 =?$
- $(4325 + 67982) * -11768 = ?$

The students hailed from various majors, some of which emphasize math skills more than others. I kept this in mind as I analyzed results. The figures at right summarize the background and average brain activity for three students. All three majored in the physical sciences and tackled math daily in their courses.

The first student, per Figure 9-6, worked quickly and accurately and drew upon only three brain regions even for the harder problems. She learned math in the Japanese school system, which focuses on step-by-step methods and rote memorization. She had no problem working even as other people talked around her to generate a small amount of distraction. She identified with ENTJ, so we might not be surprised that she used her neocortex in an efficient way.

The second student, per Figure 9-7, worked slowly and with numerous mistakes and drew upon four brain regions. He learned math in a French school system that emphasized an auditory method where students sound out the numbers and operations. Indeed, he mainly utilized auditory regions. He reported that he had difficulty doing math in noisy environments and usually needed a quiet place to solve math problems. He identified with ENFJ, which is fairly auditory compared to most other personality types.

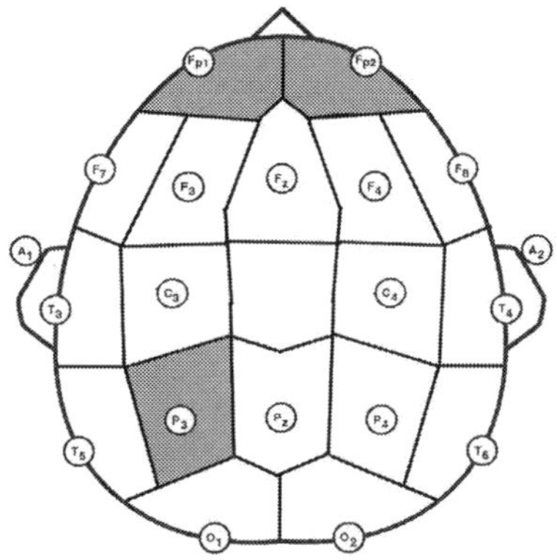

Figure 9-6: Japanese Subject

- Japanese school system
- Rote memorization method
- Solved quickly and accurately
- Used three brain regions
- Personality type ENTJ

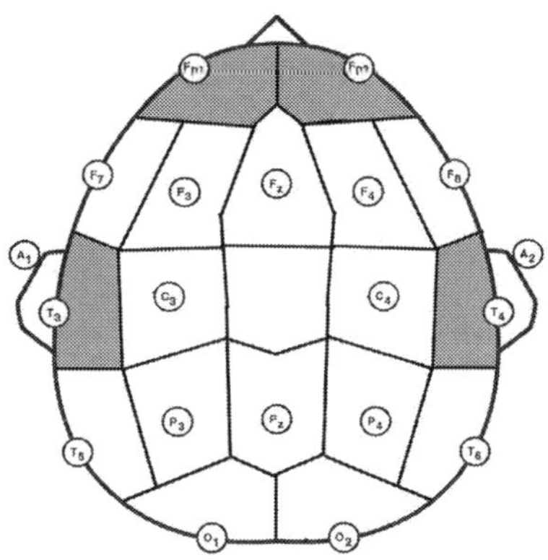

Figure 9-7: Lebanese Subject

- Lebanese/French system
- Auditory method
- Solved slowly and poorly
- Used four brain regions
- Personality type ENFJ

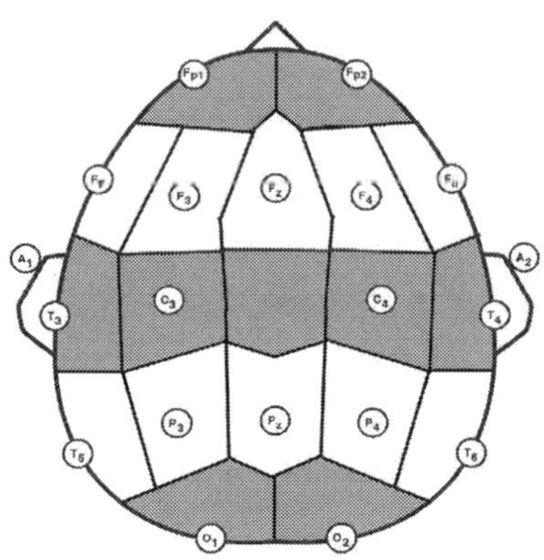

Figure 9-8: American Subject

- California public system
- "Whole math" method
- Solved quickly and accurately
- Used eight brain regions
- Personality type ENTP

Finally, the third student, per Figure 9-8, worked quickly and accurately but drew upon half of her brain to do so. She learned in a USA school that applied a whole math approach. She reported drawing upon memories of problem solving, visualizing the problems, and considering ways to proceed, particularly for the harder problems. She identified with ENTP, so we might expect her to show a lot of asynchronous brain activity to explore problems in various ways.

What does this sample of results imply for math education?

First, the amount of brain activity roughly indicates the amount of energy the student is burning to solve problems. The first two students will likely be able to keep working longer on homework problems than the third student, who may quickly experience burn out and wish to rest. However, during short timed tests, the first and third students are likely to do better, though a quiet testing environment could really help the second student. Either way, the first student did the best overall.

Second, top math performers, such as graduate students in the sciences and engineering, tend to use posterior reasoning regions (P3 and P4) in order to quickly and accurately solve math problems with referring to general principles. These mathletes can construct a system of equations based on text data and then locate a best-fit solution or a comparative advantage. This sophisticated reasoning reflects the kind of reasoning we might wish to install in future citizens to help them think in complex ways. Only the Japanese student drew upon a region associated with logical reasoning.

Third, unlike speaking or walking, learning how to do math calculations requires active instruction. All the students showed a pattern that matched their personality, though the ENTP failed to show use of reasoning centers as expected for her type, at least in a support role, suggesting she did not iternalize general math principles as whole-math advocates would hope. She could have been an outlier or her education was insufficiently rigorous.

By the way, across all tasks, few lab participants utilized key reasoning regions (F3, F4, P3, and P4). Is this okay? In the USA, both traditional and modern educational methods seem to focus on developing region Fp1, which helps us explain and decide. Using Fp1 can provide a semblance of reasoning, but explaining oneself does not equal true use of logic. It appears practicing math is not fulfilling its potential to truly hone students' reasoning skills.

The next chapter ponders insights and hypotheses like these to improve our lives, including the quality of education.

10.
Now What?

You and your brain are now more properly acquainted. Let's reflect on and put to use what you have learned. First, review your self-assessment on page 86 and the table of eight cognitive processes on pages 88 and 89 in order to locate a best-fit personality type, at least for now. Next, answer the questions below. Of the eight cognitive processes, briefly name and *describe* which process:

1. Plays the lead role?

2. Plays a support role?

3. Also often fits for you?

4. Attracts your interest to develop?

5. Acts as a pitfall/blind-spot?

Now, let's explore three application areas: learning, work, and relationships. After each area, use what you wrote above to help you develop an action plan.

In Our Classrooms

Can we improve education? We can! I know first-hand what does and doesn't work. Two teaching awards also suggest I know a little something.

As a doctoral student, two experienced professors and I transformed a failing undergraduate engineering program. There was a problem—very poor retention—and we worked to fix it. Before we began, the program offered students a three-hour lecture in a dark auditorium with a relentlessly sleep-inducing slide presentation. By the end of year one, a majority of students were dropping out. Just signing up for engineering indicated interest. Truly, the instructional method was designed to truss and slay that interest.

We three instructors fixed our sights on how to best motivate students to learn. We dumped all but twenty minutes of lecture, each took one day a week, and focused on design skills. Students did one day of technical writing, practicing the finer points of composition to articulate more clearly and more imaginatively. I taught a computer lab, where students learned hands-on, individually and in small groups, to craft small computer programs. The third day exposed students to electro-mechanical tools and concepts. All of this led toward the biggest change. We met with the local community to learn real people's needs. Then students signed up to create working solutions for those needs. It was challenging and amazingly effective. After two years of ironing out the details, our revised program went from 45% retention to 95% retention.

Soon after, when I started teaching at UCLA, I launched a robotics lab where students from all majors wrote and performed stage plays with robots that they programmed using a (mostly) graphical user interface. There was a pattern: Students with a more technical background liked programming but they didn't know *what* to program. What would a robot say when it proposes marriage, runs for political office, or refuses a cup of coffee? The English majors easily offered answers. All of the students left knowing they each had skills and could work across academic cultures.

What does the brain science say? In 2008, I conducted a brief pilot study designed by my colleague Francis Steen (also at UCLA). We introduced four student subjects to an unfamiliar topic called internet packet switching. We introduced each student using a different method; afterward, we questioned them to assess what they understood and asked them to verbalize the topic as if explaining it to a child. Internet packet switching is a complex, technical

The Two-Minute Author

Sometimes people ask me, "What's your research?" Naturally, they are curious. The brain is so very personal. We all have one that is unique! Now you too know something about the neuroscience of personality. Perhaps you will find some benefit from the following two-minute elevator speech that I use.

Your brain is home to many regions. A technology called EEG can infer the activity of regions in the neocortex, which is the brain's outermost layer. The neocortex handles many quintessentially human activities that you do such as reasoning, language, perception, and decision-making.

Each region handles the same stuff for all of us (if you're right handed!) However, individuals vary by how much they use. You focus on some regions while neglecting others. Your pattern helps uniquely define you as an individual.

There are also whole-brain states. These states strongly influence every brain region at once, like how a conductor influences an orchestra. These states are nuanced and pervasive. They are hard to summarize here!

Let's look at one state called "flow". It occurs when you are awake and calm while doing a task you are really good at, which might be playing guitar, listening actively, handling crises, imagining the future, or whatnot. Your training and also your personality influence what takes you into this flow state.

I use the Jungian/Myers-Briggs framework to understand personality. It describes eight cognitive processes that all people can access. Like handedness, you prefer some processes over the others. Amazingly, each Jungian process corresponds to specific regions and whole-brain states.

The big idea: We can use the neuroscience of personality to better understand ourselves and others to enjoy more meaning and efficiency in our lives.

process. Students were taught by four methods, a:

1. Detailed, written, literal explanation with no metaphors or visuals.
2. Written explanation with a rich metaphor.
3. Written explanation with a diagram.
4. Tactile activity that guides the student to act out the ideas.

Method #4 yielded the best test results but the worst verbal explanation. The student understood the process well because she had acted it out; however, she had no verbal reference to provide an explanation, though she offered to lead someone else through the activity. Methods #2 and #3 yielded decent test results and fairly good explanations. Method #2 was problematic because the student noticed the metaphor was inaccurate, while method #3 was problematic because the diagram didn't show actual movement, which is a major aspect of packet switching. Method #1, which acted as a fine representative of a lot of textbooks and teaching, gave the worst results.

We might think a written explanation with a clear diagram and a solid metaphor would be best, along with a physical activity to act out the idea. Sounds great! Unfortunately, this means a teacher must work harder for a student to learn more. Let's explore how students and instructors can work together.

Presently, I help students to create interactive multi-media scenarios usable on mobile technology. The scenarios are like "choose your own adventure" stories, though they include scoring so that a scenario can deliver content as well as assesses a person's ability to use his or her newly acquired knowledge to make wise decisions in a context that presents consequences and demands more decisions. The students select topics and throw themselves into the design process, researching and writing and gathering media. I help with beta-testing and suggest improvements. Along with some EEG lab sessions, I have quickly learned three lessons:

1. People learn well what they use as part of a larger, meaningful project.
2. People recall well what is learned and assessed in a *narrative* manner that requires decisions, similar to how we get through life.
3. People get "in the zone" more easily when doing their own work (play their own song, do their own dance, etc.) compared to doing others' work.

In short, like a kid who loves baseball or dinosaurs and learns everything under the sun about such topics, people of all ages excel when they design.

When I reflect on successful teaching moments, I notice there has been a common theme: Students design, compose, and create with an audience or consumer in mind, as people often do in the work world. As people go through a process of researching, implementing, testing, and redesigning for others, they use various cognitive processes to master both content and process. Integrating multiple media forms helps ensure that students tap various preferences. This design-oriented approach also transforms an instructor into a knowledgeable facilitator rather than a broadcaster and disciplinarian. Most beautifully, design does not take years of expensive education. All it takes is a brain.

Your Learning Action Plan

Use the prompts below to develop your learning action plan.

1. How do you presently engage in design (product, service, etc.)?

2. What are some of your learning goals or ideals?

3. How might you fulfill your learning through a design process?

In Our Workplaces

Imagine a world not too far along from now, where any person can seek out a brain scan to enjoy deeper self-understanding. You might use EEG, or you might use another technology such as fMRI or near-infrared spectroscopy. Whatever the means, you might receive a colorfully slick, official-looking report. Perhaps it will even be a government report. How would you feel about that?

Now, who gains access to your data? What will you and others do with it? Will future employers ask to see your latest brain scan to help decide whether you are the right person for their organization, and if so, which position suits you most? People have explored these questions. Today, in some places, it is illegal to use pencil-paper psychological assessments for hiring purposes or job placement. In other places, it's all the rage. Why all the fuss?

A few years ago, a student of mine surveyed hundreds of employees and managers at a local telecom company. He documented a lot of diverse personality types among the lower-level employees. However, all seventy-two managers scored the same way. They all ranked Stabilizer as their best-fit temperament. Was this result real, due to wishful thinking, a desire to fit in, or all of the above? Was that company deliberately sorting people? Was it ready to adroitly handle surprise changes in the marketplace? Perhaps greater diversity among its management team would better prepare it for the future. Do we even have an idea whether cognitive diversity helps or harms?

A British study asked cognitive diversity helps. It set up three small groups to examine each group's performance and social life while its members busied themselves with a task. The researchers compared two types of diversity.

- Identity: Gender, ethnicity, and nationality.
- Cognition: Ways people process information and make decisions.

There were three groups. The first group was uniformly low diversity in terms of identity and cognition. The second group was home to high diversity regarding identity and middling diversity regarding cognition. Conversely, the last group was formed around high cognitive diversity and middling identity diversity.

How did the three groups perform, and did their members enjoy the experience? The first group performed poorly on the task. The second group, with its mix of genders and ethnicities performed better. However, it also demonstrated quite a bit of unpleasant conflict. The third group had the highest performance, and its members were none the worse for wear.

A possible moral of the story? If these results hold for other kinds of groups and tasks, then perhaps we might wish to spend a lot more effort understanding and encouraging cognitive diversity. All we would need is a way to document cognition. Sounds easy, right?

History suggests that good intentions can lead us astray. Here are questions you might ask yourself, your clients or others, to promote ethical use of neuroscience, particularly in the workplace. Does a piece of new information help you:

- Gain self-awareness?
- Learn or otherwise perform more readily?
- Better connect with other people to enjoy more satisfying relationships?
- Clarify a career, relationship, or life choice?
- Become more human?

The last question might sound odd. Two people have told me they don't wish to know what's going on in their brains. "It will remove all the mystery!" Others may feel neuroscience suggests we are dull automatons. Using region F3, a seat of deductive logic, might lead us to believe life is deterministic. But that's just region F3 talking! May I suggest another viewpoint: More information about ourselves challenges us to be more human, to learn to face issues and make wise choices, such as choice of career.

One of my lab students came from a traditional family of wealthy means. His two older brothers were in medical school, and his parents wanted him to take a similar route. During the free-form period at the lab's end, he asked to explore music, for which he expressed a passion. He performed some original pieces. For the first time in two hours, I witnessed a tell-tale solid bright blue pattern indicating a state of creative flow. He remained there for his entire song. He knew the EEG's meaning. His music was more than a hobby. It was a talent and perhaps a calling. Later, he spoke at graduation because he held our program's highest grade point average. The rough draft of his speech mentioned the lab and that moment. However, his final speech did not because his parents were in the audience. He worried they might blame me. I wonder how he has handled this information as he has gone on to his future. How would you handle it?

Today, a few organizations already use brain scans to assess product development, marketing campaigns, cognitive skills, and more. Technology is even emerging to actively target brain regions, to either heighten or dampen neural activity in order to induce temporary alterations. For example, when we zap left frontal regions (F7, Fp1, etc.), we boost creative problem solving and free-hand drawing ability. Normally, signals from these zapped regions turn off some marvelous abilities that we apparently already possess! Should we augment workers? Maybe. We can also zap a small region bridging T4 and P4 in order to dampen our consideration of ethics when making decisions. That's not so great.

As our future arrives, the Jungian/Myers-Briggs framework is an effective and ethical substitute that focuses on individuals' various gifts rather than pathology. As a model it asks you to be... like you. And to afford others the same courtesy. This is a solid example that is worth our trust.

Your Workplace Action Plan

Use the prompts below to boost your career satisfaction and work life.

1. What cognitive gifts are welcome (or not) in your workplace?

2. How well do your current/desired work roles fit your cognitive gifts?

3. How might you promote productive, ethnical use of cognitive diversity?

In Our Homes

Getting to know a person's brain activity over several hours is truly an amazing window to get to know him or her in a unique, fairly intimate way. Technologies like EEG promise to exceed the benefits of our current, soft self-help methods to help us deeply understand ourselves and others and thereby foster greater compassion for each other.

Practitioners of personality type models often praise one high boon: their use brings clarity and eases conflict. All of a sudden, when we better get to know someone's underlying operating system, so to speak, a lot of confusion and tension dissipate. However, more is going on. What might that be?

Students in my research course often wonder which temperaments get along well with each other, particularly for romantic relationships, as if there must be a secret formula. For the record, there isn't a magic match because people can create satisfying pairings in many ways, often commensurate with their maturity. Indeed, one student uncovered a remarkable correlation about maturity. She asked her research subjects about their relationship history. She also gave them the Interstrength Temperament Assessment. The assessment has two parts. Part I offers a set of short, discrete questions, each one tapping one small "piece" of one's temperament. A result is computed by summing up all of the individual pieces. In contrast, Part II offers a set of four holistic temperament descriptions—all presented in prose form—that subjects are instructed to "evaluate as a whole" and rate and rank to get a result. Both parts are validated, though sometimes they give different results.

What did she discover? Subjects who reported longer and more satisfying relationships scored as the same temperament on both parts of the assessment. In contrast, subjects who reported fewer and less satisfying relationships scored differently on each part of the assessment. The meaning is a little like the metaphor of seeing the forest for the trees. A person who holds a congruent self-conception is more likely to enjoy intimate relationships compared to a person who is confused about his or her own identity and behavior. Thus, the benefits of using personality type are subtle and pervasive. Beyond a general appreciation of individual similarities and differences, we better enjoy the company of others by better understanding ourselves.

Imagine you and your loved ones could read each other's minds. In a way, we already can. In Chapter 7, we met Natalie as she tried various tasks.

Her boyfriend Grant quietly watched the whole time. Later, the two switched roles and she observed his brain activity. On the surface, they were "typical" university students: eager, polite, intelligent, talented, and involved in a myriad of activities with dreams for the future. Yet they differed in many ways. She showed up as strongly analytical, kinesthetic, and visual. He showed up as a devoted listener with grounding in strong beliefs and a rich imagination. At the same time, both were more introverted than the average student and enjoyed similar use of several brain regions. They were already vaguely aware of these qualities. But the EEG allowed them to peer beyond folk psychology, personal experience, gut instincts, and the projections they cast onto each other.

One humorous moment occurred during a computerized speed-dating activity. Grant was sure that Natalie would show heightened brain activity when she met males with a similar look and interests as him. He even picked out one that reminded him of himself. But in fact, Natalie did not select that virtual date. She narrowed her preferences down to three other males, whom she evaluated on a scale of one to ten in terms of being a potential helpmate and parent. Finally, of the three, she settled for the male that all my female subjects do: a clean-cut, smiling blond young man in a football jersey; that is, an "all American" guy. Of the three, she hadn't rated him the highest, and he was unlike her boyfriend.

The result of this activity didn't surprise me. Just as all the female subjects select the same male, the male subjects all select the same female for a virtual date (males prefer the bikini-clad blonde on the beach). The EEG brilliantly sorts romantic interest: When we like someone, our brains get more active, often showing bright red on the monitor that may appear briefly as a blip or remain over several minutes as the brain recovers from its interest. Yet romantic interest does not translate into life commitments. The propensities of deep brain structures drive sexuality and desire so strongly that our short-term choices are hardly choices at all. Yet the neocortex, concerned with its civilized questions, dominates the long-term. Sometimes the two match up. Other times not. Whatever the case, Natalie and Grant gained great insight from the EEG into each other as individuals as well as romantic partners.

Sometimes EEG can address very specific questions. One subject volunteered with a conundrum in mind: He had just ended his second serious relationship of a few years and he feared he was the "cause". He wondered, was he incapable of love? Did he care about his career and hobbies more than people? Perhaps some terrible trait lurked within his brain? He hoped for answers. To no surprise, he showed tremendous activity in region T5 (social sensitivity). Conversely, he showed little activity in region F8, which helps us weigh values and importance. Perhaps the low activity there explained why he found it hard to answer his own questions; this region was not regularly in gear to resolve the questions in a satisfying way. That said, there was some activity. Region F8 showed more activity when he talked about his two previous partners and his friends and family members than it did when he talked about his career and hobbies. (Though none of them compared to his enjoyment of chocolate!) He was relieved. Some people might consider measured clarity a bad thing, perhaps dehumanizing. Might I offer an alternative? Perhaps an EEG result is like an emotion: we can treat it as an informative data point—one among many—as we continue to muddle through for ourselves.

I offer a workshop that helps people explore the various roles they may play in romantic relationships. Roles might be Provider, Courtesan, Compatriot, Mentor, and so forth among twenty total. I focus on couples as the irreducible unit of study. Through a questionnaire, film clips, and discussion, participants explore role-dynamics, including ways to re-balance their relationships. Similarly, I talk about the various neocortex regions in terms of roles such as Chief Judge, Grounded Believer, and Flowing Artist in order to quietly suggest that we may play relationship roles that fit our cognitive skills. Thus, there is no magical "relationship" brain skill-set or personality type best suited to love. Instead, we are all free to reflect and grow with each other, with promise for the future.

Your Relationship Action Plan

Respond to the prompts below to help improve your relationships.

1. Which relationship roles do you and your loved-ones play?

2. Which cognitive strengths do you rely on to fill these roles?

3. How might you shift to address unfulfilled/unsatisfying roles?

Appendix: Resources

Workshops

Come master how to use the material in this book. Add to your competencies. These workshops are aimed at coaches, trainers, counselors, and persons in the innovative business fields. After taking a workshop, participants often say:

- "I now clearly understand each of the eight Jungian functions."
- "Finally, a truly scientific basis for the Jungian/Myers-Briggs model!"
- "Thank you for the fantastic coaching tips."

In the USA and internationally, Dr. Nardi is recognized as an engaging speaker. He pairs exciting new information with practical applications. What you learn is based on research, which helps legitimize and advertise your own activities.

Photo A-1: Workshops include solo and group activities to apply concepts.

Photo A-2: Workshops include coaching activities to build skills.

Consider one of the following three workshops.

Half-Day Introduction: This three-hour event is a fast-paced lecture with time for Q&A. It includes an introduction (or reintroduction) to the Jungian model with links to the sixteen Myers-Briggs types. Stories help attendees retain the type-specific tips. Attendees gain handouts for later review.

Day-Long Practium: This day-long workshop builds off of the half-day to include three in-depth activities. Participants put into practice specific tips mentioned earlier. The activities focus on building rapport, problem solving, and modeling new skills.

Two-Day Masters Course: Truly build your comfort with skill in this advanced workshop that builds off of the day-long event to focus on both essentials of neuroscience and use of the Jungian/Myers-Briggs model. The afternoon guides you to tailor material and concepts to your needs.

Whatever your needs, you gain take-away materials and will be able to:

- Appreciate the eight Jungian functions in depth.
- More effectively motivate and influence individuals of the sixteen types.
- Confidently point to brain research behind the sixteen types.

With these secrets in hand, attendees will be able to quickly and powerfully evoke the interest and capabilities of employees, clients, and students. Participants will receive appropriate PDF take-aways.

Technology Savvy? Organizations with Apple mobile devices like iPad or iPhone can arrange for an enhanced experience using Dr. Nardi's popular "Personality Types" app, found in the Apple iTunes store.

Visit www.radiancehouse.com for more information.

Mobile Trainer App

www.apple.com/iTunes

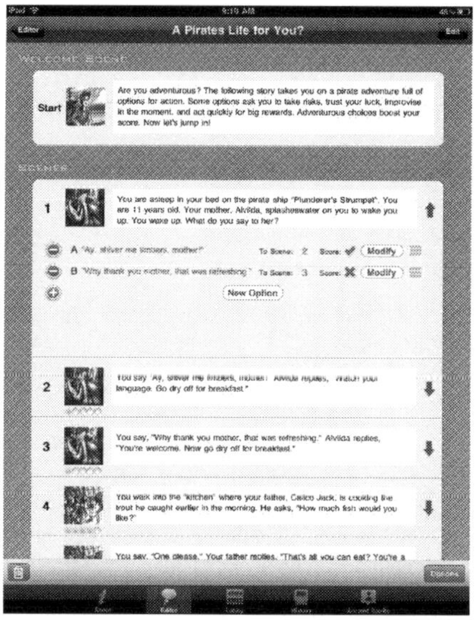

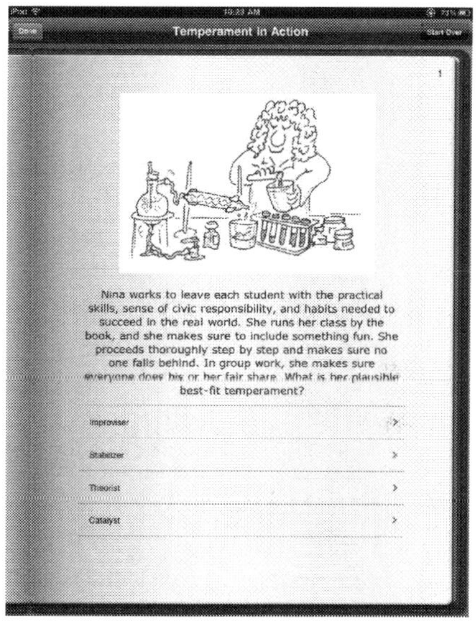

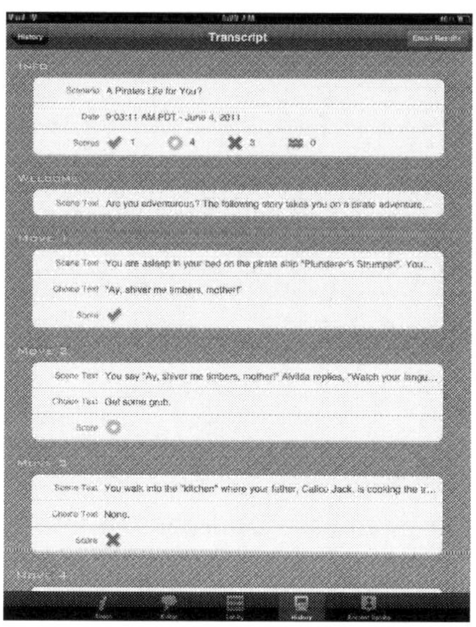

Features

This lush iPad app allows you to:

- Assess knowledge and/or decision-making ability in context!
- Engage in "choose your own adventure" style interactive stories.
- Create and publish your own training scenarios or download premade ones.
- Invite clients and friends to navigate the scenarios.
- Review performance afterward and repeat to raise performance.
- Deploy for courses, HR training, media tie-ins, and many other uses.

Apple iTunes Apps

www.apple.com/iTunes

"Personality Types"

This is a handy guide to every aspect of the sixteen Jungian/ Myers-Briggs types including special material by Dr. Linda V Berens. Includes three type assessments and allows you to do side-by-side comparisons according to type. This is a great tool to facilitate with clients using the iPad, and for folks to keep up their use of type after your sessions.

"Love Therapy"

This is a handy guide for relationship management, particularly for romantic couples. The app uses a familiar language of elements to convey essentials of temperament and twenty key roles we enjoy playing within intimate relationships. Includes three assessments and side-by-side comparison options to evaluate and troubleshoot relationships.

Popular Books

www.RadianceHouse.com

16 Personality Types: Descriptions for Self-Discovery

by Linda V Berens, Dario Nardi

The 16 Personality Types: Descriptions for Self-Discovery is an invaluable tool for users of the MBTI and related instruments. These descriptions present a living systems approach to describing the sixteen types. Dr. Berens and Dr. Nardi have captured the essence of the sixteen type patterns and crafted descriptions to be used by individuals to clarify their best-fit type.

Quick Guide to the 16 Personality Types in Organizations: Understanding Personality Differences in the Workplace

by Charles R. Martin, Dario Nardi, Linda V Berens, Linda Ernst, Marci Segal, Melissa Smith, Roger Pearman, Steve Myers, Sue A. Cooper

This guide is written by leading experts in the theory of personality type and its applications. It helps you develop your personal effectiveness within the workplace by providing two full pages of information about each of the sixteen personality types under the topics of Problem Solving, Leadership, Creativity, Teams, Stress, Learning, Career Mastery, and Personal Development. Also included is an appendix on team roles.

Understanding Yourself and Others: An Introduction to the Personality Type Code

by Linda V Berens, Dario Nardi

The personality type code devised by Isabel Myers can be a powerful tool for explaining individual differences. And while the type code embodies a simple presentation, it was meant to represent a "whole" personality pattern. We are more than the letters or the "sum of our preferences". This book introduces psychological type and the eight cognitive processes. Includes descriptions of what each process looks like within each type. These breakthrough descriptions will help your clients understand their complete type pattern in way never before available.

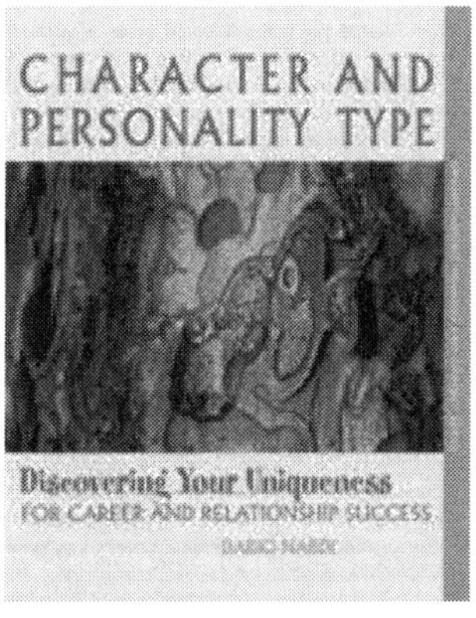

Character and Personality Type: Discovering Your Uniqueness For Career and Relationship Success

by Dario Nardi

This booklet will change the way you look at personality type and development. Contains Dr. Nardi's long-awaited sixty-four character biographies—four for each type with illustrations—gives you a new look at the differences within personality type. The self-discovery and personal self-leadership process outlined in this book is not about just making a one-time decision on a career, or "fixing" a current relationship. This book is designed to give you tools and some important organizing principles so that you can generate and maintain a life that offers sufficient choices, resources, and flexibility for you to respond to demands and opportunities over a lifetime.

8 Keys to Self-Leadership: From Awareness to Action

by Dario Nardi

Life can demand a lot if we want to be happy and successful. Wouldn't it be nice to know the keys to more insightful perception and wiser decision-making? *8 Keys to Self-Leadership: from Awareness to Action* honors your natural talents and helps you stretch yourself into new areas while keeping that sense of learning and wonder you had as a child. In this book, Dr. Nardi will guide you through the doors and show you how to unlock the eight key cognitive processes—eight ways to find greater satisfaction in all that you do.

Understanding Yourself and Others: An Introduction to the 4 Temperaments—4.0

by Linda V Berens

This essential workbook includes the latest developments in Temperament theory including four variations of each temperament, leading to the sixteen personality types. In this perennial best-seller on the application of Temperament theory, Dr. Linda V Berens introduces us to the next evolution of Temperament—the four new terms: Improviser™, Stabilizer™, Theorist™ and Catalyst™. Dr. Berens has developed a resource used by thousands to better understand themselves and others. Engaging graphics and easy-to-read text lead readers on a journey of self-discovery. Also used widely by trainers, career professionals, coaches, managers and others to lead individuals, groups and teams through the dynamics of Temperament.

EEG Specifications

EEG involves the recording of spontaneous electrical activity along the scalp produced by the firing of neurons within the outer layer of the brain, which is uniquely well-developed in humans and is associated with numerous higher cognitive functions including language, memory, thought, and consciousness.

I used the MindSet MS-1000, manufactured by Nolan Computer Systems, Inc. to conduct my research. Data was captured using the ECI Electro-Cap, which consists of nineteen electrodes that measure differences in potential beneath the scalp via a conductive gel. Sixteen electrodes are relevant to neocortex activity. The equipment setup used for each subject followed standard procedures as described in the Nolan manual. The MindSet MS-1000 has been in use since 1997, and EEG in general has been in use for over eight decades.

Although EEG cannot delve into middle or deep layers of the brain, cognitive functions unique to humans are highly represented in the neocortex. Visceral emotions, memory management, impulse control, and involuntary or semi-voluntary bodily responses such as breathing are examples of brain functions not directly accessible to EEG. However, surface brain regions are involved in integrating and processing much of what occurs in deeper layers, meaning that the activities of deeper regions linked to emotions, memory and perception are often represented indirectly. A limitation of EEG is data capture during physical activity such as sports. EEG can be used when a person is standing or using their hands or feet so long as the head remains still.

Data analysis relied on event-related potentials. That is, EEG responses were matched to complex processing of stimuli (rather than passive presentation of stimuli to a subject). This approach is typical in cognitive, psychological, and psycho-physiological research. Copious notes were taken in real time and data was played-backed and averaged using Microsoft Excel and also analysis software supplied by Nolan.

The data recorded by the MindSet MS-1000 is voluminous (averaging twenty-five megabytes per session) and the analysis software is capable of only simple statistics including averaging. For this reason, and due to this book's monochrome nature, I tend to discuss amplitude and frequency separately.

Bibliography

Here is a list of references used while preparing this book.

A D Laposky, M A Wilson, and M L Languis. "A topographic brain mapping study of electrophysiological differences between sensing and intuitive psychological types". *Proceedings of APT-IX, the Ninth Biennial International Conference of the Association for Psychological Type*, (pages 19G-24G). Richmond, VA. July, 1991.

Allan W Snyder, Elaine Mulcahy, Janet L Taylor, D John Mitchell, Perminder Sachdev, and Simon C Gandevia. "Savant-like Skills Exposed in Normal People By Suppressing the Left Fronto-Temporal Lobe". *Journal of Integrative Neuroscience*, Vol. 2, No. 2 (pages 149-158), 2003.

Alvin I Goldman. *Simulating Minds: The Philosophy, Psychology, and Neuroscience of Mindreading*. Oxford University Press, May 2008.

Andreas Fink, Aljoscha Neubauer. "EEG Alpha Oscillations During the Performance of Verbal Creativity Tasks: Differential Effects of Sex and Verbal Intelligence". *Elsevier Science*, 2006.

Annedore Hopper, Joseph Ciorciari, Gillian Johnson, John Spensley, Alex Sergejew, and Con Stough. "EEG Coherence and Dissociative Identity Disorder". *Journal of Trauma & Dissociation* 3.1 (pages 75-88), 2002.

Bart Kosko. "Fuzzy Cognitive Maps". *International Journal of Man-Machine Studies*, Vol. 24, Issue 1 (pages 65-75), January 1986.

Colin G DeYoung, Jacob B Hirsh, Matthew S Shane, Xenophon Papademetris, Nallakkandi Rajeevan, and Jeremy R Gray. "Testing Predictions From Personality Neuroscience: Brain Structure and the Big Five". *Psychological Science*, 21(6) (pages 820–828), 2010.

Colin Martindale, Nancy Hasenfus. "EEG Differences as a Function of Creativity, Stage of the Creative Process, and Effort to be Original". *Biological Psychology*, 1978. (Available online: www.sciencedirect.com).

D Erik Everhart, David W. Harrison. "Hostility Following Right CVA: Support for Right Orbital Frontal Deactivation and Right Temporal Activation". *ISNR*.

D R Belov, S F Kolodyazhnyi, N Y Smit. "Expression of Hemispheric Asymmetry and Psychological Type in the EEG Traveling Wave". *Human Physiology*, Vol. 30, No. 1 (pages 1-13), January 2004,

Dale Purves, editor. *Neuroscience, Fourth Edition*. Sinauer Associates, July 2007.

Dario Nardi. *8 Keys to Self-Leadership*. Telos Publications, October 2005.

Dario Nardi. 'Context Switching' - Meeting the Needs of All Types of Students. *Proceedings of Counter Attack: Rising to the Challenges to Education*. Gainesville, FL: Center for the Application of Psychological Type, 1998.

Dario Nardi. *The Interstrength Cognitive Assessment: Development of a validated cognitive development psychometric (Research report 2)*. Interstrength, January 2006.

Dario Nardi. *Modeling and Simulation in the Social Sciences: An Introduction to Human Complex Systems*, 2nd edition. Radiance House, January 2010.

Dario Nardi. *Multiple Intelligences and Personality Type: Tools and Strategies for Developing Human Potential*. Huntington Beach, CA: Telos Publications, 2001.

Dario Nardi. "Roots and Branches: Multiple Models of Type". *Australian Psychological Type Journal*, Vol. 2, No. 3, November 2000.

David Rock, Jeffrey Schwartz. "The Neuroscience of Leadership". *strategy + business*, issue 43. Summer 2006.

Daryl Sharp. *Personality Types: Jung's Model of Typology*. Toronto: Inner City Books, 1987.

Eddie Harmon-Jones, Jennifer S Beer, editors. *Methods in Social Neuroscience*. The Guilford Press, January 2009.

G Rizzolatti, L Craighero. "The Mirror-Neuron System". *Annual Review Neuroscience*, Vol. 27 (pages 169-192), 2004.

G Rizzolatti, L Fogassi, and V Gallese. "Neurophysiological mechanisms underlying the understanding and imitation of action". *Nature Reviews Neuroscience*, Vol. 2 (pages 661-670), 2001.

Ginette C Blackhart, John P Kline. "Individual differences in anterior EEG asymmetry between high and low defensive individuals during a rumination/distraction task". *Personality and Individual Differences*, 39 (pages 427–437), 2005.

J F Lepage, H Theoret. "EEG evidence for the presence of an action observation-execution matching system in children". *European Journal of Neuroscience*, Vol. 23 (pages 2505-2510), 2006.

J M Kilner, J L Marchant, and C D Frith. "Modulation of the mirror system by social relevance". *Social Cognitive and Affective Neuroscience*, Vol. 1 (pp 143-148), 2006.

Jung, Carl. *Psychological Types*. Reprint, Princeton, NJ: Princeton University Press, 1960.

Hannah Holmes. *Quirk: Brain Science Makes Sense of Your Peculiar Personality*. Random House, February 2011.

Isabel Briggs Myers. *Gifts Differing*. With Peter B Myers. 1980. Reprint, Palo Alto, CA: Consulting Psychologists Press, 1995.

Isabel Briggs Myers, Mary McCaulley, Naomi Quenk, and Allen Hammer. *MBTI Manual (A guide to the development and use of the Myers Briggs type indicator)*, 3rd Edition. Consulting Psychologists Press, 1998.

Jim Grigsby, David W Stevens. *Neurodynamics of Personality*. The Guilford Press, December 2001.

John Rowan. *Subpersonalities: The People Inside Us.* London: Routledge, 1990.

Joseph O'Connor, John Seymour. *Introducing NLP: Psychological Skills for Understanding and Influencing People,* 2nd ed. London: Thorsons, 1995.

Lenore Thompson. *Personality Type: An Owner's Manual*. Boston: Shambhala Publications, 1998.

Linda V Berens, Dario Nardi. *Development of a validated temperament psychometric (Research report 1)*. Interstrength, August 2004.

Linda V Berens, Dario Nardi. *Understanding Yourself and Others: An Introduction to the Personality Type Code*. Telos Publications, October 2005.

Linda V Berens. *Understanding Yourself and Others: An Introduction to 4 Temperaments -4.0*. Telos Publications [republished by Radiance House], 1998.

Linda V Berens. *Understanding Yourself and Others: An Introduction to Interaction Styles-2.0*. Telos Publications [republished by Radiance House], 2008.

Martha A Alcock. "Identity, Personality, and the EEG". *Keynote Address at the Teaching and Learning Conference*, Fairfax, VA, February 6, 1999.

Martha A Alcock, J Newman. "EEG Correlates of the Jungian Attitudes and Functions". *An Invited Advanced Research Symposium at the International APT Conference*. Boston, MA, July 9, 1997.

Marvin Zuckerman. *Psychobiology of Personality*, 2nd edition. Cambridge University Press, April 2005.

Naomi Quenk. *In the Grip*. Palo Alto, CA: Consulting Psychologists Press, 1985.

Norbert Jausovec. "Differences in Cognitive Processes Between Gifted, Intelligent, Creative and Average Individuals While Solving Complex Problems: An EEG Study". *Elsevier Science*, 2000. (Available online: www.sciencedirect.com).

Peter C Gram, Bruce R Dunn, and Diana Ellis. "Relationship Between EEG and Psychological Type". *Journal of Psychological Type*, Issue 5, November 2005.

Peter C Gram, Bruce Dunn. "The relationship of EEG to personality as measured by the Myers-Briggs Type Indicator".

Rick Dakan. "Review: Emotiv EPOC, Tough Thoughts on the New Mind-reading Controller". *Joystiq*, December 2010.

Robert W Thatcher. *Hand Calculator Calculations of EEG Coherence, Phase Delays and Brain Connectivity*. Unpublished. University of South Florida, 2007.

Sue Cooper. "How to Stop Behaving Like Yourself and Start Listening". *Proceedings of APT-X, the Tenth Biennial International Conference of the Association for Psychological Type*, (InfoMedix cassette recording no. F196-117AB). Garden Grove, CA. July, 1993.

Susan A Greenfield. *The Human Brain: A Guided Tour*. Basic Books, 1998.

Tetsuto Minami, K Goto, M Kitazaki, and S Nakauchi. "Asymmetry of P3 amplitude during oddball tasks reflects the unnaturalness of visual stimuli". *NeuroReport*, Vol.20 (pages 1471-1476), 2009.

Vincent J Monastra. Electroencephalographic biofeedback (neurotherapy) as a treatment for attention deficit hyperactivity disorder: rationale and empirical foundation. *Child Adolescent Psychiatric Clinics of North America*, Vol. 14 (pages 55-82), 2005.

About the Author

Since 1998, Dario Nardi, PhD has taught computing, general honors courses, and social science at the University of California (Los Angeles).

Dario won UCLA's 2005 Brian P. Copenhaver Award for Innovative Use of Technology In the Classroom and UCLA's 2011 annual Distinguished Teaching Award.

Dario has worked with the sixteen Myers-Briggs personality types since 1993 and is author and coauthor of numerous books including *8 Keys to Leadership*, *The 16 Personality Types: Descriptions for Self-Discovery*, and *Quick Guide to 16 Types in Organizations*, among other titles. He has also created software apps including Personality Types, Love Therapy, and Mobile Trainer for the Apple iPhone/iPad.

Dario is active in the psychological type community. He chaired the 2009 Dallas conference for the International Association of Psychological Type and is a keynote conference speaker and workshop provider for groups and companies around the world. He is founder and CEO of Radiance House, a publishing company (www.radiancehouse.com) that specializes in books, cards, software, workbooks, and other media for tabletop games, human resources, psychology, and systems thinking.

Presently, Dario conducts experiments using EEG brain-mapping technology to better understand personality.

Printed in Great Britain
by Amazon

35742947R00115